This book may be kept
FOURTEEN DAYS
A fine will be charged for each
day the book is kept overtime.

HIGHSMITH 45—226

The Reagan Revolution

Rowland Robert EVANS & NOVAK

The Reagan Revolution

E. P. DUTTON ▼ NEW YORK

Published in the United States by Elsevier-Dutton Publishing Co., Inc., 2 Park Avenue, New York, N.Y. 10016

Library of Congress Cataloging in Publication Data
Evans, Rowland,
  The Reagan revolution.
  Includes index.
  1. United States—Politics and government—1981
2. Reagan, Ronald. I. Novak, Robert D. II. Title.
E876.E93 1981   973.927'092'4   81-5553
ISBN 0-525-18970-X   AACR2

Published simultaneously in Canada by
Clarke, Irwin & Company Limited, Toronto and Vancouver

Designed by The Etheredges

10 9 8 7 6 5 4 3 2

Contents

Acknowledgments

We appreciate our exclusive interview with President Reagan for this book. We are also in the debt of administration officials who have given us time from their crowded schedules to answer our questions. The partial list includes Edwin Meese III, James A. Baker III, Alexander Haig, Caspar Weinberger, Donald T. Regan, David Stockman, James Watt, Drew Lewis, Murray Weidenbaum, Michael K. Deaver, Richard V. Allen, Martin Anderson, Lyn Nofziger, Lawrence Eagleburger, Norman Ture, Paul Craig Roberts, Richard Burt and David Gergen. Outside the administration we acknowledge many other invaluable contributors to our store of knowledge: Senator Orrin Hatch, Senator Howard Baker, Senator Jesse Helms, Senator Paul Laxalt, Representative Jack Kemp, Representative Tom Evans, Charls Walker, Richard Wirthlin, Jude Wanniski, Jeffrey Bell, George Gilder, Lewis Lehrman, Paul Weyrich, Peter Hannaford, John Sears, Tom Ellis, William Bagley, William Timmons, William Van Cleave and Tom Korologos, among others. None of these, of course, is responsible for the content of this book.

James Brady and his colleagues in the White House press office, Larry Speakes and Karna Small, plus their secretarial staff there, have been invaluable, as have departmental and agency press offices throughout the government. This book could not have been written without the patience and cooperation of the staffs of the library of the U.S. International Communications Agency and the Washington bureau of the Newhouse newspapers.

Our assistant Laura Rogers coordinated many arrangements for this book, including manuscript preparation, along with Mary Mann, the other member of our office staff, and Lesley Halpern. Our intern from Mary Washington College, Rose McCartney, was a principal researcher. We also thank our longtime friend and former assistant Helen McMaster for her help. Robert Gutwillig, our partner for fifteen years, was generous with his editing help.

Jack Macrae, publisher of E. P. Dutton, provided helpful suggestions and editing, as did our agent Esther Newberg, of International Creative Management.

ROWLAND EVANS AND ROBERT NOVAK
June 1981
Washington, D.C.

Introduction

At 8:30 A.M. on March 30, 1981, departmental assistant secretaries appointed by President Reagan and known collectively as the subcabinet filed into the Roosevelt Room in the White
House for a rare meeting with the fortieth president. The administration was seventy days old, but many of the subcabinet
officials, some barely in office, had not yet met Ronald Reagan.

Reagan was smiling, confident and soft-spoken. "I'll tell you
what I told the Cabinet at the first meeting," he began. He then
proceeded to do so:

> . . . We'll all do the job as if there will never be another election. In
> other words . . . we'll take no actions or make no decisions that are
> based on how they might bear on or affect an election. Whatever we
> do will be based on what we believe, to the best of our ability, is best
> for the people of this country.

Coming from most politicians, that might be dismissed as a
bromide. But Reagan meant exactly what he was saying, and his
subcabinet knew he meant it. Lunching with a friend that day, one
of the assistant secretaries was still struck by the force of the
president's words. He remarked that Reagan seemed to be saying
that anybody in the administration more interested in political
maneuver than in adhering to an ideological standard might just as
well leave then and there. Reagan wanted to purge his governance
of the centrist temporizing and the political maneuvering that

characterized predecessor administrations since the end of World War II. Talking at lunch, this official not only affirmed his own commitment to Reagan's ideological thrust but told how much he had been buoyed by the president's disavowal of political strategizing.

Shortly after he returned to his office from lunch, he learned that the seventy-year-old president had been rushed to the George Washington University Hospital with a bullet in his lung fired by a would-be assassin at the Washington Hilton Hotel. Remembering the Roosevelt Room lecture, the official was struck by the importance of Ronald Reagan to the fulfillment of his administration. If Reagan were lost, who was there to make the administration adhere to the standard enunciated by the president that morning?

The question would not have been asked in the same way or with the same significance in any other presidency since that of Franklin D. Roosevelt. In the post-Roosevelt administrations, the thrust and philosophy would have continued—and after the assassination of John F. Kennedy did continue, with the succession of Vice President Lyndon B. Johnson. But because Reagan came to office with a driving ideology that informed his every action, and which demanded compliance by his colleagues in government, his administration was uniquely different. Ronald Reagan *was* the administration.

The outcome of the 1982 midterm congressional election, the 1984 presidential election and perhaps elections for the rest of the century would depend on Reagan's ability to translate his standard into reality. His strategy was to win elections, not by tinkering and brooding about tactical gains and games as did Richard M. Nixon, but by changing the tone and direction of America so totally that it would establish the political dominance of Reaganism.

Reagan himself had forced that test for the 1982 and 1984 elections when, in his 1980 campaign, he asked the American people whether they were better or worse off after four years of Jimmy Carter's presidency. Voters would be asking themselves the same questions in 1982 and 1984. Are inflation rates lower? Is unemployment lower? Has my standard of living stopped declining? Do I see a better future for my children? Has the government's demand on my last dollar of income declined? Am I more confident of America's role in the world? *Are things better?*

But it would be a misinterpretation of the Reagan presidency to suppose his policies were set by calculating their effect on the answers to those questions; that would violate Reagan's advice to his subcabinet that morning of March 30. Rather, Reagan's goal was more unorthodox, indeed revolutionary: to return the republic to the status quo of an earlier day.

In foreign and national security policy, that earlier day might be fixed at 1955. The unquestioned superiority of strategic arms then prevailing surely could not be regained; seeking merely to restore the military *balance* between Moscow and Washington was task enough. The Reagan intent was a return to the international power realities of a quarter of a century earlier: a United States known as a tenacious foe and a steadfast ally; Washington as the capital of the West, unquestioned leader of the alliance; an American people supporting their leaders and confident there would be no feckless foreign adventures without clear purpose. Reagan would be satisfied on the day he left the White House if his nation's position and stature in the world approximated that of 1955.

At home, his goals were more radical: to approximate the American economic structure of fifty-five years earlier, in 1925, with selective social welfare programs of the succeeding half century retained to soften that backward leap. Reagan's role in the rehabilitation of Calvin Coolidge as an admirable and respected president reflected his desire to return to the free-market world built by Coolidge and his masterful secretary of the treasury, Andrew Mellon: radically reduced tax rates and minimal government regulation, leading to a climate suitable for high economic growth and high employment, low inflation and low interest rates. But unlike 1925, there would be protective devices—though reduced from their bloated dimensions of the seventies—for the poor, the aged and the handicapped. It was, then, a goal of 1925 with a protective social welfare shield, thick enough to protect the weak but thin enough to liberate the strong. The rehabilitation of Coolidge symbolized Reagan's dream of a new future cast from an older mold.

Those goals, in foreign and domestic policy, amounted to no

conventional agenda for a new administration. They made the Reagan Revolution.

It is the purpose of this book, written during the first four months of the Reagan Administration, to describe the origins, purposes and prospects of that revolution. This is not a biography of Reagan, either political or personal. Nor is this an attempt to describe in detail the first hundred days of the Reagan Administration.

We seek here to outline the most self-conscious effort at revolutionary change by any American president, surpassing Franklin Roosevelt in its intent if not its scope. We begin by tracing Reagan's early political career and his two serious presidential campaigns, not in detail but to distill from them the development of the ideology that guided the Reagan Revolution—tax reform, budget reform, regulatory reform, foreign and military policy and, finally, the Moral Majority social issues. We conclude with an Oval Office interview with Ronald Reagan.

The point of view in this book was shaped by sixty years of combined Washington reportage by its two authors, watching firsthand how the U.S. government and its policies have worked and not worked, how successive administrations have advanced or impeded this country's aspirations.

We began reporting on the activities of Ronald Reagan firsthand in 1965, when he made his debut as a national Republican campaigner at a fund-raising dinner in Cincinnati, a debut to which we reacted with unexpected admiration for the political skills of a Hollywood actor but with doubt whether the host of *Death Valley Days* could indeed be taken seriously. Our interview with Reagan in Cincinnati was the first of many talks with him—formal and informal, fleeting and protracted, sterile and insightful—during the intervening sixteen years. In that period, we have written uncounted columns and articles about Reagan—some critical, some admiring. We believe that our understanding of him evolved over those years; but he, too, has evolved into a more formidable political figure in the fullness of his years.

1

A New Beginning

In bright sunshine and unseasonable warmth on January 20, 1981, Ronald Wilson Reagan two weeks before his seventieth birthday became the oldest man ever to take the oath as president of the United States. Calling for "a new beginning," he talked of "rebuilding a strong and prosperous America at peace with itself and the world." Given the traumatic experiences of the previous twenty years, transforming those homilies into reality would be no easy task.

It would require a revolution.

Reagan became the first president in the republic's history to deliver his inaugural address facing west, not east—facing the Mall and the splendid monuments leading to Arlington National Cemetery, a dramatic vista rich in symbolic manifestations.

Reagan's election marked the fifth time since the end of World War II that the voters had decided to switch the political affiliation of their president. But the advent of Reagan connoted a change different not merely in degree but in kind from Eisenhower, Kennedy, Nixon and Carter replacing presidents of the opposite party. While the changes those four new presidents proposed were limited and the ideological agenda of each was obscure, Reagan came into office intent on drastic policy changes not only from his immediate Democratic predecessors but from the policy of both parties when in power over the past generation.

Those changes were so drastic that they constituted a political revolution in America. Although his advertising experts had muted Reagan's views in the past campaign's radio/television commercials, his own campaigning had left no doubt where Reagan stood. What was to come could not surprise those who had followed what he had been saying not only the past year but during the past sixteen years.

▼ For the first time in over fifty years, the federal government, propelled by the executive branch, would embark on a systematic program of income tax reduction across the board, the rich benefiting proportionately as much as other taxpayers.

▼ Simultaneously, the government would reduce its scope, both in spending and in regulation. The bipartisan notion of governmental problem-solving would diminish.

▼ These radical changes would result in a series of trade-offs. Maximum protection of the environment, of the consumer, of the worker, would all be traded off in the interest of greater energy production, of higher productivity, of economic growth. There would be more emphasis on exploitation of resources, less on conservation. Put bluntly, cleaner air and water would be sacrificed for more energy.

▼ In national security, détente with the Soviet Union would be downgraded as the nation's principal protection. Instead, there would be no flinching from confrontation with the Soviets. The nation would seek to resume a firm, unwavering leadership of the West.

▼ That would require quick restoration of the military balance between the United States and the Soviet Union. The trend toward less defense spending would end, and this country would aim for no less than equality in weaponry.

▼ Relationships with other countries would change. Abstract measurement of "human rights" again would become less important than the question of traditional friendship for the United States; South Korea, South Africa and Chile no longer would be unwelcome in Washington; efforts to court the Third World would decline.

▼ The government would change sides on a wide front of social issues: under Reagan, it would oppose abortion, favor school prayer, oppose public school busing, go much slower with affirmative action.

Not since the political threshold year of 1932 had a change of political power resonated with the promise of real change of government policy. But even the coming of the New Deal forty-eight years earlier could not compare with the arrival of Reagan in Washington in its revolutionary portents.

Preaching conventional politics in the 1932 campaign, Roosevelt offered few hints of the drama he would unfold during his first Hundred Days. During the campaign, FDR did not know what he intended to do once he assumed presidential power. His political revolution was splendidly isolated from his campaign rhetoric. Campaigner Roosevelt promised recovery, but the hows and whys of it had to await assumption of power. No "New Deal" had been visible in his nearly twenty years of public life, climaxed by four years as governor of New York. No newspapers or radios had been carrying a syndicated FDR message to millions of voters year after year. FDR's revolution had hardly been conceived before it was time to send it to the Congress.

In contrast, the fortieth president of the United States had been speaking out to the nation about the nature of his intended political revolution for sixteen years before his election. He had been proclaiming in many ways, with many examples, the peril of ever-expanding government. The nation first heard, in his nationally televised speech in support of Senator Barry Goldwater's presidential candidacy in 1964, the opening salvo of the Reagan Revolution. The culmination of Reagan's warnings came near the top of his Inaugural Address, a sentence shorn of high-flown verbiage: "Government is not the solution to our problem, government is the problem."

But what kind of a man had arrived to take power with his ideology of government defined by a single sentence?

There was no more unlikely leader of a political revolution than this septuagenarian who had become known to the nation as a Grade B movie actor. Sometimes, he seemed more improbable as a national leader viewed at first hand than he did as a personality dimly viewed through the news media.

In the midst of any one of his 1980 campaign trips, Republican political operatives brought aboard the campaign plane to meet Reagan would use a single word with uncanny frequency to describe, in private, their party's new leader: *lethargic*. He often looked every bit his years, weary from campaign demands that had taxed the energies and morale of much younger presidential hopefuls.

Not that Reagan carried on a dawn-to-dusk schedule in the modern American presidential campaign pattern. As far back as his first campaign for governor in 1966 when he was a robust fifty-five years old, schedules were adjusted so that Ron and Nancy Reagan could spend the evenings at their home in Pacific Palisades in the Los Angeles area. Political reporters exhausted from their travels that year while covering the desperate reelection campaign of Governor Edmund G. (Pat) Brown, Sr., were eager for Reagan's short hours and modest travel schedule. That set the general pattern not only for his future campaigns but for his years as governor and, prospectively, as President.

When Reagan early in his presidency attended a black tie dinner in Washington of the prestigious Alfalfa Club (boycotted for four years by Jimmy Carter because of its males-only policy), he departed at an early hour—to return to the White House, it was announced; what was not announced was that he was returning to the White House to sleep. Whereas Jimmy Carter spent late hours studying documents, Reagan went to bed. When told shortly after his election that it long had been governmental custom in Washington to hold eight o'clock breakfast meetings, Reagan replied in words to this effect: That's fine, go ahead with the breakfast meetings, but I won't be there. He was true to his word, rising no earlier than eight A.M. and retiring at an early hour. His affinity for Calvin Coolidge (whose political rehabilitation Reagan contributed to significantly by placing Coolidge's portrait at the place of honor in the cabinet room as a favorite of the new incumbent) was not limited to their similar tax policies; Reagan's sleeping time was exceeded among his presidential predecessors only by Coolidge, who normally slept at least twelve hours a day.

Over the years, many politicians and journalists who made the pilgrimage to Reagan's home in Pacific Palisades came away disappointed. Instead of engaging in a meaningful conversation, they were given canned performances straight from his platform speeches (first transcribed on 3 × 5—later 5 × 8—index cards, then committed to memory). There was little dialogue. He seemed particularly unimpressive to intellectuals. The New York intellectual/journalist Norman Podhoretz, who had traveled a long road from left radicalism to neoconservatism, liked Reagan when he met him in 1980 but had to attest that he certainly was no intellectual.

Reagan was no more comfortable gossiping about politics, a favorite pastime of Roosevelt, Truman, Johnson and Nixon, among other presidents, than he was in intellectual dialogue. What he really liked and was most comfortable talking about were the old days in Hollywood. In 1975, on a small plane ride from Jackson, Mississippi, to West Palm Beach, Florida, made long and uncomfortable by severe thunderstorms, a reporter was alone with Reagan save for the pilot and a nontalking aide/bodyguard. Naturally, the reporter thought he was in for a rich experience prospecting for news nuggets. But Reagan made it clear he was in no mood for politics. He had never enjoyed flying. In fact, for many years he refused to fly at all, traveling only by rail—a practice he was forced to discontinue when entering politics. Now clearly upset by the thunderstorms, he steadied himself with cocktails (one more than his normal maximum of one) and some reminiscences.

He started by telling the dialect jokes, especially Irish and Jewish, that he most enjoyed (but could no longer tell in public). That led to anecdotes about the old Hollywood days—about Sam Goldwyn, Harpo Marx, life on the back lot at Warner Brothers, and Ronald Reagan on the loose as a rich and handsome bachelor following the breakup of his first marriage.

But such nostalgic bull sessions with Reagan were all too unfamiliar for journalists and even friends. Reporters trailing Reagan in his first campaign for governor in 1966 were surprised to find that at day's end, Ron and Nancy Reagan often would return to Pacific Palisades and enter their home without inviting anybody in—certainly not reporters but not even aides or campaign managers. In those days, all were kept at arm's length, as befitted the Hollywood star system. The habit did not break easily as the years passed.

His close friends when he first entered politics were old buddies from the movies. Actor Robert Taylor was then considered his closest friend. As the years passed, Reagan did not cut the Hollywood ties. Actress Doris Day did not hesitate to call Governor Reagan on his private, unlisted home telephone to prod him about protection of animals. When Reagan was touring the country in the spring of 1976 in search of delegates to take the presidential nomination away from Gerald Ford, he took along old movie actors; Jimmy Stewart, a lifelong Republican of conservative vintage, was a frequent companion.

Similarly, in the late stages of his 1980 general election campaign against President Carter, superannuated actors from a bygone Hollywood era were at his side. Roy Rogers, Don DeFore and Cesar Romero appeared on the platform with Reagan four days before the election at a high school rally in Des Plaines, Illinois, a suburb of Chicago, before an audience consisting mostly of teenagers born a generation after Romero ruled the Saturday afternoon B movie screens as the Cisco Kid. Suggestions by political aides that aged actors, forgotten by the public and markedly grayer than Reagan, would do him no good politically were rebuffed by the candidate. "He just likes to have them around," one aide said.

But beginning in the late 1950s, Reagan also had developed a new set of non-show business friends: intensely conservative millionaire businessmen from the Los Angeles area. They were inextricably involved in his political campaigns and by the time of his election as president had organized themselves on a more or less formal basis as the "Kitchen Cabinet" under the leadership of chemical magnate Justin Dart, to advise him on nominations for his new administration. Not all the Kitchen Cabinet's recommendations were accepted, but all were considered. Its members were Reagan's contemporaries in age and shared with him a common social and ideological outlook. After Reagan was elected, most were content to be friends of the president, without a role in government. But not all.

William French Smith, the Los Angeles lawyer who long had been Reagan's personal attorney, was named attorney general despite his lack of any governmental experience and the fact that key Reagan advisers dismissed him as a "society lawyer." The advisers knew they could not stop Reagan from appointing Smith and did not try, but they strongly advised against the selection of Kitchen Cabinet member Charles Z. Wick as director of the International Communications Agency, the old U.S. Information Agency earmarked by Reagan for bigger things in the global propaganda war. Reagan's transition report had recommended for that post some renowned conservative journalists, specifically mentioning Pat Buchanan, George Will and William F. Buckley. Charley Wick, who had made his millions in show business, real estate and the nursing home business, was certainly not that. Ronnie (as he was called by most Kitchen Cabinet members) and Nancy in recent years had dined at the home of Charley and Mary Jane Wick each Christmas Eve. Charley wanted the ICA job badly, and Reagan told his aides he could not deny him it.

Former staffers of presidents Nixon and Ford brought in to help the Reagan campaign and transition were surprised at how unfamiliar with details he was compared to their former chiefs. As governor, Reagan had been subjected to intense criticism for instituting the "mini-memo" requirement, which limited to a single page official action memoranda submitted to him no matter how complicated the subject. Although the strict mini-memo format no longer existed, the voluminous documentary material commonly handled by all the presidents from Kennedy through Carter was not submitted to Reagan.

Reagan could do a lot with a short memo. Given a "talking paper" outlining what he might say in a meeting, Reagan would commit it to memory and deliver it verbatim—replete with planned hesitations and head-noddings. "He's just an actor," commented one campaign aide who previously had served Nixon and Ford. "Nothing substantive. It worries hell out of me."

From the foregoing, there seems to emerge a president not well grounded in issues and not prepared to commit the time usually considered necessary for presidential pursuits; a president most comfortable in the company of ex-actors and millionaires who is not averse to naming cronies to high office. But that picture of Ronald Reagan reveals only part of the truth about him.

A major part of the problem was that Reagan was being judged against the preferred presidential model established by the two Roosevelts: activist and interventionist, working feverishly around the clock with fingers on every thread of government. Yet there was a more passive presidential model, typified most recently by Eisenhower, a chief executive quick to delegate his powers, slow to react. Considering the nation's unhappy experiences in the twenty years previous to Reagan's election, the Eisenhower model was not to be despised when compared with the latter-day practitioners of the Roosevelt model that followed.

But while replicating Eisenhower's work habits and organization, Reagan was by no means a copy of the old general, the quintessential pragmatist and conciliator. Indeed, Reagan might well rank as the least pragmatic, most ideological president ever elected. He was certainly the first president ever elected who was a bona fide member of a political movement outside the regular party structure. When, on March 20, 1981, the new president addressed the Conservative Political Action Conference at the Mayflower Hotel in Washington, he was among friends. While Roosevelt was influenced by the left but never part of it, Reagan was in the vanguard of the right. As a life member of the National Rifle Association, he was an activist against gun controls. As a reader of *Human Events* and the *National Review*, he shared their dreams, as was shown in his peroration to the cheering crowd at the Mayflower: "Fellow citizens, fellow conservatives, our time is now. Our moment has arrived."

The key to understanding Reagan could be his delight in reminiscing about his acting career. "It is his real identity, the self he has neither lost nor abandoned from which he truly speaks as a man," wrote John Sears in 1980 after Reagan had deposed him as campaign manager in a manner that terminated their personal relationship. Sears added, "Reagan knows himself better than most presidents, and he has kept his identity separate from politics."[1]

The nearly thirty years spent by Reagan in the supposedly make-believe world of show business was in many ways more real than the experience of previous presidents with wide public service. He alone among recent presidents had spent his mature years in the real world, confronting daily the real bread-and-butter problems faced by his fellow citizens. But in the course of a movie career that perhaps had more downs than ups, he had learned to cope with adversity during the lean years and knew what it was to worry about where the next mortgage payment was coming from.

In the largest sense of the word, he was also an entrepreneur—one of the very few of that species so vital in the making of America ever to enter the White House. In a narrow sense, Reagan did not qualify as an entrepreneur; he never ran a business as such. But by a broader definition, his whole life was entrepreneurial. His career was deeply affected by the management and organization and financial success of a business enterprise, however personal the ventures. From his earliest days, he had lived by his wits as an independent contractor. Even when he concluded his eight years as governor at age sixty-three, retirement was out of the question. His handsome multimillion-dollar net worth hid a meager cash flow that did not provide the $400,000 or more a year needed to maintain his life-style. So Reagan became a one-man enterprise, his writing and speaking through various communications media providing income for himself, his family and a substantial staff.

That entrepreneurial background gave Reagan not only a nongovernmental view of the world but one peculiarly economics oriented for a president. Politicians are notoriously uninterested in economics, and have to be force-fed the dismal science. John Kennedy's economic advisers were delighted over the aptitude of their presidential pupil in grasping economic theory, but this was clearly a forced learning process necessitated by presidential responsibility. Other presidents scarcely went that far, preferring, as Nixon and Carter did, the headier problems of foreign affairs. Reagan was uniquely interested in economics, in the workings of the private sector as impeded or facilitated by government.

He was also uniquely receptive to new ideas in all areas, but especially in economics. His fellow septuagenarians in the Kitchen Cabinet might have locked their minds on a closed circle of beliefs a generation ago, but not Reagan. He was constantly probing, fiddling and experimenting to find a better way to reach his goals. While no intellectual, he was a voracious magazine and newspaper reader, searching always for new facts and new ideas. The result was often politically embarrassing, as Reagan prematurely surfaced radical, untested and often unworkable schemes for reforming Social Security or the tax system. But it also meant that he was not wedded to theories that perpetuated policies of doubtful success or proven failure.

Reagan's receptivity was only superficially similar to Nixon's passion for innovation. In adopting wage and price controls he had abhorred for a lifetime, Nixon demonstrated the absence of an ideological base underlying his special policies. In contrast,

Reagan's changes in policy directions on taxation or Social Security were directed by an overriding ideology, less flexible and more rigid than any president's since Coolidge.

Senator Howard Baker, the Senate Republican leader, had not known Reagan all that well until he became president. After frequent contact, Baker was impressed by how "pragmatic" Reagan was. Similarly, commentators and politicians after the election predicted Reagan would abandon much of his campaign dogma once safely within the White House. They were all wrong—Baker confusing Reagan's friendly personality and his innate and conciliatory willingness to compromise on small matters with the pragmatism of his predecessors; the commentators and politicians wrongly assuming that Reagan had not meant what he said on the campaign stump any more than other presidential candidates.

In fact, Reagan was rigid in his overwhelming suspicion of government and his faith in the private enterprise system. That informed all his policies, including his foreign policy. It derived from his faith in what he perceived to be American principles. In 1978, while addressing a Republican audience, Reagan declared: "At the heart of our message should be five simple, familiar words. No big economic theories. No sermons of political philosophy. Just five short words: *family, work, neighborhood, freedom, peace.*"

This was no mere campaign oratory. While Reagan might wrestle with and switch positions on such socially troublesome questions as women's rights and abortion, his belief in those five words never wavered. That meant a constancy of adherence to reduced government, reduced taxation, a superior national defense and a nationalistic foreign policy. A *Washington Post* headline in the spring of 1980 spoke of Reagan's philosophy as "A Vision of America Frozen in Time." That is a description he would not reject.

This "frozen" view was shaped not in the tinseled unreality of Hollywood but in Reagan's boyhood in the small towns of northern Illinois. He has been called a cultural Democrat, and that set him apart not only from his rich friends in the Kitchen Cabinet but from the greater world of corporate business. As the candidate of Main Street rather than Wall Street, his affinity for big business was an unrequited love; the corporate boardrooms preferred others in every year he sought the presidency (Nixon in 1968, Ford in 1976, John Connally in 1980).

But Reagan was certain the great mass of the people was with him, sharing his ideology that intended a revolution in Washington.

After pollsters and politicians had graded the outcome too close to call, it was an electoral landslide on November 4, 1980— 489 electoral votes for Reagan to 49 Carter. The popular vote was less clear: 43,195,000 (50.9 percent) for Reagan; 34,911,000 (41.1 percent) for Carter; 5,581,000 (6.6 percent) for independent candidate John Anderson. Accepting the conventional wisdom that Anderson's votes would have otherwise gone to Carter, it was a squeaker on the order of 1948, 1960, 1968 and 1976, with the winner barely getting half the vote. But many polls indicated less than half of Anderson's vote would have ended up with Carter under any circumstances, indicating a Reagan mandate that, if not the landslides of 1964 and 1972, was close to those of 1952 and 1956.

However, the question of Reagan's mandate depended less on raw numbers than on the motive of the great rush of voters to Reagan the last weekend of the campaign. That they were expressing dissatisfaction with the current state of affairs in the nation and Jimmy Carter's responsibility for it could not be denied. But whether the voters were also consciously accepting Reagan's alternative was less clear.

One distant vote for the latter alternative came from an unlikely source. On December 7, 1980, on a snowy, windswept plain on the outskirts of Gdansk, Lech Walesa, hero of Poland's free labor movement, talked about world politics and quietly turned to the recent American election. "It was intuition, perhaps," he said, "but one year ago I envisioned what would happen. Reagan was the only good candidate in your presidential campaign, and I knew he would win."

But why would this devout Catholic layman, a political liberal and economic socialist who had extracted unprecedented concessions from Poland's Communist regime, be moved to support the likes of Ronald Reagan? Walesa spoke cautiously, aware that he led a movement accused by his government of consorting with Western "imperialists." "Someday the West will wake up," he said, "and you may find it too late, as Solzhenitsyn has written. Reagan will do it better. He will settle things in a more efficient way. He will make the U.S. strong and make it stand up."

There, from within the restive European empire of the Soviet Union, came the answering echo to Reagan's warning that national weakness would inevitably lead to national humiliation and even defeat at the hands of ruthless adversaries who knew the meaning of power. In his Inaugural Address, Reagan put the capstone on what he had been proclaiming so long, using a word— the noun *will*—not used in such context by any recent president. In addition to military power, Reagan said, "we must realize that no arsenal or no weapon in the arsenals of the world is so formidable as the *will* and moral courage of free men and women"(emphasis added). The word *will* had become the metaphor for the worries and fears of citizens who saw the systematic decay of America's once impregnable position in the world; it was heard in the think tanks and study groups of conservatives, moderates and ex-liberals, and it was voiced quietly by military leaders. It was what Walesa was talking about. First *will*, then a rebirth of power.

On May 10, 1980, the small homes with their neatly tended lawns in Warren, Michigan, were full of surprises for the inquiring political reporter.[2] Although the sample of opinion would not be completed until sixty-four households had been visited and the questionnaires prepared by pollster Pat Caddell had been filled in, a shocking fact was apparent from the start: Reagan was cutting beyond the 50 percent mark into a vote that normally went Democratic by a 3-to-1 margin.

The revolution of the sixties and seventies was over; counterculture had withered; the three-piece suit was back, and getting a college education and a good job was in. The talk in the cluttered living rooms dominated by the constantly playing television sets was of Soviet troops in Cuba and Afghanistan and Cubans in Africa. It was about American hostages imprisoned in Tehran in what their countrymen believed was an unprecedented humiliation visited on their country.

On one question after another, the voters of Warren, Michigan, expressed rising contempt for their president, preferring Reagan over Carter to rebuild U.S. strength, to deal with the

Russians, to handle inflation, taxes and the economy, to restore America's image.

That image was especially tarnished on February 14, 1979, fifteen months before the voters of Warren told a reporter of their contempt for Carter's handling of affronts and insults to their country. The bleak events on that Valentine's Day started with the first invasion of the American Embassy in Tehran.

Within hours of the Iranian takeover of the American Embassy on Taleghani Avenue in Tehran, Telex machines in the State Department's operations center announced the kidnapping of Adolph (Spike) Dubs, the U.S. ambassador in Kabul, Afghanistan. Dubs stayed alive four hours more. The Soviet-dominated government of Afghanistan rejected the appeal of Secretary of State Cyrus Vance and stormed the room in the Hotel Kabul where Dubs had been taken by the terrorists. He was killed in the "rescue" attempt supervised by Soviet advisers. Almost simultaneously, the marine guards at the embassy in Tehran were ordered to surrender, a decision dictated both by the circumstance that faced the one-hundred American Embassy officials caught in the seizure and by the presence of seven thousand other Americans throughout Iran. It proclaimed the decline of American power from its postwar peak, when the CIA in 1953 had helped oust a leftist demagogue from power in Iran and restored a pro-American government.

It upset voters beginning for the first time to concentrate on the 1980 presidential election and to take the measure of Carter and Reagan. In Warren, Michigan, voters were asked: Which candidate, Carter or Reagan, would be stronger in handling defense? Reagan won, by 4 to 3.

The anti-Carter resentment was widened by more dramatic disasters closer to the election: the second takeover of the Tehran embassy in November 1979, resulting in the hostage crisis; the Soviet invasion of Afghanistan in December; Carter's acquiescence in the existence of a Soviet combat brigade in Cuba, after momentary bluster following its discovery (belated or not) in December 1978; the grudging acknowledgment by Carter that the Russians really had been testing a whole new generation of dreaded long- and intermediate-range nuclear missiles that soon could threaten U.S. and European safety with a knockout blow. The hobgoblins that Ronald Reagan had been conjuring up all those years were suddenly reality, and Reagan was there not just as a polemicist to say "I told you so," but as the presumptive Republican presidential nominee.

Foreign troubles were bad enough for the incumbent president, but they did not pack the political punch of the domestic variety. Not since the Great Depression had American wage-earners been so confused and distracted by economic events neither they nor their government fully understood or could come to grips with. Here, too, Ronald Reagan had been sounding the alarm for sixteen years.

In Warren, Michigan, that day in May, voters picked Reagan by 2 to 1 over Carter on ability "to handle the economy" and by 3 to 1 on tax policy. Among these auto-worker Democrats, Reagan had become digestible in a community where ten years earlier his kind of Republican was as popular as a Hoover soup kitchen. One pro-Reagan Chrysler production-line worker, asked to define what Reagan stood for, showed by his answer how deeply etched was the Reagan imprimatur: "If you don't know what Reagan stands for, you shouldn't be taking this poll." What Reagan stood for in Warren was lowered taxes, lessened government, reduced welfare, higher defense spending. The perception that cut deepest was less definable and more inflammatory: "We just can't go along this way any longer, mister, things gotta change in this country."

The task of making things change in the America of the 1980s was profound, and not just because of Jimmy Carter. Reagan was a chosen instrument of change in policies made by administrations of both parties—for foreign policy dating back a dozen years and for domestic policy all the way back to the beginning of the New Deal a half century ago.

The sixteen years of Republican rule since Franklin Roosevelt (Eisenhower, 1953–1961, and Nixon-Ford, 1969–1977) had never intended to effect revolutionary change and certainly had not done so. General Eisenhower was the establishment's choice over Senator Robert A. Taft as the Republican less likely to roil the waters. While Nixon was no establishment favorite, neither was he interested in radical change; he took the word of his Democratic adviser Daniel Patrick Moynihan that he should reassure the nation and fortify social stability by continuing most of the policies of the preceding Johnson Administration.

The unmistakable decline of U.S. power in the world began in the Nixon Administration. Unable in the latter days of the Vietnam War to sell adequate defense programs to Congress, Nixon retreated to his policy of détente with the Soviet Union, replete with treaties that critics insisted were unequal in favor of the Kremlin. What followed in the Carter Administration was not a new direction but acceleration of the old.

Like Eisenhower, Nixon disdained a massive assault to trim down the federal government. By 1971, he decided to cure the problem of too much government with more government by imposing wage and price controls. Simultaneously, he severed all remaining links between gold and the dollar (for the first time since 1876), ensuring that (contrary to the expectations of his advisers) gold would rise and the dollar would fall. Chronic inflation was at hand.

As government spending and government regulation expanded, Uncle Sam's share of the citizen's dollar rose—the steeply graduated income tax system ensuring ever greater revenues as inflation climbed. Belatedly awakening to the threat of inflation, Carter would not take Nixon's disastrous route of wage-price controls but neither would he come to grips with the soaring federal budget. Fighting all tax rate reduction plans, he proposed annual revenue increases of more than $100 billion in each of his last two years in office, thereby perpetuating the "stagflation" of Nixon and Ford—a stagnant economy amid rising inflation. Indeed, Carter had even less success than Nixon and Ford in slowing the engines of inflation.

Carter's pledge of a balanced budget by the end of his first term became a multibillion-dollar embarrassment: nearly $60 billion of deficit, the third largest in all history, in fiscal 1981 (the year ending September 30, 1981). Voters had lost any fiscal respect they might have had for Carter. While chafing under ever-rising tax rates, they were most visibly angry at the extraordinary speed with which entitlements had grown from almost nothing to multibillions: food stamps, one of those Great Society ideas backed both by farmers (glutted with overproduction) and the poor (wanting federal food subsidies), started modestly at a few millions of dollars. Carter's last budget put the cost to taxpayers at nearly $13 billion. Among the grateful recipients: well-heeled students.

Social Security, the granddad and foundation of social welfare programs—supposedly self-financed by contributions from both wage-earners and employers—had exploded to the point where it was consuming 30 percent of the entire federal budget. Social Security liability was far beyond the wildest dreams of the New Dealers who established the system's tax at 1 percent for both employee and employer on a maximum wage base of $3,000 in 1935. The steady increase in the tax burden to almost seven times that rate, on a maximum wage base of $29,700, contributed to the tax revolt of the seventies.

The growth of entitlements—legal obligations of the federal government to pay cash for one purpose or another directly to citizens—kept narrowing the slice of budget pie that was cuttable. Carter, wiser in January 1981 than he had been four years earlier, spoke in uncharacteristic words when he sent his final budget to Congress January 15, 1981. Noting that entitlements, interest on the national debt and other "mandatory contracts" now consumed 75 percent of the total budget, he appealed for restraint in words reminiscent of the language Reagan had been using for almost two decades: "We can no longer, as individuals or groups, make special pleas for exceptions to budget discipline. Too often we have taken the attitude that there must be alternative sources for reduction in programs that benefit our particular group. That attitude is in part responsible for the rapid budget growth we . . . can no longer afford."

That accurately represented what Reagan had been promoting for so long: the concept that for every problem an answer lay in the Treasury in Washington, D.C., did not work any longer.

The voters on November 4, 1980, declared that they felt the impact of an overpowering weight of big government with growing malice. Reagan was the identified enemy of big government. Coupled with the public perception of him far in front of Carter on the question of neutralizing Soviet pressure around the world, the result of the 1980 election should not have been in doubt.

But Reagan assumed power at a moment of vulnerability and challenge to the institution he inherited. The presidency was reeling from repeated shocks unknown to it since the turn of the century and since its recovery from the legislative tyranny of Reconstruction and subsequent congressional government described by Woodrow Wilson.

"By any of the usual criteria, presidents of the postwar era have not enjoyed political good fortune despite the [modern] aggrandizements of the office," a student of the modern presidency has written.[3] Starting with Harry Truman, the seven postwar presidents—almost one fifth of all the men who have served in the office—encountered greater political misfortune than any group of presidents in history, including the unfortunates who immediately preceded and followed the Civil War. Two (Harry Truman and Lyndon Johnson) declined to run for a second term because of unpopular wars; one (John Kennedy) was assassinated; one (Richard Nixon) was driven from office; two (Ford and Carter) became the first incumbent nominees to be denied election since Herbert Hoover. Only Dwight D. Eisenhower survived two full terms, during a presidency repeatedly savaged by the intellectual left as quiescent, passive and ineffective (a judgment likely to be revised by history).

The thirty-five postwar years contained repeated exercises of presidential power. Truman, who in wartime had ordered the atomic bomb dropped on Japan without consulting Congress, in 1950 dispatched troops to South Korea without asking the approval of Congress. Kennedy's handling of the Cuban missile crisis was an executive decision with only fragmentary and belated word to Congress. So was Nixon's incursion into Cambodia in 1970, justified by his legal advisers as "a valid exercise of his constitutional authority as commander-in-chief to secure the safety of American forces" in Indochina.[4] Under Nixon, national security assistant Henry Kissinger undertook secret diplomatic negotiations with not a word to any congressional leader. Kissinger obtained from Nixon unprecedented powers to influence Pentagon actions, including even the makeup of the defense budget.

This aggrandizement of the president's power was a long time coming. When John Tyler succeeded William Henry Harrison after Harrison's death in 1841 on his thirty-first day in office, his holdover Cabinet insisted, unsuccessfully, that all presidential decisions must be by majority vote of the Cabinet. That was not so ridiculous a notion in 1841 when the Cabinet contained party, regional and factional political leaders almost as powerful in their own right as the president himself. That a Cabinet member then could vie with a president shows the immense distance that rising presidential power was to travel in 150 years.

The president's power soared during Franklin Roosevelt's

tenure. FDR's Brain Trust, not Congress, wrote the first New Deal legislation during the Hundred Days. Congress, reeling under the Depression, accepted most of it on sight. That established Roosevelt as the first president who could claim to be "the nation's chief legislator."[5] Earlier presidents had devised legislative targets and even drafted precise blueprints. But it was Roosevelt who, during five days of frenzied draftmanship after his inauguration, sent his banking bill to Congress, the first of the New Deal emergency bills, and established that the White House had seized authority over the legislative process.

Roosevelt learned quickly how to build presidential power, and by 1939 his reorganization act institutionalized that buildup by moving the Budget Bureau into the White House and setting up, for the first time, an Executive Office of the President. FDR's executive staff, considered immense at the time, numbered about 200. Reagan's Executive Office numbered about 1,700 at the outset, and at that it was smaller than Carter's.

The election of Dwight D. Eisenhower in 1952 as the first Republican president in twenty years did not reverse the flow of presidential powers. He made clear in his first months in office in 1953 his resolve not to let Congress govern when he intervened to block a tax-reduction bill adopted by the Republican-controlled House Ways and Means Committee. Eisenhower's dispatch of marines to Lebanon in 1958 was a bloodless rerun of Truman's Korean intervention.

Reaction began to set in as Lyndon Johnson widened the war in Vietnam without taking Congress into his confidence and Nixon victimized himself and the presidency with the manifold abuses of Watergate. Vietnam and Watergate unloosed a withering political assault on the institution of the presidency, as much as the two men in it. Besides public demonstrations reacting against the war, the two crises produced an increasingly embittered Congress that set out to reverse the flow of power to the presidency and went far toward restoring congressional ascendancy.

The congressional targets were twofold: first, rein in the president's foreign policy powers, particularly his power to make war; second, choke off the Executive's growing budget powers, especially the impounding of congressional appropriations. Under the guise of putting controls on the president at a time when the American people were hostile to him, Congress in truth was set on its own power grab.

The high-water mark of the foreign policy grab was the War Powers Act, passed over Nixon's veto in 1973 as Watergate raged. It required congressional approval for any commitment of American troops abroad beyond sixty days. Congress erected many lesser barricades against presidential power: for the first time, the Senate Foreign Relations Committee rejected—not just pigeonholed—an ambassadorial nomination. A law enacted in 1972 required the president to submit the text of every international agreement to Congress within sixty days. The Senate began an overhaul of all wartime emergency legislation giving presidents special powers.

Congress most effectively hobbled and cut down the president by specific actions: drastically limiting his power to export nuclear fuels to foreign countries; shackling his uses of the CIA; denying him (in the amendment of Senator Dick Clark of Iowa) the right to give assistance of any kind to the anti-Marxist, pro-Western UNITA guerrilla movement in Angola. "The post-World War II pattern was based on the assumption that the legislative branch of the government will always support a chief executive who moves against Communism," wrote George Reedy. "The record now says that there are times when Congress will not grant such support . . . and future presidents must take this record into account before moving."[6]

The presidency was in decline, so much so that Gerald Ford had felt obliged to *ask* Congress for the right to do what he wanted to do in Angola; his predecessors would have explored the files and come up with "some document that could be interpreted as an American commitment . . . and the marines would have been on their way."[7] Perhaps because of his own long tenure in the House of Representatives, Ford declined to take that initiative.

That helped set the stage for the most passive of all postwar presidents, an executive who seemed powerless in the face of Soviet expansion from the Caribbean to the African continent, to the tip of the Arabian peninsula and east to Afghanistan. Carter came to power with a profound but immature conviction that the Russians wanted the same decent kind of world that he did, and he reached the White House as the Soviets were on the point of surpassing the United States in nuclear weapons (having long since exceeded the United States and Western Europe in conventional arms).

When 85,000 Soviet troops stormed into Afghanistan in December 1979, Carter felt personally betrayed. He had been wrong about the Russians, as he told ABC anchorman Frank Reynolds: The intervention "made a more dramatic change in my opinion of what the Soviets' goals are" than anything else during his administration. His belated conversion to higher defense spending, after campaigning in 1976 for a lower budget and using his power for the next three years to resist higher arms spending, came too late.

Even with a weakened presidency, Reagan at age seventy set about revolutionizing American policy. Whether or not he had a true mandate from the people, he *performed* as though he did, setting clear priorities for both the long and short range. He was the first president since Roosevelt acting on a clear agenda.

In the short run: to cut taxes, to halt the runaway growth of spending, to relax regulation of business, to accelerate military spending, to present a face to the world more resolute against the Soviet Union and more dependable to allies.

In the longer run: to stabilize the size of the federal government (rather than merely to limit its growth), to stimulate greater productivity, to increase production of energy, to pull equal with the Soviet Union in military power, to resume full leadership of the Western world.

Other items on the Reagan agenda—antibusing, antiabortion, proschool prayer—would not come until later.

This was indeed a revolutionary agenda for the septuagenarian who had traveled a road to the White House unique in the annals of American political history.

2

Hollywood to Sacramento

The tall, skinny broadcaster from Radio Station WHO in Des Moines, Iowa, accompanied the Chicago Cubs to spring training in California in February 1937 as he had for several years, but his mind was not on baseball that spring training season. Now twenty-six years old, "Dutch" Reagan had planned to use the trip to satisfy his deepest ambition: to get into show business.

Sports announcing was only a temporary substitute for the bright lights of the theater. While working his way through tiny Eureka College in northern Illinois with the help of a football scholarship, Reagan viewed the stage as his future. He joined the Eureka College Dramatic Society, which in his junior year finished second in the collegiate one-act play competition sponsored by Northwestern University. When the head of Northwestern's drama department suggested he consider acting as a career, Reagan's ambition was kindled. "Show business," was his quick reply in college when asked what he wanted to do.

Graduating from Eureka in June 1932, Reagan announced to friends that he would be earning $5,000 within the year and set off to Chicago to find a job in radio to make good his boast. But not a single door opened to the inexperienced young man, and he hitchhiked back to his hometown of Dixon, Illinois. At his father's suggestion, he next set off in the family car to find a job in some small-town radio station, and talked his way into a sports broadcaster's job with WOC in Davenport, Iowa, across the Mississippi

River from Illinois. WOC soon merged with WHO in Des Moines, an NBC outlet, and Reagan's play-by-play accounts of college football were sent coast to coast.

Reagan also broadcast Chicago Cubs games for WHO, sitting in the Des Moines radio studio and melding terse teletype accounts of the game with his vivid imagination. Reagan talked WHO into sending him to Catalina Island with the Cubs each spring so that he could familiarize himself with the team for the coming season. He had made several such trips when in 1937, just before the Cubs were to return home, Reagan decided to pursue his old dreams.

He looked up singer Joy Hodges, who once had worked for WHO and now was performing at the Biltmore Bowl in Los Angeles, and asked her out to dinner. He poured out his ambitions to her, and she arranged a meeting with Hollywood agent William Meiklejohn. Claiming that "I have another Robert Taylor in my office," Meiklejohn sent Reagan over to Warner Brothers for a screen test. Reagan put his eyeglasses in his pocket and did a scene from Philip Barry's play *Holiday*, after which he was told to stand by until Jack Warner could see the screen test; Warner was out of town. "No," replied Reagan, "I will be on the train tomorrow—me and the Cubs are going home."[1]

On the long train ride east, Dutch wondered whether he had lost the great chance of his life. Writing about his early years a quarter of a century later, Reagan gave the answer: "I had done, through ignorance, the smartest thing it was possible to do. Hollywood just *loves* people who don't need Hollywood."[2] But was it ignorance or an entrepreneur's intuition that propelled him to the correct decision? On his first day back in Des Moines, he received this telegram: "Warners offer contract seven years, one year's option, starting at $200 a week. What shall I do? Meiklejohn." Reagan wired back: "Sign before they change their minds."[3] Returning to California, Ronald Reagan was typecast as a brash young radio announcer, the starring role in a B movie called *Love Is on the Air*. It would be the first of fifty-two full-length motion pictures in which he would appear over the next twenty years.

No previous president of the United States had so bizarre a preparation for political office, and few in recent years had so long a career in the private sector of American life. Most postwar presidents had entered public life in one form or another immediately after college. Only Jimmy Carter had spent an appreciable time in the private sector (a family business), and even he put in nine years as a naval officer before entering business.

Reagan alone among recent presidents, without benefit of special education or capital resources, had hitchhiked, wandered from town to town, begged, pleaded and finally talked his way into a job. He alone had lived by his wits, parlaying his intelligence and talent into an increasingly better living. He alone had to make the decisions "on the margin"—when his choice would be decisive. At age twenty-six, he had a classic marginal choice: whether to stay in Los Angeles as Warner Brothers asked or risk losing all by making himself seem more desirable and taking the train home to Iowa.

Not until thirty years later did he enter public service, as the fifty-six-year-old governor of California (apart from four wartime years in the army). Those thirty years polished the intuitive judgment so indispensable to the entrepreneurial and capitalist system. They would profoundly affect his public policy, all the way to the White House.

Democrats were annoyed and Republicans taken aback when Ronald Reagan, in his acceptance speech at the Republican Presidential Convention in Detroit in July 1980, quoted Franklin D. Roosevelt. There should have been no surprise. He had quoted FDR often in his Republican campaigner's career, betraying the hero worship of a Democratic household in rural, rock-ribbed Republican Illinois. His father, Jack, was unemployed when Roosevelt ran against President Herbert Hoover in 1932. The New Deal provided instant help: a job for Jack Reagan as a local official of the Works Progress Administration.

In his early adulthood as a broadcaster and later Hollywood actor, Reagan was, in his own description, a "near hopeless hemophilic liberal." His membership on the left would seem to confirm that self-appraisal: Americans for Democratic Action, United World Federalists, American Veterans Committee, Hollywood Independent Citizens Committee of Arts, Sciences and Professions.

How was it possible that this liberal young Democrat could in his riper years become the hope of the right?

To begin with, Reagan was never quite so "hopeless" a bleeding-heart liberal as he later pronounced himself. His idolatry for Roosevelt, apart from inherited Democratic loyalty and natural gratitude for his father's government job, was less a matter of ideology than admiration by a prospective radio performer for the president's use of the still novel electronic communications medium. Reagan's mind was on his dream of a show-business career, not the great political revolution underway that he would seek to duplicate in reverse direction a half century later.

Even then, Reagan's liberalism was limited. From the start in 1937 as a $200-a-week Warner Brothers contract actor, rising quickly to $500 within two years, Reagan was appalled at the share taken by the government under steeply graduated income-tax rates. At first privately and later publicly, he spoke out against the progressive tax system as a debilitating force that drains creativity—presaging the economic concepts that would help take him to the White House. Thus, there was no dramatic conversion from left to right, as Reagan himself later described it. Rather, his evolution to conservative Republicanism was easy, considering the soggy foundation of his Democratic liberalism.

His working-class, Democratic background made trade unionism congenial and he was a vigorous working member and later leader of the Screen Actors Guild. Testifying before the House Un-American Activities Committee during its 1951 circuslike hearings on Communism in Hollywood, Reagan declared that "I hope that we are never prompted by fear of Communism into compromising our democratic principles."

But he preceded that by asserting, "I abhor the Communist philosophy." While Hollywood colleagues were taking the Fifth Amendment, Reagan treated the committee and its outrageous chairman, Representative J. Parnell Thomas, with the utmost courtesy. He had long since resigned from the American Veterans Committee and the Hollywood Independent Citizens Committee because of their leftist philosophy and had long been a vocal anti-Communist, though still an avowed liberal, within the Screen Actors Guild. At that 1951 Hollywood hearing in Washington, actor Sterling Hayden described the difficulties faced by a pro-Communist cell in the union: "We ran into a one-man battalion named Ronald Reagan," Hayden testified. As early as 1948, ADA member and liberal Democrat Reagan was telling the Los Angeles Rotary Club of his fight against Communism in the Guild: "We are for the free-enterprise system. We are against statism. We have fought our little Red brothers all along the line."

That speech was delivered four years before Reagan's second marriage, to actress Nancy Davis—an event that, in Reagan folklore, carried him across the left-right dividing line. Nancy's stepfather, Dr. Loyal Davis, a millionaire neurosurgeon and militantly conservative Republican from Chicago, is supposed to have converted Reagan. Whatever Davis's influence, Reagan clearly had traveled most of the distance on his own before the marriage. His anti-Communism and attacks on high-tax government were then and subsequently remained the focus of his political philosophy.

By the time of his 1952 marriage, Reagan felt his anti-Communism had damaged his career and deprived him of movie roles just as it had Adolphe Menjou and Pat O'Brien. In his memoir written at the end of his years in film and before his political career had been truly launched, Reagan wrote, somewhat elliptically: "Probably the most tragic thing [about show business] is to be denied the chance to practice your profession when someone handing out the parts decides against you—this too I have known."[4] A few years later, as governor of California, he bluntly told an interviewer about his postwar movie career: "There is no question my career suffered from anti-Communism. There are the outright Communists, of course, but many people are influenced who never realize it. . . . All one of the influential ones has to say is something like, 'Ronald Reagan, you must be kidding!' and that's enough."[5]

Whether it was the attitudes of the left in Hollywood, his inability to revive his popularity after four years of noncombatant duty (due to poor eyesight) during World War II, or a combination of both, Reagan at the outset of his second marriage was hard pressed financially. Having purchased for $100,000 the home in Pacific Palisades where he was to live until his election as president, he was deeply in debt and without any steady source of income. It was then that a job came along that was inextricably linked with his changing political philosophy.

In 1954, Taft Schreiber of the Music Corporation of America selected Reagan as host of the new half-hour television dramatic series sponsored by the General Electric Corporation. He would make only three more full-length films for the big screen (the last in 1957, costarring wife Nancy). His new career had two sides: hosting and occasionally acting in the *General Electric Theater* and, more important to his future, spending one-quarter of his time for the next eight years speaking to 250,000 GE employees across the country. GE chairman Ralph Cordiner was preaching a muscular defense of the capitalistic system to the company employees, and Reagan's services were highly valued. It was during this time that Reagan developed, honed and perfected The Speech, which was to play an incalculable part in his own and his nation's life. As first delivered to GE employees, The Speech hammered away at the growth of government and warned against communism.

It was in fact Reagan's political debut. As a former GE executive recalled it twenty-five years later, "Reagan had to spend eight weeks a year glad-handing GE workers at over one hundred plants around the country, and giving endless talks to the Elks, the Moose, the American Legion and soap box derby contestants." It was a return to Reagan's small-town working-class roots after the past sixteen years in Hollywood, an experience that shaped him for elective politics. "GE people changed Reagan," said the former executive, Edward Langley, adding:

> Year after year, in smoky factories, he let himself be forklifted into the air to jabber with welders, or he bounded onto cafeteria tables to talk with clerks. In the beginning he tried to woo them with Hollywood jokes. But they weren't buying. They wanted, and in time forced him, to hear and respond to their concerns, their growls against government. A lady coil-winder hit him with, "Do you know how many licenses I need to open a part-time beauty parlor in my house? The government is running my life. Why?" A reluctant Reagan listened. He was nose-to-nose with middle America—and changing in the process. No other politician I can think of has been so steeped in the native conservatism of working America.[6]

By 1962, GE's militancy had waned. Company executives were anxious about their TV host's public attacks on the income tax and welfare state, which generated publicity GE did not particularly like. They were not pleased by national news stories in 1961 describing how the St. Paul, Minnesota, Federation of Teachers unsuccessfully attempted to stop Reagan from addressing a high school assembly. In 1962, *GE Theater* was canceled, ostensibly because it had lost its Sunday night dominance in the ratings to *Bonanza*. But protests about Reagan's political bluntness played a part in killing the program.

It was not until 1964, two years later, that Reagan caught on in a similar host/actor dual role on *Death Valley Days*, sponsored by the U.S. Borax Company. He was to be gone in less than two years, by his own choosing, to seek public office. For the past decade, his political activity had been steadily intensifying as he moved from soft left to hard right.

"No, it should be Jimmy Stewart for governor, Ronald Reagan for best friend," Jack Warner is reputed to have said of his old contract actor when he learned of Reagan's plans to run for governor of California. In truth, despite frequent second-banana movie roles in which he lost the girl (more likely to Errol Flynn than to Jimmy Stewart), Reagan had always gravitated toward leadership. Within a few weeks of his arrival at Eureka College, he was named freshman representative on the student strike committee which eventually forced the resignation of the college president because of budget-cutting plans to reduce the curriculum. He quickly became the public spokesman of the student movement. The 6-foot-1, 175-pound seventeen-year-old "delivered a ringing dramatic speech" to both student body and faculty assembled at the college chapel near midnight on November 27, 1928. "It was heady wine," Reagan said years later. "Hell, with two more lines I could have had them riding through 'every Middlesex village and farm'—without horses yet.'"[7] He was the obvious selection for class president his senior year.

His principal outlet for leadership in his early career was union work. In his second year in Hollywood, the Screen Actors Guild put Reagan on its board as representative of the young contract actors. He served the guild for twenty-two years, six as president. His immersion in union activities was cited by his first wife, actress Jane Wyman, as a reason for their divorce in 1951. But it proved to be more satisfying than his often frustrating acting career. *Where's the Rest of Me?*, the title of Reagan's 1965 autobiography, was taken from the line uttered by the legless Reagan in *King's Row* (described by Reagan as "my best movie");

in real life, the question was asked to find the rest of his personality and aspiration beyond the Hollywood sound stage. He found it in union work.

Reagan's move into partisan politics came at a much slower pace, particularly while he maintained his Democratic registration. As a recent college graduate in the fall of 1932, he had enthusiastically supported Roosevelt over Hoover, but he was considerably more interested in getting his career launched than in party politics. He was a similarly passive Roosevelt supporter in the next three presidential elections, and despite his rightward ideological trend, he headed the Labor League of Hollywood Voters, backing Harry Truman in 1948. At about that time, he turned down Democratic pleas to run against a right-wing Republican congressman from California named Donald Jackson, notorious as a member of the House Un-American Activities Committee. As late as 1950, Reagan campaigned for liberal Democratic Representative Helen Gahagan Douglas, a former actress, in her unsuccessful election campaign against the abrasive bid for the Senate by young Representative Richard M. Nixon (though Reagan years later told a biographer he could not "actually recall ever doing anything particular for her as an individual").[8]

But by 1952, Reagan was a Democrat for Eisenhower, as he was in 1956. In 1960, he was an activist in the Democrats for Nixon organization, delivering over 200 speeches for the Republican nominee—essentially The Speech, as perfected on the General Electric circuit. In 1962, he at long last cut the umbilical cord and changed his voter registration from Democratic to Republican. Reagan entered his new party on its right wing, intent on nominating candidates who would echo his own views. While quickly rejecting bids from the right that he personally challenge liberal Senator Thomas H. Kuchel in the 1962 California Republican primary, Reagan did serve as honorary campaign chairman for the candidate of the right, lawyer Loyd Wright (who collected only 15 percent of the vote against Kuchel).

It was natural, then, that Reagan join the grass-roots revolt of Republican party workers who in 1964 destroyed decades of eastern establishment control over the party's national machinery and nominated Senator Barry Goldwater for president. Reagan became cochairman of the California Citizens for Goldwater-Miller. In September, as the featured speaker at a $1,000-a-plate fund-raiser for the Goldwater campaign in Los Angeles, Reagan polished The Speech to near perfection for the event. Holmes Tuttle, a millionaire Ford dealer in Los Angeles who had organized the dinner, was so impressed by Reagan's oratory that he proposed The Speech be delivered over national television as an eleventh-hour boost for the hopeless Goldwater campaign.

No national political debut since William Jennings Bryan's Cross of Gold speech in 1896 was to have such impact. Goldwater's closest advisers, Denison Kitchel and William Baroody, Sr., tried their hardest to keep the speech off the air; they called Reagan's approach "unscholarly" and specifically objected to his criticisms of Social Security, the issue that had caused Goldwater so much trouble in the campaign.[9] But Reagan's friends felt the real reason Goldwater's handlers objected to putting Reagan's speech on national TV was that Reagan would outshine Goldwater.

Outshine him he certainly did. He turned to the idol of his youth, FDR, to deliver this peroration: "You and I have a rendezvous with destiny. We can preserve for our children this last best hope of man on earth or we can sentence them to take the first step into a thousand years of darkness. If we fail, at least let our children and our children's children say of us we justified our brief moment here. We did all that could be done." On that October 27, 1964, Republicans and conservatives across the country, all too sadly prepared for the coming electoral debacle, were lifted and exhilarated by this spokesman of the right who they felt could sell their doctrine as Goldwater could not.

After the election, Tuttle quickly joined two Southern California oil millionaires, A. C. Rubel and Henry Salvatori, in asking Reagan to run for governor of California in 1966. "Friends of Ronald Reagan" was formed by the millionaires (the nucleus of Reagan's Kitchen Cabinet), and the Los Angeles political management firm of Spencer-Roberts & Associates was hired for the campaign.

Like others on the right, Reagan was enraged by the general election campaign defection of moderate-to-liberal Republicans, who had supported Governor Nelson Rockefeller of New York for the nomination. In a postelection speech to the Los Angeles County Young Republicans, Reagan was unforgiving about the Rockefeller wing of his new party: "We don't intend to turn the Republican Party over to the traitors in the battle just ended. The conservative philosophy was not repudiated [in Goldwater's loss]. We will have no more of those candidates who are pledged to the same socialist philosophy of our opposition." The professional politicians hired to run his campaign, Stu Spencer and Bill Roberts, had been intimately connected with those "traitors"— managing Kuchel's reelection in 1962 and Nelson Rockefeller's race against Goldwater in the 1964 California presidential primary.

The upshot was a confrontation in April 1965 between Reagan and Spencer and Roberts at Cave de Roy, a private club in Los Angeles. The two political managers made clear that an "ultraconservative" campaign could not win in California and that they were not interested in joining another Goldwater debacle. Neither was he, rejoined Reagan. In the course of this and other meetings, Reagan implied he would tone down the rhetoric of The Speech to Spencer-Robert's specifications in order to get elected.[10]

This was the first sign, to be followed by many more over the years, of Reagan's determination to do what was needed to win—whether diluting his rhetoric or dropping old friends. There was no more talk about Republican "traitors." Following Spencer-Roberts guidelines, he did what Goldwater could not bring himself to do: deliver a limited denunciation of the John Birch Society, the then expanding right-wing group whose ranks contained many supporters of Goldwater and Reagan.

There was more than a touch of cosmetics to Reagan's softened posture. Throughout the 1966 campaign, Reagan was a far departure from all recent Republican candidates in California. To the consternation of Republican moderates, he opposed a state fair housing law, called for an investigation of the University of California, endorsed an antipornography initiative and refused to get involved in the far-ranging governmental "problem-solving" favored by Rockefeller. Capitalizing on growing distrust of Big Government, Reagan was a landslide winner for governor without betraying any of the principles he had enunciated as General Electric's political troubadour.

At fourteen minutes after midnight on January 3, 1967, Ronald Reagan was sworn in as governor of California in a dramatic ceremony in the state capital rotunda. After taking the oath, he

turned to Senator George Murphy of California, another Hollywood actor-turned-Republican politician, and said: "Well, George,
here we are on the late show again." It was an exotic introduction
into public life, but not by any stretch the most exotic signal to
come from the Reagan Administration.

This was the California Reagan Revolution. It emphasized
reducing the role of government and resisting upward pressure on
taxes, two dramatic departures both from California's recent past
and from the nation's present. Reagan was breaking the progressive succession of governors of both parties, going all the way back
to Republican Earl Warren twenty years earlier. Elected as Republican governors on the same day as Reagan were "problem-
solvers" dedicated to making big government work rather than
tearing it down: Nelson Rockefeller in New York, George Romney
in Michigan, Ray Shafer in Pennsylvania, John Chafee in Rhode
Island, John Love in Colorado, John Volpe in Massachusetts.
Reagan was swimming upstream, historically at home and currently in the nation.

While enjoying Republican majorities in the state legislature
for only the first two of his eight years as governor, Reagan did
have more than modest success in slowing the runaway growth of
government under his Democratic predecessor, the genial, big-
spending Pat Brown. The state work force was cut in half, and
the capital outlay budget by 40 percent. Overall, state spending
did no more than keep pace with inflation—in sharp contrast to the
other major industrial states.

Yet it was not quite the revolution that Reagan and his
supporters wanted. A major change, yes; revolution, no. Reagan
soon found that mandated federal programs imposed legal limits
on changes he wished to carry out. More important, public opinion
was not attuned to radical change during a time of high employment and modest inflation. Reagan himself was soon swept up into
the traditional and prevailing mood of Sacramento, where
budget-cutting violated the laws of good government.

One of those laws sanctioned tax increases and prohibited tax
cuts. Through the 1950s and 1960s, raising taxes was applauded at
all levels of government, including the state, in the press and by
the academic community as a demonstration of courage and good
government.

Thus it was that Ronald Reagan, having preached for a generation about the ills of high taxation, became the greatest taxer in California's history (though he distributed $1.2 billion of income-tax surpluses in three one-time rebates and pushed through another $4.5 billion in property tax relief). Unable and ultimately unwilling to cut the budget enough to prevent tax increases, Reagan was forced into periodic tax increases—beginning with a $942.2 million income tax increase (still the largest ever adopted by any state) in 1967. Each odd-numbered (that is, nonelection) year, the Republican governor and the usually Democratic legislature collaborated after much confrontation in a tax increase of some kind. "Taxes should hurt," said Reagan in adamantly opposing tax withholding in his first term (weekly withholding softened the pain of paying taxes all at once); he endorsed its passage in his second term. When he left office, the California tax system was far more progressive than he had found it, with upper-income individuals, corporations and banks paying a markedly higher share of the state's revenue than they had under Pat Brown.

Had Reagan abandoned his old conviction that tax progressivity sapped initiative and growth? Not at all. He had been trapped. Unable to achieve or even seriously propose radical budget cuts, Reagan had to search out new sources of revenue where available and easiest to obtain. That meant tax withholding and high progressivity of rates.

Similarly, welfare reform, the pride of his governorship, was also a surrender to the conventional wisdom of problem-solving government. In attempting to limit aid to the "truly needy" (by enforcing work rules and fighting fraud and waste), Reagan enraged the welfare establishment and won conservative plaudits for dramatic reduction of welfare costs and control of skyrocketing welfare spending. He forced able-bodied welfare recipients to work, removed cheaters from the rolls and ferreted out delinquent fathers to pay for child support. All this cut the runaway annual growth in welfare from 25 percent to 5 percent.

But Reagan also increased by 43 percent benefits for the "truly needy"—that is, those who could meet the new, more rigorous qualification standards. As putative welfare recipients caught on to the new system, the costs rose and rolls expanded; they were moving out of control soon after Reagan left office. In the words of one critic: "By 1978, California—a sunny state with relatively low living costs and a buoyant economy—was running only behind Massachusetts in the continental United States in the percentage of its budget devoted to welfare, the level of payments to each family, and the amount of welfare spending and number of recipients in proportion to its population."[11]

California's reduction in welfare costs during Reagan's tenure in Sacramento is partially attributable to a decision he later publicly repented: his approval, after much anguish and indecision, of a state abortion law (at the urging of his otherwise conservative father-in-law, Dr. Davis). Without all those abortions, which Reagan later regretted having permitted, aid-to-dependent children welfare would have been far higher. Thanks to the Reagan-signed law, California's state-financed abortions increased from 518 in 1967 to 135,762 in 1974; the total during his eight years as governor was 276,940. Since most if not all of those abortions prevented additions to welfare rolls, they are responsible for a large share—perhaps half or more—of the 200,000 to 300,000 fewer state welfare cases during Reagan's tenure.

Reagan's eight years as governor became an exhibit in later years to prove his moderation and flexibility and repudiate the charge that he was really an extremist. His administration was not exactly the revolution he had promised, the "prairie fire" for the rest of the nation to follow. A close reading of Reagan's weekly press conferences in his second term reveals a fairly conventional, albeit conservative, governor immersed in the minutiae of government—highly knowledgeable about its details but seldom delivering great philosophical propositions. It was precisely opposite to the model Reagan had promised.

On March 23, 1971, at his weekly press conference, Governor Reagan was asked whether he intended to pursue a plan to remove $72 million from the state teachers retirement fund, "in view of the objections." He replied:

> Yes, because the objections just aren't well founded. This state is responsible totally for any contingency. So . . . if there was a contingency we'd have to meet it anyway. . . . We ourselves support a program that would replace this money. . . . It is necessary to put that program on a sound actuarial basis. It is not on such a sound basis now. It is one of the most ridiculous programs in the manner in which it has been allowed to drift over the years that anyone could imagine.

The crisp authority and certainty with which he answered this routine question about state government in the fifth year of his governorship would not have been possible when he first came to Sacramento. Reagan had learned state government on the job. Not in 1967 would he have spoken as he did on March 23, 1971, when he told a questioner he was open to possible compromise on a tax-withholding proposal being fashioned by Assemblyman William T. Bagley, then chairman of the Social Welfare Committee.

Not only did Reagan know little about state government in 1967; he knew nothing about the need to conciliate the legislature. His was the imperial governorship, far removed from the raucous legislators just one floor above him in the State Capitol. Nothing so typified his sour relations with the legislature than the coolness between him and Bagley.

Bagley, a colorful San Francisco Bay Area lawyer-politician, was in the liberal Republican tradition of Earl Warren, trying to swim against California's conservative tide. He had fought against the nominations of Barry Goldwater for president in 1964 and Ronald Reagan for governor in 1966. In 1967, as chairman of the Assembly Labor Committee, Bagley confronted the new governor with unconcealed animosity. He did not hide his low opinion of Reagan's competence to handle the office, referring publicly to "a Gipper gap in Sacramento" (a reference to Reagan's best remembered movie role, as Notre Dame football immortal George Gipp—the "Gipper"). For their part, Reagan and his closest aides treated Bill Bagley as a nonperson. Correspondence from the governor's office was addressed to Bagley's Democratic predecessor at the Labor Committee. Bagley was neither invited into Reagan's office nor called by him on the telephone. Such a hostile relationship was common between Reagan and state legislators in 1967.

By the end of Reagan's first term, all had changed. During his second term, he collaborated closely with Bagley on his welfare reform and later (after Bagley became chairman of the Revenue and Taxation Committee) on tax reform. To cut down the welfare rolls and win his "workfare" program, Reagan agreed with Bagley's insistence that he must sacrifice his top goal: a permanent annual welfare appropriations ceiling. Such compromises represented a dilution of Reagan's revolutionary fervor but also an accommodation to the ways of statehouse politics.

The accommodations were facilitated by the two chief aides of his second term: Edwin Meese III as executive secretary (the top job in the governor's office) and Verne Orr as finance director (roughly equivalent to budget director in the federal government). Meese, a deputy district attorney in Oakland when Reagan was first elected, had come to the governor's office to handle paroles and pardons, and quickly climbed the ladder to the top rung in 1969. Orr was an auto dealer who (at the recommendation of fellow auto dealer Holmes Tuttle) first was named Reagan's director of motor vehicles and became finance director in 1970. In contrast to the tone of Reagan's first staffers, Meese and Orr preferred conciliation to confrontation. Orr (who was to become President Reagan's secretary of the Air Force) liked to stop by Bagley's office late in the afternoon for a highball and political chatter, a concession to political reality that would have been unthinkable in the first term.

The spirit of accommodation also reflected Reagan's revised attitude toward the legislature. He never became one of the boys, but he was no longer the aloof grandee of the early Sacramento years. Reagan increasingly was directly involved in negotiations with legislative leaders of both parties, occasionally raising his voice. Robert Monagan, Republican leader of the Assembly, later described such a session to Reagan biographer Bill Boyarsky: "There would be a few profanities. 'Goddamn it, we aren't going to horse around with this crap anymore, that's it, you don't want to do anything, the hell with you. We just won't do it.' Fifteen minutes later, he'd be telling some kind of anecdote, something about James Cagney, movie stories and things. He'd have a gag or something to tell, then pretty soon everyone was talking easier again."[12]

By his second term, Monagan and Bagley agreed, Reagan had educated himself in the details of government and had no need for the notorious "mini-memos" that compressed the most complicated problems into a single sheet. "The Gipper gap was closed," said Bagley. Reagan never even attempted mastery over the many aspects of the California state government, but nobody denied he was making his own decisions and, said Monagan, "knew as much as" his staff about the issue of the moment.[13] Whatever the losses in Reagan's revolutionary spirit during eight years in Sacramento, he had learned much about the allied arts of politics and government.

Reagan and his friends, with some justice, blamed the federal leviathan in Washington for blocking genuine revolution in Sacramento. Despite the election of Republican Richard M. Nixon in 1968, Reagan's struggle with Washington over federal rules and regulations grew into the most nationally visible aspect of his state administration, particularly after his reelection as governor in 1970.

The symbolic focus in 1971 was Governor Reagan's veto of a rural legal assistance program approved and funded by President Nixon's Office of Economic Opportunity. For months, Reagan fought that struggle as a rear-guard action against federal intervention in state affairs. In his January 28, 1971, press conference, Reagan was asked whether there was "a philosophical difference between you and the Director of Federal OEO," a civil servant named Frank Carlucci, who a decade later would be president Reagan's deputy secretary of defense.

A. I think it is just that Washington—various departments and agencies in Washington—sort of have a built-in reluctance to believe that state or local governments can be right. You have seen this in . . . bipartisan, both parties. . . . They think out here in the provinces that we—we aren't quite up to standard.

Q. . . . Did you take your case directly to the president— personally to the president when you were back there [in Washington]?

A. . . . Without asking for any answer or reply from him, I simply explained to him what the case . . .

Q. You said you didn't ask for any answer?

A. Didn't ask for any answer, no.

Q. But he didn't give you one either?

A. No.
   (Laughter)

Nixon could not take much potshotting like that from across the continent. On the next day, January 29, Carlucci announced in Washington that the president would not override Reagan's veto for at least six months, and Reagan interpreted this as a victory. He was right. Nixon, believing defections from the right had defeated him in his losing race for governor of California in 1962, wanted no Reagan-led revolt on the right to disrupt his reelection plans for 1972. On the legal affairs dispute, as on other antipoverty and welfare questions, Nixon gave in to Reagan. The governor and his chief of staff, Ed Meese, took credit (with some degree of plausibility) for talking Nixon into dropping his ill-fated family assistance plan of additional cash for the poor and (with somewhat less plausibility) into launching a modest budget-cutting operation in 1971 when they met. Reagan took an overt tutorial role, using "reading sheets" prepared by his staff to lecture the president on runaway government.

That could not have been easy for Nixon to take. But high as the psychic price might have been, the payoff was worth it: by the late summer of 1971, Reagan had stopped sniping at the president. More than that, he defended Nixon after his August "shocks" of 1971—the overtures to Communist China, wage-price controls, decoupling gold from the dollar—had sent the right reeling. When Representative John Ashbrook of Ohio took up the cause of the right against Nixon with a symbolic presidential candidacy, his Kitchen Cabinet and other California conservatives stayed with Nixon.

All this had diminished Reagan's standing on the right as Nixon swept the 1972 election against George McGovern. Suddenly, he was in danger of being eclipsed by Vice President Spiro T. Agnew. Reagan clearly needed something new, showy and workable.

It came on February 8, 1973: a statewide referendum (Proposition 1) to appear on the November ballot that year. Proposition 1 would turn back the clock and erase six years of Reagan's conciliation on tax increases. A permanent constitutional limitation on spending from tax revenues would be imposed, forcing an immediate 20 percent tax rebate. Reagan was back on the cutting edge of revolutionary change. Once California adopted Proposition 1, he would peddle it across the country—combustible new fuel for the prairie fire that had died out.

But the conditions for political revolution at home in California were not ripe. The entire establishment—newspapers, radio-television, business, organized labor, the educational system, the bureaucracy, all Democratic politicians and a great many Republican politicians—opened fire on Proposition 1. It would mean an end to responsible government, voters were told. Not yet desperate for relief from taxes and big government, they rejected it.

Reagan had lost the weapon he intended to carry across the

country once he left office in January 1975. Nor was that his only liability. Although he had infuriated Nixon loyalists by more than two years of flanking attacks against his moderate welfare policies in Washington, Reagan suddenly—and perversely—became an intense Nixon loyalist and defender, now that the president was in real trouble over Watergate. Much to the dismay of his political advisers, he never would make a public break with Nixon over Watergate even to the day of the president's resignation. Agnew had left in disgrace, but his appointed successor as Vice President, Gerald R. Ford, who each day seemed more likely to succeed to the presidency before the 1976 election, quickly surpassed Reagan in popularity among the Republican faithful.

Reagan would be sixty-five years old as he left office, his ideological thrust blunted and with no visible prospect for 1976, universally perceived as his last chance for the presidency. That was depressing for Reagan and his inner circle, who had eyed the White House these past eight years—eight years that did surprisingly little to advance his cause.

On June 9, 1965, the host of television's *Death Valley Days* flew east from Los Angeles to Cincinnati to address a $100-a-plate dinner at the Cincinnati Gardens and put himself on display for some of Washington's political correspondents, who had flown west from Washington to see the new hero of the Republican right.

A bit ill at ease, Reagan told the newsmen about himself in a rambling press conference. As reported in a syndicated column at the time: "Reagan stumbled into the same ideological traps that undid Goldwater. He equivocated on the John Birch Society, refused to say yes or no about a voluntary approach to Social Security and declared his opposition to the most important provisions of the 1964 Civil Rights Act."[14] Reagan was immaculately groomed in blue blazer and gray slacks and looked twenty years younger than his fifty-four years. He finally excused himself by saying he had to "freshen up." The sweating, disheveled newsmen could only grin.

His speech that night showed that here was no Barry Goldwater. His style was more reminiscent of John Kennedy than of Goldwater, his conservative doctrine sugar-coated with statistics, wit and literary allusions (including a quote from Hilaire Belloc). The faithful attending, shaken by the electoral catastrophe the previous November, watched and listened carefully. They believed Reagan could present Goldwater's doctrine more skillfully than the senator. Unlike Goldwater, Reagan transcended country-club Republicans and appealed to FDR's "forgotten American."

The same syndicated column that wondered whether Reagan would fall into old Goldwater traps also reported this from Cincinnati: "Many militant conservative Republicans who paid $100 a plate to swelter at Cincinnati Gardens and hear Reagan excoriate the welfare state have all but forgotten Barry Goldwater. They talked to us quite seriously of Ronnie Reagan running for president in 1968 (though some would prefer Richard M. Nixon as a sacrificial lamb against President Johnson in 1968, saving Reagan for 1972)."[15]

So, even before he had formally announced for governor, Hollywood's Reagan was a putative presidential contender. The question was not if, but when. If not in 1968, then 1972. Perhaps 1976 might be possible (but he would be sixty-five years old then). 1980? Preposterous!

The intimations of these future plans were not masked in the 1966 campaign for governor. Both Reagan and his press secretary, Lyn Nofziger, used the prairie-fire metaphor frequently to give national coherence to his state campaign. But once elected, it was no easy task to launch a national campaign for president while trying to deal with a balky legislature and an intractable fiscal headache. As Governor George Romney and the ubiquitous Nixon geared for a head-on clash in the primaries, Reagan was concerned with provincial business.

Still, Nofziger was absolutely convinced that Romney and Nixon would destroy each other in the primaries, and persuaded Reagan to believe it too. F. Clifton White, the suave New Yorker who had built Goldwater's campaign for the 1964 nomination, was quietly retained by the Kitchen Cabinet to plan Reagan's nomination in 1968. Like Nofziger, White saw inconclusive primaries, with Reagan winning a battle of maneuver on the floor at the 1968 convention in Miami Beach.

Instead, Nixon knocked Romney out in the very first primary in New Hampshire, swept through the remaining primaries without incident and came to Miami Beach apparently the unstoppable front-runner. Under Clif White's tutelage, Reagan engaged in an eleventh-hour campaign that started two weeks before the convention (leaving so distasteful a memory that twelve years later Reagan vociferously denied at a press conference in Iowa that he had sought the 1968 nomination). The prairie fire had burned out. Far from convincing the party that he was the true voice of the conservative revolution, Reagan could not even convince the party's most respected figures on the right that a repudiation of Nixon in Reagan's favor would not result in the nomination of the hated Nelson Rockefeller. Senators Barry Goldwater, Strom Thurmond, John Tower and other leading conservatives stuck with Nixon.

Yet it was an incredibly close affair. So magnetic was Reagan's pull on rank-and-file delegates, despite his failure to have campaigned at all, and so unappealing was Nixon to those delegates after four years of nonstop campaigning, that (by Clif White's expert calculation) a switch of only six votes in the unit rule (winner-take-all) states of Mississippi and Florida would have deadlocked the convention on the first ballot and led to Reagan's nomination on the third ballot.

To the unhappy Reagan faithful, it seemed that those six delegates might keep Reagan and his revolution permanently out of the White House. Nixon's win over Hubert Humphrey almost certainly would close the presidency to Reagan until 1976 when he would be sixty-five—and two years out of office, assuming he would serve only two terms as governor. Would he still be viable then?

Reagan and his men were just beginning to ponder that question in the spring of 1973 when Watergate smashed all conventional political speculation and indefinitely postponed presidential planning. When in the summer of 1974 Gerald R. Ford became the republic's first appointive president, the question was unavoidable: Should Reagan challenge this suddenly popular new figure on the national scene or forever abandon his dream of carrying his revolution to Washington?

3

1976: Defeat

There was no clear warning signal that Ronald Reagan's address to the Chicago Executives Club on September 26, 1975, would likely cost him the Republican presidential nomination by intensifying the conflict between his dreams for an American revolution of the right and his ambition to be elected president.

Over the past year, Reagan's attitude toward challenging President Ford for the Republican nomination had been transformed from a probable no to an almost certain yes. But he trailed Ford badly in the polls, and his political pronouncements lacked impact. He was in need of a new philosophical thrust to ignite his dormant revolutionary impulse. Not since his ill-fated Proposition 1 in 1973 to cut California taxes had Reagan offered a radical solution to government-induced "stagflation" in the economy.

The answer came from a thirty-one-year-old speechwriter in Reagan's Washington office named Jeffrey Bell. A former staffer for the American Conservative Union, Bell had joined Reagan's staff in Sacramento during his last year as governor. His ill-advised proposal in the governor's inner councils that Reagan lead a new conservative party into the 1976 campaign against both Ford and the Democrats had diminished Bell's stature among practicing politicians around Reagan. When the organizing of Reagan's campaign for the Republican presidential nomination finally began, Bell was placed in the Washington office. From his fertile mind came the most radical initiative yet proposed by Reagan.

Helping to translate Bell's proposal into a formal speech were columnist M. Stanton Evans, then chairman of the American Conservative Union, and John McClaughry of Lyndonville, Vermont, nationally known as a Republican operative and theorist. The speech arrived at Reagan's Los Angeles office in August. Reagan's political advisers routinely approved it as a badly needed political initiative that fully conformed to Reagan's overriding philosophy. Reagan himself was most enthusiastic, amending the Bell-Evans-McClaughry speech with his own flourishes.

The speech to the Chicago Executives Club (called "Let the People Rule") conformed to Reagan's theories developed as General Electric's celebrated circuit rider (and would continue beyond his inauguration as president). Noting that the federal government now dominated all sources of taxation, Reagan said:

> This absorption of revenue by all levels of government, the alarming rate of inflation and the rising toll of unemployment all stem from a single source: the belief that government, particularly the federal government, has the answer to our ills, and that the proper method of dealing with social problems is to transfer power from the private to the public sector, and within the public sector from state and local governments to the ultimate power center in Washington. This collectivist, centralizing approach, whatever name or party label it wears, has created our economic problems. By taxing and consuming an ever-greater share of the national wealth, it has imposed an intolerable burden of taxation on American citizens. By spending above and beyond even this level of taxation, it has created the horrendous inflation of the past decade. And by saddling our economy with an ever-greater burden of controls and regulations, it has generated countless economic problems—from the raising of consumer prices to the destruction of jobs to choking off vital supplies of food and energy.

Here was a succinct and eloquent summary of Reagan's economic ideology, substantially different not only from past Democratic administrations but from the Republican administration in power under Ford, as Reagan himself hinted in condemning the centralizing approach "whatever name or party labels it wears."

But what to do about it? "What I propose is nothing less than a systematic transfer of authority and resources to the states—a

program of creative federalism for America's third century."
Whether it was systematic, it was certainly sweeping, as Reagan
went on to tell the Chicago Executives Club:

> The sums involved and the potential savings to the taxpayer are
> large. Transfer of authority in whole or part in all these areas would
> reduce the outlay of the federal government by more than $90 billion,
> using the spending levels of fiscal 1976. With such savings, it would
> be possible to balance the federal budget, making an initial $5 billion
> payment on the national debt, and cut the federal personal income tax
> burden of every American by an average of 23 percent. By taking
> such a step, we could quickly liberate our economy and political
> system from the dead hand of federal interference, with beneficial
> impact on every aspect of our daily lives.

Here was the nucleus of the idea that, against intense opposition, Reagan would champion four years later and carry into the
White House against undiminished opposition: to free the
capitalistic system from the dead hand of government through
income tax rate reduction. But this nucleus was buried in a concept
so large that it was inoperable as governmental policy and vulnerable as a campaign proposal. Functioning without the benefit of
what later would become widely known as "supply-side" tax ideology, Reagan had stumbled over a scheme that posed more questions than it offered solutions: How would all these $90 billion
worth of federal programs be transferred to the state level? How
would they be paid for by the states, particularly the poorer
states? How would tax reduction be coordinated with the massive
transfer? Worse yet, the flaws would soon be compounded by
Reagan's own blunders in explaining the program.

What became known as the $90 billion blunder may have cost
Reagan the 1976 nomination. What is certain, it highlighted the
conflict within his own team between ideological theoreticians and
pragmatic politicians—a conflict that would dog him until he was
eventually elected as president. That conflict had begun as Reagan
considered whether to challenge Jerry Ford in 1976.

Reagan based his defense of the Watergate-doomed Nixon on
"veneration for the presidency." How then could he possibly attack President Ford with the animus that would be needed to deny
him nomination?

The answer was provided by two aides on his staff as the

eight-year Reagan governorship neared an end: Robert Walker, a veteran political activist who had been a regional coordinator for Reagan's eleventh-hour 1968 attempt for the presidency; and Jeff Bell, brought to Sacramento by Walker in the summer of 1974 to plan Reagan's national campaigning for Republican candidates in the 1974 midterm election. Walker and Bell began to interest Reagan in a truly radical political departure: a conservative third party, brandishing a compelling ideology, to replace somnolent, complacent Republicans as the Republicans had supplanted somnolent, complacent Whigs more than a century earlier. Reagan was so enthralled by this novel idea in the autumn of 1974 that he actually broached it at an October 15 press conference in Sacramento.

That brought Reagan's money men down hard on him. Holmes Tuttle, so important in Reagan's entrance into politics, urged the governor to stop all talk about a third party on the ground that it was alienating his future as a Republican. Reagan agreed, ruling out a third party in an interview with *U.S. News & World Report*, published just after the election.[1]

But the option of running against Ford as a Republican was not closed. Reagan talked privately of the strange attitude toward Ford he had found among the Republican faithful as he campaigned across the country in a vain effort to revive the party's prospects: nobody mentioned the name of Jerry Ford. Why, said Reagan, it was as if there were a Democrat in the Oval Office. If that were the case, Reagan had an easy pretext for ignoring his "veneration for the presidency" and challenging Ford. With Ford's popularity plunging after his pardon of Nixon, might it not be possible to seize the nomination?

William Timmons, a senior Ford aide inherited from Nixon and an experienced Republican practitioner, did not agree with Ford's advisers that Reagan would never dare challenge him. Timmons was ignored for nearly three months. At this early point in Ford's presidency, a principal political adviser was his friend and close colleague in the House, Melvin R. Laird. A senior member of the Republican establishment, Laird was a master of the details of government and politics and as such did not disguise his contempt for Reagan as a media creation without substance. Laird typified the solid Republican professional who could not appreciate Reagan's appeal. After succeeding to his father's seat in the Wisconsin legislature, Laird was elected to Congress and developed into one of the supreme craftsmen in the House, capping his political career as Nixon's secretary of defense with a curtain call as a senior White House aide during the Watergate crisis. Laird viewed Reagan as a poseur, straight off the Hollywood sound stages. Consequently, he advised Ford soon after taking office to disregard Reagan. Learning of this, Jeff Bell wrote Reagan a memo on "Lairdism" in hopes of pushing the governor toward a presidential race.

Not until Reagan's abortive third party talk in mid-October did Ford's inner council take warning. Timmons arranged two secret meetings between Reagan and Ford when the president was in Los Angeles the last weekend of the 1974 campaign. Ford was conciliatory, seeking Reagan's advice on several appointments and hinting that he would continue to be consulted after leaving the governorship in just one month. The relationship between the two Republicans became warmer.

The result following the 1974 election was unaccustomed passivity by Reagan. To make a living following his governorship, his views would be on public display—in syndicated radio commentaries and newspaper columns and on what he called the "mashed potato circuit" (giving lectures at $5,000 apiece). He intended to be an ideological policeman, watching carefully for leftish deviations by Ford. But there would be no attempt to build an organization. In fact, Reagan was telling confidantes that the only way he could be induced to run for president in 1976 would be if Ford's record in the next year was so poor that he would not even seek the party's nomination for himself, bowing out as an appointive president who had nobly fulfilled his obligation.

All this was nonsense to Reagan's political advisers, who saw 1976 as his last chance and wanted him to get started without further soul-searching: Bob Walker, who left Reagan's payroll January 6, 1975; Jeff Bell, who went on Reagan's private payroll; ex-press secretary Lyn Nofziger, who had been off the payroll for some time; and a newcomer named John Sears who had never been on the payroll.

Unlike Walker, Bell and Nofziger, Sears was no right-wing ideologue. As a twenty-eight-year-old junior member of Nixon's Wall Street law firm, Sears had done the preliminary political groundwork in Nixon's 1968 delegate hunt and had gone into the

White House in 1969 as a political aide. But hostility between Sears and a senior partner of the Nixon firm who had managed the 1968 campaign, Attorney General John Mitchell, proved too intense, and Sears was forced out—his political aspirations large but unfulfilled. He would wait for a future campaign over which he, not Mitchell, would have full charge. It was a long wait through the presumed eight years of the Nixon presidency until 1976, but Sears used the time wisely to grow closer to the man he believed had the best chance for 1976: Vice President Spiro T. Agnew. Did Sears really feel Agnew's vulgar conservatism made him presidential timber? To friends, Sears indicated that neither ability nor ideology had anything to do with it. "I'm a jockey looking for a horse," he confided as early as January 1971. "Agnew's the best horse around."

But the horse was scratched. The successive resignations of Agnew and Nixon and the possibility of Ford holding office through 1980 made Sears' wait seem endless. Now the only new horse available was Reagan, and Sears moved. Urbane and articulate, he ingratiated himself with Ron and Nancy Reagan. He had become prematurely gray and wore a year-round pallor, looking a decade older than his thirty-six years. Sardonic to the point of cynicism, the mirthless chuckle and biting wit of John Sears endeared him to the Washington press corps and made him a man to reckon with. He groomed Reagan into a measurably more acceptable figure to the media and he promised he would similarly entice party regulars committed to Ford.

Sears was on a collision course with Nofziger and the other hard-line conservative aides dedicated to a challenge against Ford. Nofziger felt that Reagan's great chance for the nomination was mass support from grass roots conservatives who nominated Goldwater in 1964; therefore, Reagan must maintain a high rightist ideological tone. Sears, who had preempted the party regulars for Nixon in 1968, wanted to duplicate the feat for Reagan eight years later, which would compel rubbing off the hard ideological edges from Reagan's reputation to make him acceptable to Republicans of all varieties and indeed to the electorate in general. This conflict undercut Reagan's 1976 campaign, carrying into his campaign of 1980 as well.

Reagan was the philosophic mate of Nofziger, not Sears. But as in 1965 when he told Spencer and Roberts at the Cave de Roy that he did not want to be another Goldwater, once Reagan decided he wanted to run for president in 1976, he would follow whatever course he felt would nominate and elect him, no matter how distasteful.

What almost certainly decided him to run was ideological conviction, although that was not alone in propelling him to the decision he finally took. There was also a personal factor, the conviction that ideology or not, he was a better man than Ford and deserved the right to prove it. Reagan betrayed that sentiment in a conversation with a reporter in the back seat of his campaign limousine driving across the lush San Joaquin Valley ten days before the 1976 California presidential primary.

If the top twenty-five Republican leaders had been asked to list their 1976 presidential preferences before scandal drove Agnew and Nixon out of office, how many mentions, he asked the reporter, would Jerry Ford have received? Not waiting for an answer, Reagan gave his own: probably not one. But how many mentions would Reagan himself have gotten? Reagan pondered only a second longer: almost surely, he said, more first-place mentions than any other potential nominee. He spoke not with vanity—or with contempt for Ford—but with total assurance. That, too, played a role in his decision, even though ideological conviction thrust him into the race.

The conviction grew in February with Ford's appointment of several liberal Republicans to high office, particularly Los Angeles lawyer Carla A. Hills as secretary of housing and urban development. Reagan was not consulted about his fellow Californian, contrary to Ford's implicit promises three months earlier. His speeches, commentaries and columns attacked Ford's budget deficit and approval of a modest tax cut (an ironic criticism in light of what was to follow in 1980).

By early spring, Reagan attacked what essentially was the same détente policy for which he had praised Nixon. Now, however, it was being administered by Ford. "If the Communists get the prestige and material aid they want without having to change any of their own policies," he said in a speech in London on April 17, "the seeds of future conflict will be continually nourished, ready to sprout anew with little or no warning."

That statement crept into the peroration of Reagan's speeches as he traveled cross country in May, never mentioning the president's name to Republican fund-raising dinners. The point of no return may have come when Russian dissident Alexander Solzhenitsyn's Fourth of July visit to Washington was snubbed by the Ford White House for the sake of détente. In his syndicated newspaper column of July 15, Reagan wrote:

> Press Secretary Ron Nessen gave out a succession of reasons why there wouldn't be a meeting between Solzhenitsyn and the president. First, the president couldn't attend the dinner because he was scheduled to be at a party for his daughter. Then, it seems, there wouldn't be a subsequent meeting because Solzhenitsyn hadn't requested one. Next, Nessen said, the president doesn't ordinarily meet with *private* personages (he met that very week with Brazilian soccer star Pele). Then, "for image reasons, the president does like to have some substance in his meetings. It is not clear what he would gain by a meeting with Solzhenitsyn." For substance, the president has met recently with the Strawberry Queen of West Virginia and the Maid of Cotton.
>
> Finally, the real reason for the snub surfaced: a visit with Solzhenitsyn would violate the "spirit of détente."

From that time on, nobody had any real doubt that Reagan would run. But he must have something new to say, and in that summer of 1975, Jeff Bell started preparing his economic speech.

Only one Washington correspondent attended Reagan's speech to the Chicago Executives Club on September 26, and he buried the Reagan economic proposal at the end of a dispatch analyzing Reagan's presidential ambitions. The speech itself received little attention (except for a story by the *Washington Post's* Chicago correspondent, Joel Weisman, buried deep in the paper). The right was overjoyed that Reagan was about to launch a radical campaign in contrast to the frequent compromises of his governorship, particularly in its first term. Sears, by now Reagan's de facto campaign manager, was in the audience at Chicago and much later professed to be taken by surprise by "the damn thing," contradicting all others in the Reagan campaign who said that Sears had read it in advance and heartily approved. Even if he was as upset by the speech as he later claimed, there is no evidence that Sears did anything about it. Fully one month later, on October 27, 1975, Reagan repeated his "Let the People Rule" address to an appreciative audience of Republicans at Hauppauge, New York, on the Eastern tip of Long Island; indeed, it had become standard fare for him on the "mashed potato" circuit.

But the Sears game plan had no room for such radical proposals. When Reagan at long last announced his candidacy on November 20 at the National Press Club in Washington, Bell's rhetoric was gone. Instead, there were two clear signs of Sears' success in moving Reagan toward the center: First, in his announcement speech, Reagan listed "big business" along with "the Congress, the bureaucracy, the lobbyists and big labor" among the nation's worst problem-makers; second, while attacking Ford's foreign policy as too compromising, he promised to "continue" seeking peace "through détente."

It seemed to be working. While second thoughts about Ford by conservative Republicans were being reinforced, Reagan seemed to be making himself more acceptable to the mainstream Republican voters. To the surprise of both camps, pollster George Gallup put Reagan ahead of Ford at the beginning of December as the first choice of Republicans for their presidential nomination. That closely followed Ford's wholly unexpected dismissal on November 2, 1975, of James Schlesinger as secretary of defense, a move criticized by Reagan and highly unpopular with the Republican faithful. Partly because of his semi-public feuding with Secretary of State Henry A. Kissinger, Schlesinger was perceived by party conservatives as a hard-line foe of détente. Kissinger was becoming an untouchable for the Republican right, providing an opportunity for Reagan now and complications for him later.

Despite Reagan's lead in the polls, there were the beginnings of problems that would cast long shadows. Following Sears' blueprint, Reagan no longer talked about the $90 billion fund transfer except when asked (which at first was infrequently). But on November 30, on ABC's *Issues and Answers*, he was asked about it by ABC correspondent Bob Clark, with calamitous results:

CLARK: In candor, wouldn't you have to tell the people of New Hampshire that you are going to have to increase your [New Hampshire] tax burden and that probably as either a sales tax or a state income tax?

REAGAN: But isn't this a proper decision for the people of the state to make?

Bell could not believe his ears. Reagan had been briefed to explain that the "resources"—that is, the tax base—would be transferred to the state to finance the old federal programs. Reagan said nothing about that or about the reduction of federal income taxes under the program. Instead, he implied that the nation's first primary election state might have to end its cherished freedom from income and sales taxes.

Less than two weeks later, addressing the Southern Republican Conference in Houston on the evening of December 13, Reagan again fumbled Bell's directions. Insistent that Reagan's campaign must contain new initiatives, Bell had convinced Reagan to suggest—though not actually propose—a complicated Social Security reform plan involving retirement bonds. As his political debut in his 1964 nationally televised speech showed, Reagan was more than eager to discuss long-apparent shortcomings now beginning to mature in the Social Security system. Taking questions from the audience, Reagan was asked if he had "any comment at all on what I think is the biggest rip-off the federal government has going for them now, and that's the Social Security system." Reagan's reply:

> Young people in the room, perk up your ears, because you're the victims of this. Social Security, for a number of years—Barry Goldwater, God bless him, tried to warn the people years ago and nobody paid any attention (cheers)—and now it happens that Social Security, on an insurance actuarial basis, is about two and a quarter trillion dollars out of balance. . . .
>
> There are plans that are being discussed by a number of economists. One very interesting plan is one that would legitimize that imbalance by simply—well, here's roughly what the plan would do. I just offer this as an example of the thinking of some knowledgeable people. This one would stop the payroll tax, and make the employer's share of Social Security be given in the paycheck to the workers, so that he would have in effect a raise of pay. He's no longer paying the tax. But then you create retirement bonds that have an annuity effect, in other words an insurance feature with them. Retirement bonds, and the worker would have to buy 10 percent of his income in bonds or $2,500 worth, whichever was less. . . . Under this plan, it proposed that they could if they saw a better chance to invest those bonds in, say, a private pension, they could do it, which would make the government competitive with private pension plans—and there's

never anything wrong when you've got competition instead of monopoly (applause).

"Cheers" and "applause" aside, it is doubtful that the audience knew exactly what Reagan was talking abut. The hideously complicated scheme was shortly thereafter scrapped on the mundane grounds that it was too expensive even for the federal government. But the politicians understood that without using the forbidden word *voluntary*, Reagan was actually talking about voluntary Social Security. If anybody forgot that such talk helped doom Goldwater in 1964, Reagan reminded them with his "God bless Barry" opening. Finally, Reagan neglected Bell's advice that he must preface any discussion of Social Security with an ironclad promise to "save" the system so that the aged would continue to receive their checks.

A fascinated observer of all this was Stu Spencer, the professional political manager from Los Angeles who had managed Reagan's campaigns for governor for 1966 and 1970, then gradually drifted away from him over the years. Now, in 1976, he was called by Ford to save a campaign that was moving toward defeat. The *Washington Post* dispatch on the "Let the People Rule" speech, unnoticed by most politicians and journalists, immediately attracted Spencer's eye. So did Reagan's stumblings over the Social Security issue. When Reagan arrived in New Hampshire on January 5, 1976, to campaign for that state's first-in-the-nation primary less than two months hence, the Ford campaign had begun a remorseless barrage on the "$90 billion boondoggle" and Social Security. Spencer soon found better ammunition on Social Security when Reagan, during a campaign appearance in Florida, began musing out loud about another unexplored notion: putting the program's trust fund into the stock market. Instead of attacking a less than popular incumbent, Reagan was on the defensive from the start.

Martin Anderson, a cool-headed professor of economics at Stanford who had been a junior member of the White House staff under Nixon, joined the Reagan campaign in the fall of 1979 and soon began scaling down Bell's $90 billion plan to manageable dimensions. From his first day in New Hampshire, Reagan backed away from his most radical, though patently unworkable, proposal. Thus, Anderson and Bell fell into competition with each

other for Reagan's mind in a struggle of radicalism versus orthodoxy, a pattern that would persist into the presidency five years
later. By the time Anderson had completed his surgery, "Let the
People Rule" was merely a transfer to the states of $8 billion in
federal excise taxes on cigarettes, liquor and other unspecified
items. Nevertheless, Ford pounded away at Reagan's "tax increases" and tinkering with the Social Security system, contending that his opponent's position on the issues put him too far to the
right to be President. It was a burden Reagan carried all over New
Hampshire.

Although Reagan's own polls showed him comfortably ahead
a week before the election, Ford won the February 24 primary by
1,317 votes. The virtual deadlock was trumpeted in the press as a
Reagan debacle, with profound consequences for the future.

The Sears strategy for the winning nomination had been to
avoid Goldwater's experience of 1964 when he roughhoused his
way to the top and alienated half the party in the process. Sears
wanted not only to snatch the nomination from an incumbent
president but also to end up with a united party. Consequently,
Sears did not contest the regular party organization for delegates
in such major states as New York, Pennsylvania, New Jersey and
Ohio. Instead, Sears would use his considerable skills of persua-
sion on his old friends dating back to 1968 and convince them that
Reagan was a winner and Ford a loser.

Obviously, that was possible only if Reagan began the campaign with a string of primary victories, beginning with New
Hampshire on February 24 and continuing with an encore in
Florida on March 9. Ford's Waterloo would come in Reagan's
native state, Illinois, March 16. After that triple drubbing, the
president presumably would bow out of the race. The big state
Republican leaders would endorse Reagan, bearing no grudges
since he had not challenged them for control of their delegations.

That strategy called for a centrist stance by the candidate that
would convince those politicians that here was no madman of the
right. So, Reagan had little new to volunteer of substance during
the New Hampshire campaign. An exception was a tough attack
on Ford's détente policy delivered at Phillips Exeter Academy in
Exeter, New Hampshire, but its impact was muted by its odd

setting (a restless audience of schoolboys) and Reagan's failure to mention Ford's name. His television commercials were dull, bland and purposely clumsy (purposely, to avoid stirring memories of the candidate's Hollywood background). All this would look like a prescription for defeat to Reagan's staunchly committed conservative activists, such as his state chairman in North Carolina, Tom Ellis. A tough trial lawyer and rigidly doctrinaire conservative from Raleigh, North Carolina, Ellis had managed to elect a conservative television commentator named Jesse Helms to the U.S. Senate as a Republican in 1972. Now, Helms and Ellis were confronting moderate Republican Governor Jim Holshouser of North Carolina, one of Ford's most important Southern supporters.

In Washington in early February, Ellis met Sears for the first time, beginning what was to be a relationship of unremitting hostility. When Ellis complained about the inept Reagan commercials and pleaded for an undiluted version of the Reagan gospel, Sears chuckled and reassured him that the forthcoming triumph in New Hampshire would take care of all that.

Ford's narrow win in New Hampshire immediately fractured the Sears strategy. Now the only way to win the nomination was grass roots combat for every delegate, the strategy that had won for Goldwater a dozen years earlier. But it was far too late to launch delegate fights in the big states. There was, moreover, a deeper problem. The fight now required a highly ideologized Reagan appeal to the right. But Sears read the results in New Hampshire as showing the defects of radical initiatives.

As Reagan left New Hampshire, he was on the defensive and displaying little contrast to Ford on the issues. The result was landslide Ford victories in Florida and Illinois. The race seemed over, and on March 20, Sears—acting without Reagan's knowledge and authorization—met with Rogers Morton, Ford's campaign manager, to begin discussions of a possible peace settlement in anticipation of yet another loss in the North Carolina primary March 23.

But that reckoned without Tom Ellis, who insisted that North Carolina could and would be won if the unvarnished Reagan were presented to that state's conservative voters. When Sears and Nofziger still refused, Ellis threatened to put an old Reagan speech, anachronisms and all, on the air. Nofziger finally relented and agreed to air a thirty-minute tape cut a few weeks earlier for a single Florida television station. It was, in effect, an updated version of The Speech: pure ideological Reagan. "To continue on the present course," he said, "is to recognize the inevitability of a socialist America." Fifteen of North Carolina's seventeen television stations showed it on prime time.

Ellis was right. To the amazement of both Ford and Reagan professionals, Reagan won North Carolina, 52 percent to 46 percent.

The victory not only kept Reagan in the 1976 race; it preserved him as a viable national politician for the future. While Reagan's win on March 23 might well have doomed Ford for the November election by forcing him into a debilitating and protracted race for the nomination, it indisputably made possible Reagan's reemergence four years later. Without his North Carolina victory, Ronald Reagan at age sixty-five would surely have drifted into political oblivion.

It also buttressed Ellis's argument against Sears: Reagan could not effectively campaign as a centrist. On March 31, he delivered a national fund-raising speech that repeated the themes of the North Carolina tape. The gloves were off with attacks on Ford foreign and defense policies, hitting Ford and Secretary of State Henry Kissinger for weakness and retreat. Kissinger, though one of the most popular Americans among the general populace, had become a negative symbol of dismay and frustration for conservatives. To them, Kissinger typified a tendency, contrary to national tradition, to temporize with adversaries and seek to outwit them by stealth instead of strength. Attacks on Kissinger now became central to the Reagan campaign.

The combination of the North Carolina upset and the national television talk brought a deluge of needed contributions to replenish Reagan's empty war chest for the later presidential primaries.

Texas was ideally suited for Reagan's new themes of attacking Ford for his proposed turnover of the Panama Canal and price control of domestic oil. Reagan swept Texas May 1 and on May 4 swamped the president in three more conservative states: Indiana, Alabama and Georgia.

But Sears' strategy had yielded a bitter harvest. While Reagan's late victories guaranteed a fight to the finish right down to the convention floor in Kansas City, they were not convincing enough to persuade those big state Republican leaders, hostile in any case to Reagan's toughened rhetoric, to abandon Ford. The party regulars would deliver nearly all the delegations of New York, Pennsylvania, New Jersey and Ohio to Ford.

How then could Reagan possibly win this long endurance race? Here again, the opposite strategies of Tom Ellis and John Sears came into play. Ellis envisioned an ideological battle at Kansas City in which Reagan would struggle for a conservative platform that more closely reflected the mood of the convention than Ford's centrist policies, weaning delegates away from the president on ideological grounds. Sears not only took a directly opposite route, but one that made Ellis's plan untenable.

Sears could not even conceive the rationale for ideological struggle, much less plan it as an effective course for winning a nomination. Instead, he still had his eyes on those hundreds of delegates from the big states who were being directed by their leaders toward Ford but had not yet formally committed to him. Sears' unique tactic: woo them by selecting in advance a liberal-to-moderate vice presidential running mate for Reagan. His first choice was William Ruckelshaus, the Indiana moderate who was ousted by Nixon as deputy attorney general in the Saturday Night Massacre that ultimately sealed Nixon's Watergate fate. But Ruckelshaus was despised by party regulars, and Sears ended up with a little-known and essentially colorless liberal Republican: Senator Richard Schweiker of Pennsylvania, whose voting record during eight years in the Senate was reflected in the 89 percent favorable rating of the Americans for Democratic Action and 100 percent favorable rating of the AFL-CIO, two of the most conventionally liberal political groupings in the country.

Jesse Helms, who with Tom Ellis had prevented Reagan from slipping into oblivion back in March, noted that on Sunday evening, July 25, at precisely 9:05 P.M., he was telephoned by Reagan personally to inform him of Schweiker's new role. He had noted the hour, Helms said later, because "I wanted to record for posterity the shock of my life." Representative Steve Symms of Idaho, one of the few Republican House members to support Reagan against ex-congressman Ford, said: "I thought it was some kind of practical joke. I'm sick." Another of those rare

Reaganite congressmen, Representative Philip Crane of Illinois, responded harshly when he received his personal call from Reagan by attacking Schweiker's record. Reagan "seemed kind of stunned," Crane reported.[2] Clarke Reed, Mississippi's Republican national committeeman, who earlier had considered defecting to Ford but decided against it, was actually pushed into the president's camp. South Carolina Governor James Edwards, a strong conservative and all-out Reaganite, was almost speechless at lunch with a reporter in Washington the next day. "What's gotten into him?" he asked.

Indeed, all of Reagan's backers on the right were asking: How could he do this to us? The answer was easy. Reagan had shown before and would show again that neither ideological scruples nor personal affection would get in the way of victory, and Sears had convinced him that Schweiker was the only way to achieve it.

But whether Sears really believed that Schweiker would turn the tide is less certain. He had been claiming to newsmen for months that there were forty or more potential Reagan delegates, enough to change the outcome at Kansas City, sequestered in those big-state delegations. Now, on the morning of July 26, he told newsmen: "Did you think I didn't have a plan in mind?" But months later, after it became clear that the Schweiker ploy produced no delegates at all for Reagan, Sears claimed that the idea was merely to keep Reagan alive at a time when there was nowhere to go for delegates.

Yet there was an alternative strategy for keeping Reagan alive into Kansas City. On Sunday, July 25, before Reagan began placing those fateful telephone calls, Senator Helms had convened a meeting of Reagan backers in Atlanta to draft twenty-two separate platform planks for Kansas City as a basis for ideological warfare. Helms and Ellis correctly reasoned that only if they themselves initiated such action would there be a real opportunity for an ideological struggle at the convention. Marty Anderson, who long ago had shunted aside Jeff Bell, had no taste for such struggles. Nor, certainly, did John Sears. By instinct, Nofziger was inclined to back Ellis, but he was in no position to dispute Sears, thanks to precautions by Sears. Following Sears' recommendations as he almost always did, Reagan finessed the issue by dropping Nofziger as press secretary in April and shipping him back to California to manage what could only be certain primary election victory there. In Kansas City, Nofziger was in charge of physical arrangements far removed from strategy.

The Helms-Ellis rationale was that the convention could not reject their platform planks and that if they accepted them over Ford's opposition, the convention could not nominate Ford. But the Schweiker shock had badly diminished the enthusiasm of the conservatives who gathered in Atlanta that last weekend of July. For all his subtlety, Sears never truly understood the genius of the Reagan campaign—the ideological fervor that led Phil Crane to defy his state party leadership and Tom Ellis to defy not only his president and governor but to confront Reagan's own campaign manager on strategy questions. The Schweiker ploy had irrevocably weakened that feverish zeal and fervor. It was reported at the time that "the Phil Cranes and Tom Ellises will go to Kansas City as the walking wounded of a lost war rather than militant acolytes of a sacred cause."[3]

The opposing strategies of Sears and Ellis collided at Kansas City. Now admitting that the Schweiker ploy had failed to unlock big state delegates for Reagan, Sears was still unwilling to launch what he considered ideological warfare. Martin Anderson, running Reagan's platform operation, kept a tight rein on efforts to provoke a serious fight over issues. Instead, Sears wanted a test of strength on the floor that would change Convention Rule 16-C to require Ford, as well as Reagan, to name his vice president in advance. It never had a chance, winning public support but private contempt from Reaganite delegates. The situation was later described by David Keene, a conservative political operative in charge of the southern states for Reagan: "We were asking our troops to fight battles that were important, but were not the kind of battle they came to Kansas City to fight."[4]

The kind of battle they came to fight was on the platform. Domestic differences between Ford and Reagan were muted, but conflict over foreign policy questions was harsh and obvious on such issues as détente, Kissinger, the Panama Canal, Africa and China. However, efforts by the right to entice Ford into confrontational battle were thwarted by the Ford camp's shrewd acceptance of very nearly any foreign policy language the conservatives offered and by the Reagan camp's refusal to go as far as Ellis wanted with hard-line Panama Canal and Taiwan planks that Ellis believed Ford simply could not swallow. Yet, Ellis might have been wrong. The rank and file of the convention was so much closer ideologically to Reagan than Ford that the president surely would have lost any test vote on the platform. Therefore, even specific mention of the Panama Canal and Taiwan likely would have been accepted by James Baker, Ford's shrewd campaign manager. Baker later could think of only one two-word plank that he would have been forced to fight: "Fire Kissinger."[5] Ford probably would have lost that fight, Baker added, and Reagan might have been nominated.

By the testimony of President Ford's own campaign manager, John Sears was wrong in failing to exploit Ronald Reagan's ideological kinship with the delegates, including many pledged to Ford, at Kansas City.

Ronald Reagan's first serious attempt at the presidential nomination was seriously flawed. His attempt to codify his lifelong opposition to big government and high tax rates spawned the ill-conceived $90 billion blunder, which quietly died in its crib and was not replaced. Lacking an overriding domestic issue, he campaigned essentially on foreign policy issues so abrasively that he alarmed nonconservatives. He conceded hundreds of delegates in the big Northeastern states after Ford's win in New Hampshire doomed Sears' strategy. Finally, Sears sought confrontation at Kansas City on the wrong issue, fighting over procedure when he should have been fighting over ideology.

Yet, such was Reagan's identity with the rank and file of the Republican Party that he very nearly pulled it off anyway against an incumbent president. The timely correction of those mistakes might have won him the 1976 nomination, and their future correction would put him in good position to challenge Jimmy Carter in 1980—except that 1980 seemed to pose a wholly different problem that lent itself to no correction at all: the fact that, by any logical calculation, his age would rule him out.

4

1980: Victory

While Ronald Reagan was being driven from his home in Pacific Palisades to a television recording studio in Hollywood on Sunday afternoon, January 27, 1980, his long quest for the presidency was in jeopardy. On the previous Monday, he had suffered a humiliating upset loss to George Bush in the Iowa caucuses, the starting line in the long process of selecting delegates to the Republican National Convention. It was bad enough that Dutch Reagan had been rejected in the state of his young manhood and that the flaws of the cautious strategy devised by his campaign manager, John Sears, had been exposed. More serious was the widespread interpretation of the Iowa results as evidence that a man nearing his sixty-ninth birthday and carrying so much right-wing ideological baggage was not the Republican who could beat Jimmy Carter. Reagan's Iowa loss was followed by public opinion polls showing that his early status as favorite among Republican voters had vanished in the wake of defeat on the prairies. Bush had moved ahead of him in key primary states—especially New Hampshire, whose first-in-the-nation primary was a month away, February 26. Losing New Hampshire in 1976 had ruined Sears' strategy and prevented Reagan's nomination; losing New Hampshire in 1980 would almost surely write the end of Reagan's political life.

Without announcement and unattended by any newsmen, Reagan was in the Hollywood studio that January 27 to tape television spots for the crucial New Hampshire campaign. Two young men who had flown across the continent to make the spots were with him. The producer was Elliott Curson, a Philadelphia advertising man with a reputation for innovative political commercials. The director was tall, brooding Jeffrey Bell, still blamed for Reagan's New Hampshire defeat in 1976 because of the fatal $90 billion federal transfer plan he authored.

Bell's relations with Reagan had grown distant. Shunted aside from the candidate's inner circle in 1976 after the "$90 billion blunder," Bell launched a seemingly quixotic 1978 campaign for the U.S. Senate from New Jersey against the veteran liberal Republican Senator Clifford Case, one of the state's all time great vote-getters. Reagan, seeking to show the Republican regulars still appalled by his 1976 challenge to President Ford that he was no wild man from the right seeking to turn Republican incumbents out of office, gave no help whatever to Bell's Republican primary campaign against Case. Neither did the Citizens for the Republic, a Reaganite front run by Lyn Nofziger which was dispensing campaign funds to other conservative Republican candidates. Nofziger himself wanted CFR to help Bell and personally contributed fifty dollars. But Senator Paul Laxalt of Nevada, who had been nominal chairman of Reagan's 1976 campaign and would hold the same post in 1980, served as head of CFR's steering committee and insisted that candidates challenging Republican incumbents should get no aid.

Running a highly ideological campaign based on tax reduction, Bell stunned the political world by upsetting Case. He ran an effective, intellectually stimulating campaign in the general election but could not match the popularity of his Democratic opponent, former professional basketball star Bill Bradley.

No wonder Bell was not on the scene when Reagan's try for the 1980 nomination began. But in December 1979, Sears asked for his help. Charles Black, a Sears lieutenant, telephoned Bell to ask for the same kind of television spots for Reagan that Bell and Curson had produced for Bell's New Jersey Senate race. Agreeing to help, Bell had the commercials written and ready for production before year's end, but Sears could not find time for Reagan to shoot them until after the Iowa caucuses. Now, in the wake of the Iowa debacle, they were being taped in a mood of alarm within the Reagan camp.

Those seven television spots shot that Sunday in Los Angeles received little attention from the press, but proved critical to Reagan's 1980 victory. Three of them, embodying a vital new phase of the Reagan Revolution, were different in nature from all the countless words that Reagan had uttered in years gone by. One thirty-second spot opened with a voice declaiming that "President Carter says to fight inflation, we have to keep tax rates high. Ronald Reagan doesn't agree." Reagan, on screen, then said:

High tax rates don't lower prices. They raise them. In the 1970s, taxes grew faster than any other item in the household budget— including the price of energy. High tax rates discourage work and production. They add to the cost of living. If we make a deep cut in everyone's tax rates, we'll have lower prices, an increase in production, and a lot more peace of mind.

Another thirty-second spot began with the voice saying, "Ronald Reagan believes that when you tax something, you get less of it. We're taxing work, savings and investment like never before. As a result, we have less work, less savings and less invested." Reagan then followed:

I didn't always agree with President Kennedy. But when his 30 percent federal tax cut became law, the economy did so well that every group in the country came out ahead. Even the government gained $54 billion in unexpected revenue. If I become president, we're going to try that again.

Almost a carbon copy of Bell's New Jersey speech campaign was a sixty-second spot in which, after a voice talks about "the largest tax increases in history" and mentions claims by "our leaders" that "to have lower prices, we have to keep federal tax rates high," Reagan says:

If there's one thing we've seen enough, it's this idea that for one American to gain, another American has to suffer. When the economy is weak—as it has been in recent years—everybody suffers, especially those who have the least. If we reduce paperwork and unnecessary regulations, if we cut tax rates deeply and permanently, we'll be removing many of the barriers that hold everyone back. Those who have the least will gain the most. If we put incentives back into society, everyone will gain. We have to move ahead. But we can't leave anyone behind.

The dramatic promise not to "leave anyone behind," which caused this widely used spot to be called "The Good Shepherd," seemed downright un-Republican. It was perhaps the most revolutionary note in some truly revolutionary material. Here was the leader of the American conservative movement talking positively about growth instead of austerity, about pleasure instead of suffering, even talking positively about John F. Kennedy, while stressing tax reduction in terms never heard before from a presidential candidate.

Within a few days after the Sunday taping session, the Curson-Bell commercials were coming into New Hampshire living rooms (using the "Good Shepherd" spot more than any other), transferring votes from Bush to Reagan. The spots were used heavily in all early primary states until the nomination was clinched. It is no exaggeration to say that those Curson-Bell spots, unpublicized though they were, were indispensable to Reagan's solution of his basic political and ideological problems—a solution necessary for him to win the presidency. The development of those commercials and their acceptance by Reagan began years before that Sunday taping session in Hollywood—including early developments that did not touch Reagan and of which he was not aware.

When Jeff Bell was called in December 1979 to write the new Reagan television commercials, he made pains *not* to call his two closest political collaborators: Representative Jack Kemp of New York, a professional football player turned politician, and Jude Wanniski, a newspaper reporter turned business consultant. Bell had been warned by the habitually secretive Sears to keep the new operation secret, and Bell felt Kemp and Wanniski had trouble keeping secrets. Indeed, it was the propensity of these two young men to preach from the housetops that made it possible for a collection of nonconformist economic ideas to be absorbed as the cutting edge of the Reagan Revolution.

Wanniski, a registered Democrat who as a teenager campaigned for Adlai Stevenson in 1952 and 1956 and voted for John Kennedy in 1960 and Lyndon Johnson in 1964, was the unlikely sharpener of this cutting edge. It began in 1974, that fateful year when the nation's social and political systems were malfunctioning amid the resignation of a president, galloping inflation and business stagnation. As an editorial writer for the *Wall Street Journal*, Wanniski had been closely collaborating the previous three years with a spectacularly innovative young economist named Arthur Laffer, who argued that removal of government obstacles—especially taxation—could revive the economy. Laffer, a professor at the University of Southern California, by 1974 was preaching that tax rate reduction was indispensable.

In May 1974, at a Washington conference on global inflation, Wanniski met Robert Mundell, a Canadian economist teaching at Columbia University. While the Ford Administration was insisting that only a tax increase could fight inflation, Mundell argued that an immediate $10 billion *reduction* was essential to avoid even bigger budget deficits fueled by "stagflation," the lethal combination of inflation and stagnation inherited from Nixon by Ford. Dining with Mundell and Laffer at a Georgetown restaurant that night, Wanniski became totally converted to their heretical economic views.[1]

But Wanniski could not yet convert *Wall Street Journal* editorial policy to the heresy of tax reduction amid inflation. Shedding journalistic objectivity and assuming the advocate's role for the first but certainly not the last time, Wanniski tried to reverse Ford Administration policy. He was no more successful than he had been within his own newspaper. William Simon, secretary of the Treasury, and Alan Greenspan, chairman of the president's Council of Economic Advisers, showed no interest. The only glimmering of attention came from President Ford's chief of staff, Donald Rumsfeld. At Rumsfeld's suggestion, Laffer hurried to Washington from Los Angeles to sell his iconoclasm.

Laffer accomplished no more than Wanniski in affecting Ford policy, but did provide Wanniski with a marvelous propaganda tool. Dining with Wanniski and Richard Cheney, Rumsfeld's deputy, Laffer tried to explain how higher tax rates can produce less revenue by reducing incentive and discouraging initiative and how lower rates may actually increase revenue by increasing incentive, initiative and, therefore, taxable income. When Cheney seemed mystified, Laffer impulsively grabbed a napkin and drew a curve, demonstrating the variable relationship between tax rates and revenues. Thus was born what Wanniski popularized in his writings as the Laffer Curve.

A monograph by Wanniski on these new ideas ("The

Mundell-Laffer Hypothesis—A New View of the World Economy") appeared in the spring 1975 issue of the *Public Interest*. While principally arguing the Mundell-Laffer call for a return to the gold standard, Wanniski also wrote that the two heretical economists "go back to an older style of economic thought in which the incentives and motivations of the individual producer, consumer and merchant are made the keystone of economic policy."[2]

That article did not receive general attention, and the politically pregnant comment on taxes was buried in the discussion of monetary affairs. But it nevertheless caught the eye of Jeff Bell, then preparing for Reagan's assault against Ford. He contacted Wanniski, beginning a long and intimate political collaboration. Bell's ill-fated $90 billion transfer plan for Reagan's campaign was partially inspired by this contact, the first political manifestation of Wanniski's advocacy.

A more successful manifestation was around the corner. In January 1976, Wanniski was walking down the corridor of the Rayburn House Office Building in Washington when he noticed the office of Jack Kemp. A former star quarterback for the Buffalo Bills, Kemp had been elected to Congress in 1970 from a predominantly Democratic, blue-collar district in Buffalo. Seeking a Republican approach to helping his economically blighted constituency, Kemp had introduced a package of complicated tax benefits for business. Wanniski did not like the approach and decided to tell Kemp where he had gone wrong. The result was a day-long seminar on economics, ending late that night at Kemp's home in the Maryland suburbs. Kemp was converted to the teachings of Mundell and Laffer.

All this came to fruition in 1977, the first year of the Carter Administration. The *Wall Street Journal* had been aboard the movement for the past year with its editorial page editor, Robert Bartley, an enthusiastic convert. But what to call the movement? Oddly, the answer came from one of its archfoes: Dr. Herbert Stein, the orthodox conservative economist who had been chairman of the Council of Economic Advisers under presidents Nixon and Ford, in a November 15, 1976, article in the *Wall Street Journal* identified the Kemp-Roth school of tax-cutters as "supply-side fiscalists." It was faintly derisive, but Wanniski liked the sound of it. He soon wrote a column for the *Journal* called

"Supply-Side Fiscalism," a designation he repeated at every opportunity.

Simultaneously, Dr. Paul Craig Roberts, a young conservative economist who had been Kemp's aide and now was a Republican minority staffer on the House Budget Committee, for the first time elevated tax reduction to the level of party policy. Although most Republican members of the House scarcely appreciated what was happening, Roberts succeeded in attaching an across-the-board tax reduction as a Republican amendment to the budget. Soon afterward, Kemp met with Senator William Roth of Delaware and devised a new tax bill based on what he, Roberts and Wanniski had been plotting for the past year: a three-year, across-the-board tax reduction at 10 percent a year, based on the Kennedy tax reduction bill of the 1960s.

In 1977 and 1978, Kemp was a tireless, itinerant preacher of tax reduction gospel to party audiences, business groups and even labor audiences. For the first time in a half century, a Republican had a positive response to big-government liberalism. Although Republican politicians tended to doubt the validity of "supply-side" economics, they recognized its political utility for a party out of power. The Kemp-Roth bill was endorsed as party policy, a highly unusual move, by the Republican National Committee late in 1977. House Republicans sponsored a Kemp-Roth amendment to the 1978 tax bill, with Representative John Anderson of Illinois—who in the 1980 presidential election was its scornful detractor—going to the well of the House to deliver an impassioned oration in its support.

As Kemp traveled the nation on behalf of Republican candidates in 1978, party leaders asked him to consider running for president in 1980. Some dauntless Reagan supporters of 1976—such as Governor James Edwards of South Carolina—wondered whether a younger man might be needed against Carter.

The supply-siders around Kemp had no doubts. Under relentless assault from the Carter White House and Democrats generally, many Republican candidates in 1978 had retreated from tax reduction positions. To supply-siders, a Republican nominee for president congenial to their ideas was essential to keep the movement going. As 1979 began, only Kemp, who would be forty-five in 1980, seemed to fill that description. Wanniski, Bell and Irving Kristol, editor of *Public Interest*, urged him to run. They had lined up pollsters, advertising experts and political technicians, ready to go to work at a word from Kemp.

The word never came. Kemp was as cautious in plotting his personal career as he was audacious in grasping new ideological concepts. Whether he would have challenged Reagan under any circumstances is doubtful. But all doubt was removed when Reagan in 1979 gradually began to unveil himself as the political leader of the supply-side movement—a development attributable in no small part to backstage maneuvers by the enigmatic John Sears.

It is doubtful that Sears, following Reagan's defeat at Kansas City in the summer of 1976, thought he ever would be managing another Reagan-for-president campaign. He was ready to take on the presidential campaign of Senator Howard Baker of Tennessee, the Senate Republican leader. Other political professionals associated with Reagan also had picked out new clients. Lyn Nofziger, elbowed aside by Sears in 1976, was ready to manage a campaign of his own, that of Senator Robert Dole of Kansas. David Keene was advising William Simon, who then harbored presidential ambitions.

They were not defecting from Reagan. They simply did not believe it possible or plausible for a sixty-nine-year-old to try for the presidency. Nor did many of them think it advisable. It was the presumed improbability of another Reagan campaign that led Representative Philip Crane of Illinois, the ardent Reaganite of 1976, to get the jump over all other Republican hopefuls in announcing his own candidacy for 1980.

But the decision to run was made quickly and irrevocably by Ron and Nancy Reagan. They had resisted pleas from Sears, Nofziger and Keene that he run in 1976. This time out the Reagans were telling Sears, Nofziger and Keene that he *would* run. He also wanted their help.

Once that became clear, Sears signed on for the duration. But his authority was considerably murkier than in 1976. Nofziger had spent 1977 and 1978 building national contacts as head of the Citizens for the Republic and wanted to run Reagan's campaign this time, avoiding the errors he believed Sears had committed in 1976. Michael Deaver, Reagan's long-time aide and adviser, had subordinated himself to Sears in 1976 because of unfamiliarity with national politics; now he felt confident that he too could avoid Sears' mistakes if given the authority to run the 1980 campaign.

But there was a new face not present in 1976: Edwin Meese III, a quick-witted, deceptively bland lawyer from San Diego who as chief of staff during Reagan's last six years as governor commanded his confidence as no other man. Committed to private employment in 1976, Meese had returned for 1980. Sears insisted on retaining his title of 1976, executive vice chairman of the Reagan committee (its nominal chairman was Senator Laxalt, a noncompetitor in far-off Washington); but Meese soon referred to himself as chief of staff. Keene prophetically believed that Sears ultimately could not overcome the competition from such old Reaganite retainers as Nofziger, Deaver and Meese and that those perceived as Sears' lieutenants—including Dave Keene—would fall with Sears himself. So, after it became clear that Simon was not serious about a presidential campaign, Keene left Reagan to sign on as George Bush's national political director.

But for now, Ron and Nancy Reagan saw in Sears the innovative political strategist that Nofziger, Deaver or even Meese never could be. They were willing to take his advice, indeed to do almost anything he demanded.

Sears was not seriously troubled by Reagan's age, considered by almost everyone his greatest liability. Once Reagan displayed his remarkable physical vitality on the campaign stump, Sears felt such misgivings would fade away. Nor did Sears believe there was any real possibility that after coming so tantalizingly close to taking the nomination away from an incumbent president, Reagan could lose to the likes of Baker, Bush, Crane, Dole or ex-Democrat John B. Connally. Rather, Sears worried about the same thing he had in 1976: whether Reagan's identification in the public mind as Mr. Right would destroy him against Carter. The problem was how to convince the ordinary American that Reagan was no extremist but the friend of the forgotten American he had talked about in the famous 1964 speech; not the creature of corporate boardrooms but the populist of the right.

Predictably, Sears as a backroom politician immediately began courting some of Ford's 1976 supporters who had done so much to rough up Reagan. A prize acquisition was Drew Lewis, the formidable Pennsylvania Republican leader who signed on to tie up his state for Reagan in 1980 as he had for Ford in 1976. With considerably less success, Sears courted moderate-to-liberal Republican governors—especially the highly esteemed Robert Ray of Iowa. By the same token, Sears lost no sleep over defections from the right, such as Phil Crane's candidacy or the nonsupport of the North Carolina partners, Senator Jesse Helms and Tom Ellis. What did worry Sears was Kemp and the prospect that he might run. Although a favorite of the right, Kemp's support ran far beyond it. In Kemp, Sears saw a rare Republican who actually could break out support beyond Wall Street and Main Street to blue-collar workers. More than any other professional politician, Sears was intrigued by the political potential in the tax reduction movement.

He had rebuffed Kemp in August 1976 at Kansas City. Spurred by Wanniski, Kemp—neutral in the Ford-Reagan race—had gone to the convention city to offer his help in trying to move upstate New York delegates from Ford to Reagan if tax reduction were written into the platform. Tax reduction was not on anybody's political agenda in 1976, and Sears showed no interest. Certainly, he did not relay the remarkable offer to Reagan.

Characteristically keeping his intentions to himself, Sears was seeking two 1980 goals simultaneously: to neutralize Kemp as a potential rival and to co-opt the tax reduction movement, which Sears perceived as the instrument for making Reagan acceptable to the ordinary voter. In this, he had an influential ally in Peter Hannaford, a Reagan adviser and speechwriter dating back to his days as governor and now a partner with Mike Deaver in the firm that marketed Ronald Reagan as a syndicated commentator and platform lecturer. Alone among Reagan's old California hands, Hannaford was interested in the supply-side movement as a vehicle to broaden Reagan's support.

On May 6, 1978, conservative syndicated columnist James Jackson Kilpatrick wrote that Reagan was "getting a little long in the tooth" and that Kemp ought to run instead. For Kemp, under unwanted pressure from his supply-side friends to run, this was too much. A few days later, he saw Hannaford in a meeting at Kemp's Rayburn Building office requested by Hannaford. Kemp confided he had no intention of running for president and would support Reagan. After all, Reagan had been Kemp's first mentor in politics as governor of California, when Kemp had served him as an aide during the National Football League off season. Moreover, in the spring of 1978 before the Kemp-Roth tax bill was officially endorsed by the Republican National Committee, Reagan was the only nationally prominent Republican backing the bill. But had Reagan genuinely embraced this radical concept? In truth, he was ambivalent.

On the one hand, the Kemp-Roth bill appealed to Reagan's tax-cutting instincts dating back to his early days at Warner Brothers. Unlike many politicians who had spent their entire careers in public service, he understood the incentives and disincentives that affect the private entrepreneur; he knew how the prohibitively high tax rates after World War II deterred him from making more than one or two films a year and how the progressive tax system had ruined the movie industry by discouraging production. He was well aware of supply-side arguments authored regularly by Bartley and Wanniski on the editorial page of the *Wall Street Journal,* but probably was even more aware of pleas for Kemp-Roth in the right-wing weekly *Human Events,* perhaps Reagan's favorite periodical.

On the other hand, Reagan could not quite sever his affection for what Laffer called "deep root-canal" economics—that is, economics based on the theory that like deep root-canal oral surgery, economic austerity *must* be good for you if it is truly painful. For half a century, sadomasochistic Republican orators had promised pain and suffering to voters and, appropriately, had been rewarded with defeat at the polls. After the 1976 election, Reagan's special version of this was to warn that the nation faced a big "bellyache" of unemployment and recession as punishment for its inflationary binge. By 1978, Hannaford was doing his best to remove the "bellyache" from Reagan's repertoire, but it would periodically reappear.

One such occasion was a chilly Southern California evening in mid-May of 1978 when Reagan entertained a visiting newsman from Washington over cocktails in his Pacific Palisades home. "Frankly," he said, "I'm afraid this country is just going to have to suffer two, three years of hard times to pay for the binge we've been on." Not one word was said of the regenerative effect of lower tax rates.

At about the same time, Kemp telephoned Reagan to ask his help for what then seemed Jeff Bell's quixotic effort to seize the Senate nomination from Senator Case in New Jersey. Laxalt had impressed on Reagan that under no conditions should he or could he support Republican challengers against Republican incumbents no matter what the ideological or personal considerations. Reagan told Kemp he could not endorse Bell or, as Bell requested, even raise money for his threadbare campaign.

Wanniski, in California on a final assignment for the *Wall Street Journal* before leaving the newspaper to run his own consulting firm, lunched with Hannaford in Los Angeles on May 12. Wanniski contended, backed neither by logic nor by Kemp's approval, that Reagan's refusal to support Bell had voided Kemp's promise to support him. But Bell's candidacy aside, Wanniski continued, a force majeure was building behind Kemp, an irresistible tide that would eradicate his personal pledges of support.

While disowning any connection between Reagan's nonsupport for Bell and his own support for Reagan, Kemp did not completely dismiss the force majeure argument. Wanniski and others urging him to run had been furious when they learned of his commitment to Reagan, and they had persuaded him to shift position. When a report of his promise to Hannaford appeared in print June 3, Kemp annulled his promised support for Reagan on grounds even more dubious than Wanniski's.[3] Kemp telephoned Hannaford to inform him that disclosure of a "private" discussion had made his commitment null and void.

Sears now redoubled his efforts to win over Kemp, promising him the eventual campaign chairmanship, replacing Laxalt. No other politician was accorded more time by Sears in the second half of 1978. Partly to win over Kemp and partly as a means of broadening Reagan's support, Sears joined Hannaford in pressing Reagan to join the supply-side camp.

The calendar was on Reagan's side. As Kemp protested to his friends that he could not launch a long-odds campaign while there was still a prospect that short-odds candidate Reagan would embrace their cause, time was running out on a Kemp candidacy. The campaign technicians reserved by his friends could wait no longer and were committing themselves to other campaigns.

Reagan promoted Kemp-Roth as the Republican key issue in the midterm campaign of 1978, as did most leading Republicans (but not Bush and Connally). Unlike most leading Republicans, Reagan by this time meant it. Others might have seen it as a convenient gimmick, but he viewed it as serious policy. That became clear after the election when, on January 4, 1979, Reagan took Kemp and his wife, Joanne, to lunch in Los Angeles. "I was wrong," said Reagan, disavowing deep root-canal theory. He praised Kemp's recent speech to the longshoremen's union in which he had preached supply-side economics to reach the Democratic-oriented blue-collar worker. From that point on, the battle was truly over even though Wanniski did not acknowledge it.

Trying to make sure that Reagan was not only in the supply-side camp but would stay there, Kemp did not commit himself as the year wore on. With Reagan enjoying an immense early lead in the public opinion polls, Sears ordered a cautious policy through the year in which the still unannounced candidacy reached back for speech material up to ten years into the past. Nothing in his speeches displayed the increasing depth of Reagan's genuine commitment on taxes.

This temporary noncommittal stance by Reagan was encouraged by his research director, Martin Anderson, an economist who harbored grave doubts about supply-side doctrine. That reflected the opinion of Anderson's mentor, Arthur Burns, and Anderson's friend, Alan Greenspan. Sears was starting to grumble to other Reagan campaign staffers that Anderson, with whom he had collaborated effectively in the 1976 campaign, closed his mind to new ideas and was not fulfilling his mission of discovering exciting new positions for the candidate.

But when Reagan returned to the campaign trail that September after a summer respite, something new had been added to his basic oratory. In each speech, he would mention the tax proposals of "a young congressman from New York—Jack Kemp," then launch into fifteen minutes or more of Kempian prose. Pointing to President Carter's ephemeral balanced budget which was commended by other Republicans, Reagan would note that "anybody can balance the budget by raising taxes, and inflation is a tax." Tax rates rising because of inflation constitute "a penalty imposed on working men and women." Tax rate reduction is "another way to balance the budget and another way to end inflation. . . . I do not believe inflation is caused by too many people working." The last sentence was lifted verbatim from Kemp's speeches.

Kemp heard his own words played back to him by his former mentor for the first time in a speech at a dinner in his Buffalo constituency on October 5. Reagan and Kemp conferred on economics for a half hour that night in Buffalo. Four days later in Washington, Sears met with Kemp to pin down the deal. Kemp would be at Reagan's side after he announced his candidacy November 13, probably as chairman or cochairman (with Iowa's Governor Ray) of the campaign, supplanting Laxalt.

A fateful decision had been taken. Reagan had separated himself from his Republican rivals who had applauded Carter's budget-balancing attempts through higher taxes and higher unemployment, leading insensibly to higher inflation. The party's leaders had cheered that autumn when Carter's secretary of the Treasury, G. William Miller, addressed the World Bank meeting in Belgrade, Yugoslavia, with a call for "austerity"; Reagan condemned it. Chatting with a newsman on a private plane traveling from Owensboro, Kentucky, to Washington on October 18, Reagan said Miller "is voicing the old-fashioned economics that the choice is between inflation and recession."[4] He had prepared the ground, as no Republican had since the coming of the New Deal, to attack the Democrats for the "immoral" act of curing inflation by putting working men and women out of work—an approach that enabled him to run a fifty-state campaign including the industrial workers of the Northeast as Kemp wanted, not just the Sun Belt states where Reagan was strongest. Whether John Sears realized it or not, he had found the tactic for broadening Reagan's appeal, with a year to spare before the election.

But there was a full month of tedious negotiation before Kemp officially endorsed Reagan. A major reason for the delay was Senator Laxalt. He had learned of Sears' plans to install Kemp in his place and immediately protested to Ron and Nancy Reagan, who assured him he would remain as chairman. Sears promised he would find a way to get rid of Laxalt eventually, but for now Kemp would have to be satisfied with the title of chief campaign spokesman.

Sears also had another compensating benefit for Kemp. At the height of negotiations over Kemp's endorsement, Charles Black confided to him that Sears had fired Marty Anderson, who would return to the Stanford faculty under the cover story that he had resigned. Since Anderson was viewed by Kemp, Wanniski and Bell as a major ideological foe of supply-side economics, sacking him looked like a significant triumph to them.

That did not solve the problem of the speech to be delivered by Reagan in announcing his candidacy at the New York Hilton the evening of November 13, 1979. It raised the question of what Sears really sought in his long courtship of Kemp. Was the true interest in the back of Sears' mind to eliminate Kemp as a threat to Reagan's nomination by enlisting him as a Reagan supporter? Or was it, as he claimed, Kemp's exciting new philosophy?

As so often with John Sears, nobody could be quite sure. Kemp was not pleased by Reagan's announcement speech. In contrast to Reagan's protracted discussions of Kemp-Roth and supply-side economics on the campaign trail over the past six weeks, the announcement speech contained only a brief, relatively unspecific reference to the tax cut movement. Calling for "reducing federal tax rates where they discourage individual initiative —especially personal income tax rates," Reagan added rather lamely: "Proposals such as the Kemp-Roth bill would bring about this kind of realistic reduction in tax rates." The centerpiece of the New York Hilton speech was a "North American accord" between the United States, Mexico and Canada—the type of campaign proposal that is forgotten after one headline. The suspicion that Sears intended to run Reagan on gimmickry instead of radical supply-side ideology was inescapable.

But it was neither the slighting of Kemp-Roth nor the introduction of the North American accord that truly bothered Kemp and the supply-siders. It was a suggestion in Reagan's announcement speech that Carter's "windfall" profits tax on oil might be desirable after all: "I don't believe we've been given all the information we need to make a judgment about this [oil profits]. We should have that information. Government exists to protect us from each other." Kemp had been denouncing the Carter tax proposal as a menace equivalent to the depression-making Smoot-Hawley Tariff of 1930.

Kemp finally accepted the conditional acceptance of the oil tax in return for the announced role of chief campaign spokesman and the unannounced role of drafting an imminent major economic policy speech by Reagan.

In effect, Sears and Kemp were going after the same problem from different directions. Neither saw any help in the preconvention campaign from corporate business (which favored Connally, Nixon's secretary of the Treasury, for president); both considered it desirable to separate Reagan from the corporate boardrooms. Sears felt an arm's length from the unpopular oil industry would be a dramatic gesture, but Kemp considered the oil tax a demagogic retreat from supply-side ideology and insisted that across-the-board tax reduction, disliked by corporate business, was the correct neopopulist route.

Kemp used his new proximity to Reagan quickly, urging him to attack the windfall profits tax. Reagan did so the first day after his announcement, contending in Boston that the tax eventually would cost the consumer ("You're going to pay for it"). In answer to a question, he said he would have voted against the tax approved by the Senate Finance Committee and supported by Senate Republicans under Howard Baker's leadership.

But Jack Kemp was a sitting congressman, unable to be at Reagan's side each day. The tone of the campaign was set by Sears: dull, noncontroversial sameness—sitting on the immense Reagan lead in the public opinion polls. Once Kemp had been signed on, Reagan said little about tax rate reduction, little about anything.

Seemingly fearful that too much exposure would erode Reagan's massive lead, Sears had devised a strategy of caution. Reagan did not appear at any of the joint appearances with other Republican candidates. Naturally, then, he did not accept an invitation to debate six other Republican candidates prior to the Iowa caucuses. While John Sears was giving press conferences at the Fort Des Moines Hotel those first three weeks of January, Reagan was seldom in evidence. All told, he spent six days campaigning in Iowa (where Governor Ray stayed neutral).

George Bush, who had held five high federal offices climaxed by director of the Central Intelligence Agency the last year of the Ford Administration, campaigned in Iowa no less than twenty-seven days. The virulent Reagan-Ford foreign policy disagreements of 1976 had given way to an antidétente consensus among Republicans. There was but one serious disagreement between Bush and Reagan: taxation. Relying exclusively on the same orthodox economists who had advised Ford, Bush opposed Kemp-Roth. But with Reagan nowhere to be seen (not even deigning to debate), Iowans could be excused for assuming that Bush was a younger, more vigorous, more interesting version of Dutch Reagan. The tax issue was dormant in Iowa.

Reagan's candidacy on January 21 moved from inevitability to desperation when Bush swept the Iowa caucuses. It was under those circumstances that the Curson-Bell commercials retrieved Reagan's campaign.

Until the Iowa disaster, Sears' control of the Reagan campaign had been unchallenged. In the summer of 1979, Nofziger lost another power struggle with Sears and was shunted off to fundraising duties, for which he was ill suited; Nofziger left the campaign soon thereafter. Deaver had helped convince Reagan that he must follow Sears' advice and get rid of Nofziger. That was followed by a Sears-Deaver power struggle that climaxed in a tense meeting at Reagan's Pacific Palisades home on November 26. Sears and his two principal lieutenants, Black and press secretary James Lake, all threatened to quit unless Deaver was fired. "Governor," Deaver told Reagan, "you don't have to make that decision." He resigned, and Reagan accepted it. Only Meese, seemingly an ineffectual "issues adviser," was left of Reagan's old staff from the Sacramento days. So intense was Reagan's appetite for the White House that he had thrown overboard his oldest, most trusted political aides and friends in the belief that John Sears was best qualified to lead him to victory.

That belief was shaken by Iowa, but the Curson-Bell commercials did the necessary recovery work in New Hampshire. Abandoning the cautious tactics of Iowa, Reagan campaigned as heavily as Bush and, of course, joined the whole mob of Republican candidates in a televised debate. But polls showed it was the television spots that were winning Reagan blue-collar support. The finishing touch was the February 22 debating coup in Nashua, New Hampshire, engineered by Gerald Carmen, Reagan's New Hampshire chairman. In a scheduled two-man debate between the two front-runners, Bush was maneuvered into the position of denying access to the other Republican candidates while an amiable Reagan opened the door to them. Badly shaken, Bush was devoured in the debate, which once and for all underlined their differences on the tax question. Reagan flatly condemned Bush's acquiescence in the Carter budget's income tax increases, which Bush could not and did not deny.

Reagan's New Hampshire sweep on February 26 by twenty-seven percentage points saved the Reagan candidacy, but not Sears. Shortly before primary day, Sears began his move to purge

Meese, the last obstacle to his total control. But Meese was special. This was one old friend that Reagan could not bring himself to throw overboard. Or perhaps it was more a case of losing confidence in Sears. Meese had briefed Reagan on the financial plight of the campaign resulting from Sears' profligacy. As in 1976, Sears' strategy was based on a Reagan triumph in the early primaries; no funds were held in reserve for a comeback later should Reagan lose the early tests. Besides, Iowa had shaken Ron and Nancy Reagan's faith in Sears. Unknown to Sears, Reagan had made a promise to Meese: in the wake of the elimination of Nofziger, Deaver and Anderson, there would be no more purges. Thus, when a supremely confident Sears went after Meese, he made his fatal mistake.

On primary day in New Hampshire as voters went to the polls, Reagan fired Sears, Lake and Black. The nonideological political tactician who had been midwife for Reagan's acceptance of the Reagan Revolution's most radical economic ideology was gone. Would supply-side economics survive?

Although neither Reagan nor his opponents realized it at the time, victory in New Hampshire effectively ended the chase for the 1980 nomination far more surely than his defeat there had ended the 1976 contest. Bush was finished. Whereas in Iowa and New Hampshire he had painted himself as a solid conservative who was in truth a younger version of Reagan, now he sought to emphasize their great disagreement on taxation. "Voodoo economics" was Bush's memorable description of supply-side theory. It proved politically disastrous. Bush lost to Reagan in successive primaries in South Carolina, Florida, Illinois and Wisconsin, and then it was too late for anything to change the result—even the prospect of a belated candidacy by Gerald R. Ford (who conferred with Sears, now publicly critical of Reagan). But Ford's best friends (including Stu Spencer) told him not to run, and his acceptance of their advice ended the last small element of suspense.

The departure of Sears aborted his plans to replace Laxalt with Kemp as campaign chairman. Instead, Kemp's role as principal policy spokesman atrophied, and he spent less and less time with Reagan, either privately advising him or publicly by his side, as the year progressed. The economic speech in the early weeks of the campaign over which Kemp had been promised control as part of his agreement to support Reagan never was given. One draft of that aborted speech, pulled together by Jeff Bell at Kemp's request, was submitted to Reagan's new political high command—and promptly disappeared from sight. Bell's last participation in 1980 Reagan campaign planning was a strategy session in New Hampshire plotting the Nashua debate trap for Bush. Similarly, Wanniski, who had been summoned to Los Angeles in January for precampaign issues planning, was struck from future invitation lists.

The last function Bell performed in the national Reagan campaign was delivery of that doomed economic speech draft over dinner at the University Club in Washington to Sears' successor as campaign manager: distinguished Manhattan lawyer William Casey. At age sixty-seven, two years Reagan's junior, he had run U.S. espionage operations on the European Continent for the Office of Strategic Services in World War II and had served the Nixon Administration in several high posts (including undersecretary of state for economic affairs). But Casey, one of three triumvirs now overseeing the campaign, had little to do with either long-range strategy or day-to-day issues. He concentrated on restoring a semblance of order to the administrative and financial shambles left by Sears. The second triumvir was Reagan's pollster from Los Angeles, Dr. Richard Wirthlin, who was put in charge of long-range strategy. Ed Meese was the third and most powerful triumvir, traveling with the candidate and running the campaign's daily affairs.

The triumvirate replacing Sears substituted stability for flair and quickly reduced commitment to the supply-side movement at high levels of the campaign. All three followed Republican orthodoxy in suspecting the economic and political effectiveness of Kemp-Roth—particularly Wirthlin, who interpreted his polls to show public hostility to it. As late as mid-April, Meese was privately contending that Reagan's commitment to radical tax reduction might have to be withdrawn as a political liability.

But two factors perpetuated Kemp-Roth as part of the Reagan campaign.

One factor was those Curson-Bell television spots which turned the tide in New Hampshire. Thanks to Sears' profligate budgeting which had left the campaign destitute, they were the only available television commercials for the primaries immediately following New Hampshire. Although the triumvirate liked neither the style nor the content of the Curson-Bell spots, there was no alternative. They would be put on the air in the closing days of each primary campaign, and invariably would be followed by a Reagan spurt in the polls. Frank Donatelli, a conservative young Washington lawyer running the Wisconsin campaign, pleaded for the Curson-Bell spots to get Reagan off the ground there. As usual, they worked. After Wisconsin on April 16, with the nomination virtually clinched, there was neither need to use the commercials again nor money to put them on the air.

The second factor perpetuating Kemp-Roth in Reagan's campaign was Reagan himself. Although he never approached Kemp's mastery of supply-side theory, he had become nearly as committed to its principles.

Among the many drafts of Reagan's never-delivered economic speech was one written under Kemp's supervision by his aides and Wanniski. Late in March, it was resurrected by Hannaford as the text of Reagan's April 8 appearance in Washington before the American Society of Newspaper Editors. Reagan was delighted with it. The speech was one long cheer for Kemp-Roth, reaffirming the political application of supply-side politics: "Political experts used to tell us there were social issues and economic issues. Today the economic issues are the primary social issue. The economic disaster confronting the United States hurts family values, destroys family savings and eats away the very heart of family hopes and dreams."

One listener less than impressed was Dr. Charls Walker, Nixon's deputy secretary of the Treasury who was now a Washington superlobbyist representing big corporations. Like his corporate clients, Walker preferred John Connally over Reagan and liberalized depreciation for capital expenditures over across-the-board tax rate cuts. Joining the Reagan campaign as an outside adviser now that Connally had failed miserably in the primaries, Walker immediately set out to review Reagan's tax policy. Specifically, he wanted the 30 percent rate cuts of Kemp-Roth stretched out over four or even five years.

He got nowhere with either Reagan or Martin Anderson, who returned to the campaign after Sears was fired and went along with Reagan's embrace of Kemp-Roth. But Charly Walker, master of the quick double-shuffle in the back rooms of Capitol Hill, did not give up. On June 20, Reagan met in Chicago with big business supporters and economic advisers (including Walker) in what was supposed to be a ritualized stroking of financial contributors by the candidate. Marty Anderson did not deem it important enough to attend. Neither Kemp nor any other member of Congress was invited. Walker seized the opportunity. He warned Reagan that Jimmy Carter might preempt the tax issue in Congress (the anti-tax cut president actually had no such intention) and that the Republicans had better beat him to the punch before the nominating conventions by coming up with their own tax package. Walker just happened to have one handy: Why not a one-year 10 percent tax cut, with liberalized business depreciation attached? Great idea, said Reagan. It was done that easily.

Four days later in Washington, Kemp learned what had happened when he and one of his close associates, a young congressman from Michigan named David Stockman, were summoned to a conference on Republican strategy. There they were presented with a tax policy statement written by Walker that erased the Kemp-Roth label, cut off the second two years of tax reduction considered so vital by the supply-siders, and puffed up Walker's depreciation proposal ("the widely supported Capital Cost Recovery Act"). When Kemp and Stockman heatedly protested, Walker proposed that Stockman rewrite the statement. He did, making clear that this was "only the first installment of a permanent program" to cut taxes by pledging two more years of tax reduction; the commitment to Walker's depreciation measure was fuzzed over. In fact, nothing had been compromised because no bill was about to pass anyway in that election-year summer, and the one-year cut insured support from orthodox Republicans suspicious of Kemp-Roth. Nevertheless, the incident showed that Reagan, while committed to the essence of his revolutionary tax program, was vague about the details—a vagueness that would take on immense importance once he took office.

In his unremitting efforts to stretch out the tax cut, Walker was aided by Dr. Alan Greenspan, Ford's chief economic adviser who had come aboard the Reagan team as an outside adviser.

Greenspan wanted the formulation changed to 30 percent in tax rate cuts in "three years *or more.*" But Kemp and Stockman dominated the proceedings of the platform committee at the Republican National Convention in Detroit, and no change was permitted. Ironically, publicity coming out of Detroit in mid-July depicted Reagan as the candidate of the extremist right, based on sensationalized accounts of platform planks against abortion and the Equal Rights Amendment for women. In fact, the real story of the platform was Kemp's successful efforts in guiding through the Reagan Revolution manifesto of conservative populism, not hard reaction as embodied in the amendments pushed by Jesse Helms. Kemp managed either to beat down or talk Helms out of plans that would return the party to trade protectionism, revive the Panama Canal issue and attack the Trilateral Commission (a favorite issue of the paranoiac right). Reagan's acceptance speech followed the platform, with a strong flavor of supply-side economics:

> When those in leadership give us tax increases and tell us we must also do with less, have they thought about those who have always had less—especially the minorities? This is like telling them that just as they step on that first rung of the ladder of opportunity, the ladder is being pulled up from under them. That may be the Democratic leadership's message to the minorities, but it won't be our message. Ours will be: We have to move ahead, but we are not going to leave *anyone* behind [emphasis in original].

Hannaford's touch was unmistakable. So were memories of the "Good Shepherd" television commercial. Reagan's magnificently delivered acceptance also echoed Kemp's speech to an enthusiastic convention a night earlier. But there never was serious thought of a Reagan-Kemp ticket by Reagan's inner circle. Despite Bush's talk of "voodoo economics," he was the vice presidential prospect who could best pacify the defeated moderate wing of the party and please the potent Eastern press. The only realistic alternative to Bush at Detroit was Jerry Ford, who would have provided a short-term boost and long-term grief as a running mate who thought himself superior to the presidential candidate. That catastrophe was averted in the Detroit negotiations when Ford and his agents went too far in demanding a share of presidential power. The result was the Reagan-Bush ticket, which diluted the revolutionary nature of the candidacy for the sake of reassurance, an omen of what to expect in the campaign just beginning.

John Sears, who despite his sacking was keeping in the public view as a sometime lecturer and guest newspaper columnist, repeatedly forecast that Reagan's new managers would court defeat by sitting on their huge lead over the embattled Democratic president following the triumphant Detroit convention. The natural inclination of the Casey-Wirthlin-Meese troika to do precisely what Sears predicted was enhanced by Reagan's fumbles as the campaign began (over Vietnam, over China, even over evolution versus scripture). Stu Spencer, Reagan's manager in 1966 and adversary in 1976, was brought aboard the campaign plane to advise the candidate. But beyond that, there was a tendency to do nothing.

It was evident in the media campaign. Since chief strategist Wirthlin's polls showed people around the country did not know enough of Reagan's post-Hollywood record in Sacramento, the television spots produced by Los Angeles advertising executive Peter Dailey were soporific documentary-type accounts of his bygone days as governor. Night after night on prime-time television came the same sixty-second account of a fifty-four-year-old Ronald Reagan being sworn in as governor and signing a bill (ironically, the abortion bill that caused him so much embarrassment). No trace of the Reagan Revolution was evident in these spots, and not much came out of speeches that were crafted to avoid mistakes.

On September 3, Reagan conferred with his economic advisers at Wexford, the estate he had rented for the campaign in the Virginia hunt country west of Washington. Once again, Reagan had to beat down an effort by traditionalists to stretch the 30 percent tax cut over four instead of three years in an economic speech to be given before the International Business Council in Chicago September 9. The final version reiterated support for Kemp-Roth in supply-side language ("More than any single thing, high rates of taxation destroy incentive to earn, to save, to invest"). But the fact sheet distributed in conjunction with the Chicago speech reflected a decision at Wexford to project only modest revenues generated by tax rate reductions. In other words, while Kemp-Roth survived, the Laffer Curve was rejected—an apparently obscure distinction whose meaning would not be clear for nearly six months. None of the supply-siders—Kemp, Laffer, Bell, Wanniski—was present to protest. They were no longer invited to economic policy meetings.

Wanniski feared what Reagan might say when tax reduction was attacked by independent candidate John Anderson in the Baltimore debate of September 21 (being boycotted by Carter). Out of that fear came a suggestion with far-reaching consequences. Wanniski telephoned Kemp to express concern that no supply-sider would be present at the Wexford briefings of Reagan prior to the Anderson debate. Why not suggest that Stockman, once a congressional aide to Anderson, be present? Kemp snapped up the idea, and Stockman ended up impersonating Anderson in debate rehearsals and impressing Reagan with his quick-witted intelligence.

The Baltimore debate produced vintage Reagan, but that was the exception rather than the rule over that autumn. Although Dailey's media campaign was supposed to switch from the theme that established Reagan's credentials as a president to an attack-Carter theme on October 1, the Sacramento documentary spot ran endlessly on the nation's screens through the month of October, thanks to Wirthlin's cautious strategy. "If I ever see you being sworn in as governor again," Governor James Rhodes of Ohio bluntly told Reagan, "I'll be sick." Reagan was coasting.

On the weekend of October 11, a variety of public opinion polls showed a sharp drop in Reagan's nationwide strength. Carter's attacks on him as a warmonger were beginning to bite. Reagan now was not merely coasting, but coasting to defeat. James Baker, an urbane Houston lawyer who had managed Gerald Ford's and George Bush's campaigns against Reagan in 1976 and 1980 respectively, had joined the Reagan campaign after Detroit and quickly won the candidate's confidence. He argued that Reagan must debate or risk defeat, a lonely position for a time. But almost simultaneously, Spencer, Nofziger and Reagan himself came to the same conclusion. Meese and Casey agreed, but never Wirthlin.

The Carter-Reagan debate in Cleveland October 28 decided the election. Whether or not it was the Reagan issues of economic revitalization through budget reductions and strong national defense that won it for Reagan cannot be proved. But face to face, Carter's warmongering charges seemed mean and unfair.

Not until after that debate, in the campaign's closing week, did Reagan take the offensive with an attack on Carter's ability to manage the presidency. Traveling the nation that last week, Reagan won cheers everywhere with his promises of not just one, not just two, not just three years of tax reduction, but three years plus counterinflationary tax indexing after that. Political history was being made: a Republican candidate promising growth, not austerity; calling for prosperity, not sacrifice. The campaign built to a crescendo as Jimmy Carter failed to get the hostages out of Iran in time for the election. The crescendo overrode mistakes and hesitations of the past and led to a victory large enough to serve as the mandate for the most revolutionary administration since Franklin Roosevelt's. As the long-departed John Sears had hoped, the blue-collar worker joined the Reagan Revolution on November 4, 1980, in unprecedented numbers. How long he would stay in it, however, depended on what happened next.

5

The Supply Side

On February 16, 1981, the official holiday marking George Washington's birthday, Jack Kemp was in an uncharacteristically somber mood when he arrived at his office on deserted Capitol Hill. It was just then that the normally exuberant congressman was reached by a telephone call from *New York Times* reporter Steven Rattner. The conversation that ensued was reflected on the front page of the next morning's *Times* in a Washington dispatch dated February 16 that said Kemp "broke today with the White House and said he would pursue his own tax cut plan." Kemp was quoted as saying, "I am no longer bound. Obviously, I support the president but I will pursue my own program."[1]

The White House was stunned. Presidential Press Secretary James Brady telephoned Kemp that morning of February 17 to ask what in the world was wrong. Then came a call from Ronald Reagan himself, who in a fifteen-minute conversation with the congressman also expressed incredulity and reassured Kemp that both of them sought the same goals and that there was absolutely nothing to worry about. Another call from the White House that morning invited Joanne Kemp to join the First Lady in her box when the president presented his economic program to a joint session of Congress the following evening. As newsmen telephoned Kemp to confirm his unhappiness, Kemp hastily backed away from the *Times* report, contending that it grossly exaggerated what he had actually said. He made clear he was still on the

Reagan team and still supported its economic package, and that even though he wished for some improvements, he certainly was not going into business for himself.

If Kemp's performance over that twenty-four-hour period seemed ambivalent, the impression was accurate. Jack Kemp *was* ambivalent, as were other prophets of the supply-side gospel, about the fate of their movement in the hands of the Reagan Administration.

On the face of it, the wildest dreams of the pioneers in the movement that was given its name just four years earlier had been surpassed. In his speech to Congress the next night, Reagan would request what was in fact a duplicate of the Kemp-Roth bill—10 percent annual reductions in tax rates across the board for three years—plus liberalized depreciation on new plants, and equipment for business. This was the first presidential request for major tax cuts since John F. Kennedy, the first presidential policy of sustained tax reduction since Calvin Coolidge and the biggest single tax reduction ever requested by a president.

But beneath the surface, the supply-siders had suffered serious setbacks. They were less than enthusiastic about the depreciation allowances provided by the bill and were downright unhappy about delaying the effective starting dates for the income tax cuts for individuals from January 1, 1981, to July 1. Nor did the bill go nearly so far as supply-siders wanted in expanding the program's economic impact by radically reducing tax rates in the upper brackets.

But what troubled the supply-siders advising Kemp most of all was in the realm not of the program's specifics but its rhetoric. Radical supply-side language had been purged from the new president's economic report, and his speech to Congress called for Kemp-Roth without explaining its underlying philosophy. That, in turn, reflected the fact that supply-siders were not fully in control in this administration. Highly publicized supply-side domination of tax and economic policy bureaus of the Treasury Department was more than balanced by exclusion of supply-siders from other economic posts and by antipathy of key White House officials to supply-side doctrine.

Thus, there existed a curious state of affairs: Reagan was adopting supply-side theory as the economic cornerstone of his revolution but refusing to buttress it with supply-side rhetoric.

The questions raised were unmistakable. Did Ronald Reagan fully understand the theoretical basis for supply-side economics? If not, were his instincts sufficient to ensure its inclusion in the Reagan Revolution against the unrelenting assaults of politicians, businessmen, labor leaders, economists and journalists, including many who confused matters by carrying the supply-side banner themselves?

When he learned classical economics at Eureka College fifty years before his inauguration, Reagan was taught Say's Law. The French economist Jean Baptiste Say (1767–1832) theorized that purchasing power and producing power always are equal. In other words, supply creates its own demand. That means that if there is a glut of goods, it must be caused not by inadequate demand, but by some outside interference with supply. In Say's world of the early nineteenth century, that interference took the form of tariff barriers between European nations.

By the time Reagan had traveled his unlikely route to the White House, Say's Law was mentioned to college students only in derision. The revolution wrought by the British economist John Maynard Keynes (1883–1946) in his *General Theory of Employment, Interest, and Money* dominated Western economic theory. The most popular college economics textbook in the world, written by a Nobel laureate, declares unequivocally that with Lord Keynes's epic work "the simple-minded belief in Say's Law (declaring overproduction impossible) was banished."[2] In its place, Keynes—theorizing amid the Great Depression—held that unwillingness to invest in poor economic times was endemic and compounded the slump. But "effective demand" could stimulate this investment. As developed in a half century of academic and political refinement, Keynesianism was described by one of its most esteemed followers: "To dampen a boom, a budgetary surplus is desirable. There are two ways to produce a surplus: by a reduction in government expenditure, yes; but also by an increase in tax receipts. To fight a recession, there are likewise two ways open: raising expenditures or lowering tax receipts."[3] Or, as described by an anti-Keynesian writer: "Demand management simply involves increasing government spending, via deficit finance, in recession, and increasing government taxation (to reduce the deficits) when the economy 'heats up' in a boom."[4] (Keynesian tax reduction coincides with supply-side tax reduction in terms of recession, but for wholly different reasons.)

This system by the end of World War II was not only the accepted version of truth in economics classrooms but the undisputed policy of non-Marxist governments worldwide. Intent on avoiding a recurrence of the Great Depression and the world war that emerged from it, Western statesman built elaborate governmental systems of spending to cushion and shorten economic slumps. But when the economic dislocations of the early 1970s were not corrected by Keynesian remedies, the timely moment had arrived for economic heresy.

Arthur Laffer was a heretic. His Boswell, Jude Wanniski, called him a "modern Say, arguing that the supply of goods creates a demand for goods and that the supply of goods can be increased by removing government impediments to production and commerce."[5] Those "impediments" were described as a "wedge" in a 1974 memorandum written by Laffer as a consultant to the secretary of the Treasury. Calling it "a simple truth" that use of "people, machines, land and other factors of production" is based on people's "ability to earn after-tax income," he continued:

> Marginal taxes of all sorts stand as a wedge between what an employer pays his factors of production and what they ultimately receive in after-tax income. In order to increase total output, policy measures must have the effect of both increasing firms' demand for productive factors and increasing the productive factors' desire to be employed. Taxes of all sorts must be reduced. These reductions will be most effective where they lower marginal tax rates the most. Any reduction in marginal rates means that the employer will pay less and yet employees will receive more. Both from the employer and employee point of view, more employment will be desired and more output will be forthcoming.[6]

Over six years later as Reagan was inaugurated, this memo (a plea for tax reduction, ignored by the Ford Administration to which it was addressed) faithfully reflected supply-side doctrine, which by then had accumulated a substantial body of literature. Its key element remained constant: the impact on decisions made by any individual of the *marginal* tax rate—the effective tax on the last dollar he earns. "When someone is considering starting a new business, learning a new skill, investing in stock or taking a second job," Kemp wrote in 1979, "what matters is not the average tax on his or her existing earnings, *but how much of any added earnings he or she will be allowed to keep.* Without added earnings there can be no added production, and without added production there can be no growth" (emphasis in original).[7]

This mandates an effective supply-side policy that must reduce the top marginal rate, not merely rates in lower brackets that would affect all taxpayers; it also presupposes that the taxpayer will work more if taxed less, not work less as Keynesians have theorized. Instead of inducing the breadwinner to work longer and harder on his job, as maintained by the Keynesians, high tax rates are seen by supply-siders as pushing workers into an "underground" economy where income is not reported to the Internal Revenue Service—from barter transactions to moonlighting jobs paid in cash to outright criminal activity. Indeed, the supply-side theory that tax rate reduction would increase tax revenue stems from both the effect of incentives on harder work and higher production and the transfer of underground activity into the legal money economy.

This added revenue would cushion the supposed inflationary effect of tax rate reduction, but anti-inflationary supply-side arguments do not end there. They hold that the lowered marginal tax rates would so greatly expand savings that the remaining deficit could be financed with less inflationary impact than without those expanded savings. Presumably, the tax cut will be converted into savings more than consumer spending, though the percentage converted to savings will be higher in the upper-income brackets.

It naturally follows that any tax rate reduction must be across the board—equal in percentage for the rich and the poor. That is what was so remarkable in the tax cut first proposed by President Kennedy in 1963 and enacted in 1964 after his death. According to Wanniski, "Had Kennedy only cut the lower rates, thus increasing the progressivity of the system, the economic effect would have been negative."[8]

But strict adherence to across-the-board tax reduction means abandonment of a half century of using the graduated tax system to redistribute wealth. That, in turn, presupposes an economy in growth rather than contraction. So the supply-side doctrine completes the circle: to expand, there must be tax rate reduction for *all* taxpayers rich and poor; for the political system to be able to accept larger sums of tax reduction for the rich than the poor, the economy must be expanding.

The rationale for not trying to soak the rich is that it simply does not work; the higher the rates, the more the rich go into nonproductive tax shelters (the rich man's version of the underground economy). The answer, in a *Wall Street Journal* editorial of March 1977 (that could have been written by nobody other than Wanniski), was not to eliminate tax shelters, since the rich simply would not "risk $1 million and two years' hard work for $5,719 in after-tax income." Instead,

> Why not tax the rich by lowering the rates they face? They will thus be enticed back from their yachts and once again assemble widget plants in New York City, with tax revenues flowing to Washington, Albany and City Hall not only from them, but also from all those who would then be usefully employed in widget-making. By all means, tax the rich! But do it right, and in this fashion lift the burdens of taxation from those who aren't rich.[9]

That was no easy prescription, because of the way the rich handled their money to avoid subjecting it to confiscatory taxation. Besides putting it in tax shelters, they converted it to gold and other hoarded collectibles, as eloquently described by George Gilder. Four years after the Wanniski editorial, Gilder wrote that "this is the gravest peril of capitalism in our current inflationary period. As the wealthy consume more and invest less, resentment toward them increases and ignorant or demagogic politicians impose yet higher rates to punish them. The rich discover that it is easier and more gratifying to spend money than to earn it for the government, and they get a yen to travel and invest abroad. The problem becomes worse in a vicious spiral of taxation and capital flight."[10] Gilder's rich are the risk-taking benefactors of the capitalist society, "fostering opportunities for the classes below them in the continuing drama of the creation of wealth and progress."[11]

For a government in a democratic society to enable the rich to perform that role requires acceptance of Gilder's "essential insight of supply-side economics. Government cannot significantly affect real aggregate demand through policies of taxing and spending—

taking money from one man and giving it to another, whether in government or out. All this shifting of wealth is a zero sum game and the net effect on incomes is usually zero, or even negative."[12] Because of his own experience and instincts, Reagan shared Gilder's insight. But how deeply he was to share this most radical aspect of his revolution while his aides remained deeply skeptical was to be an important question in his early months in office.

Supply-side doctrine was radical but not new. What Kemp, Wanniski and Gilder were describing had been played out on the world stage a millennium earlier. Will Durant has described how the Pax Romana, built not only by arms but by equitable and mild taxation, was undermined by "the socialism of Diocletian."[13] The massive governmental undertakings of the Roman emperor Diocletian's reign (284–305) were so costly that, with deficit financing yet undiscovered, "taxation rose to unprecedented peaks of ubiquitous continuity"—accompanied by rigorous enforcement (including torture to prevent tax avoidance).

> Toward the end of the third century, and still more in the fourth, flight from taxes became almost epidemic in the empire. The well-to-do concealed their riches, local aristocrats had themselves reclassified as *humiliores* [lowly persons] to escape election to municipal office, artisans deserted their trades, peasant proprietors left their overtaxed holdings to become hired men, many villages and some towns (*e.g.*, Tiberias in Palestine) were abandoned because of high assessments; at last in the fourth century, thousands of citizens fled over the border to seek refuge among the barbarians.[14]

In analyzing the fall of the Roman Empire, Durant cites economic factors, including "the discouragement of ability and the absorption of investment capital by confiscatory taxation," that left Rome "a political ghost surviving economic death."[15] That cast an economic pall over Europe that was not entirely lifted until the late eighteenth century with the American and French revolutions, both described by Wanniski as "rebellions against the upper reaches of the Laffer Curve."[16] Both the American and French revolutionaries were protesting high tax rates, which were followed by long periods of low tax rates and sustained economic growth.

That changed for the United States with entrance into World War I. To finance it, the federal income tax (sanctioned by constitutional amendment only four years earlier in 1913) ventured for the first time into confiscatory taxation; the 1913–1915 top marginal rate of 7 percent on income over $500,000 by 1918 was 77 percent on income over $1 million. Fearful of the huge national debt left by the war, the Democratic Congress and administration would not reduce the top marginal rate below 73 percent. President Warren G. Harding, the Republican elected in 1920, pledged in his Inaugural Address to "strike at war taxation" and ensured reaching that goal by naming Andrew Mellon, the millionaire Pittsburgh banker, as his secretary of the Treasury.

Mellon's views on taxation were as modern as those of Arthur Laffer and as ancient as those of Ibn Khaldun, the fourteenth-century Arab historian who reported the phenomenon of tax revenue decreasing as tax rates increase. Tax rates were reduced by Congress in 1921 to a top marginal rate of 58 percent, but that was not nearly enough for Mellon. Calvin Coolidge succeeded to the presidency after Harding's death in 1923; no such enthusiastic tax-cutter was to enter the White House for fifty-eight years. Encouraged by Coolidge, Mellon in the election year of 1924 was seeking a top marginal rate of 25 percent. His argument evokes the supply-siders of a half century later:

> The history of taxation shows that taxes which are inherently excessive are not paid. . . . Experience has shown that the present high rates of surtax are bringing in each year progressively less revenue to the government. This means that the price is too high to the large taxpayer and he is avoiding a taxable income by the many ways which are available to him. What rates will bring in the largest revenue to the government experience has not developed, but it is estimated that by cutting the surtaxes in half, the government, when the full effect of the reduction is felt, will receive more revenue from the owners of large incomes at the lower rates of tax than it would have received at the higher rates. . . .

> An income tax is the price which the government charges for the privilege of having taxable income. If the price is too low, the government's revenue is not large enough; if the price is too high, the taxpayer, through the many means available, avoids a taxable income and the government gets less out of a high tax than it would get out of a lower one.[17]

This preconception of the Laffer Curve proved accurate. Although in 1925 the top marginal rate fell to 25 percent, revenue increased for the year. So did returns filed by the rich. While 44 percent of all taxpayers (in the lower brackets) were removed from the rolls, the percentage of the rich increased dramatically (a 67 percent increase of taxpayers earning over $100,000). Precisely this had been predicted to the National Republican Club by Coolidge when he declared: "I agree perfectly with those who wish to relieve the small taxpayer by getting the largest possible contribution from the people with large incomes. But if the rates on large incomes are so high that they disappear, the small taxpayer will be left to bear the entire burden. If on the other hand the rates are placed where they will get the most revenue from large incomes, then the small taxpayer will be relieved." The Coolidge-Mellon tax reduction program generated not only high federal revenues but growth and prosperity.

There has been speculation that if Coolidge had sought and gained a third term in 1928, he and Mellon would have recommended even more reduction. As it was, serious tax reduction was finished for another thirty-five years. Under President Herbert Hoover, the dominant force at the Treasury was his hand-picked anti-tax-cutter Ogden Mills, first as undersecretary to Mellon and in 1930 as secretary. The Hoover-Mills team, while barring the door to further tax rate reduction, agreed to a tax increase of catastrophic consequences: the Smoot-Hawley Tariff Act. Whether or not Wanniski and the other supply-siders are correct in attributing the stock market crash of 1929 to Hoover's acceptance of Smoot-Hawley's progress through Congress, the inexorable workings of the Laffer Curve reduced customs revenue from higher tariffs. Faced with the advent of the Great Depression and a widening budget deficit, Hoover and Mills committed a fatal act that condemned their party to fifty years in the wilderness: a tax increase. In 1932, the top marginal rate was raised to 63 percent. As Mellon knew all too well it would, it further depressed the economy without bringing in new revenue.

Hoover had sought higher taxes to balance the budget. Franklin D. Roosevelt, the initiator of a political revolution, wanted higher tax rates to finance New Deal spending. In 1935, the top marginal rate was pushed up to 75 percent. In 1936, Roosevelt won from Congress tax increases on corporate profits. What followed was the 1937 recession, from which the nation never fully recovered until World War II. Wartime financing requirements raised the top marginal rate to a peak of 94 percent. It was still 86 percent after the war's end in 1946. The Republican Eightieth Congress elected in 1946 tried to turn back the clock to Coolidge-Mellon with a 20 percent across-the-board tax reduction, but President Harry Truman vetoed it twice. In 1948, on the third try, Senator Robert A. Taft finally got through a tax reduction, but with the top marginal rate cut only four percentage points to 82 percent, increasing rather than decreasing the progressivity of the system. The start of the Korean War in 1950 brought massive tax increases anyway, with the top marginal rate back to 91 percent.

Nor did the election of a Republican in 1952 bring Taft, the vestigial preservator of the Coolidge-Mellon tradition, any greater success. President Dwight D. Eisenhower followed the advice of George Humphrey, a Cleveland steel magnate who was secretary of the Treasury, and Dr. Arthur F. Burns, a Columbia University economics professor who was chairman of the president's Council of Economic Advisers, both of whom opposed tax rate reductions while the budget was out of balance. In 1953, Eisenhower blocked efforts by the only Republican Congress in his administration to cut taxes across the board. In 1955, Humphrey changed his mind and pushed for tax reduction (on Keynesian countercyclical grounds to fight recession); Burns still opposed cuts, and Eisenhower backed him. In 1958, Burns (now back at Columbia) changed his mind, and backed tax reduction (also on Keynesian grounds to fight recession); Humphrey's successor at the Treasury, Robert Anderson, convinced Eisenhower to oppose it. Incredibly, Eisenhower's eight years ended with no major tax cut and the economy stagnant.

What Eisenhower's young Democratic successor next did earned him a niche in the supply-side pantheon. The posthumous passage of Kennedy's tax reduction, the first determined presidential effort for across-the-board tax reduction since Coolidge, brought the top marginal rate down to 70 percent and generated an expansionary surge in the economy. Surprised business audiences across the country in the 1970s heard Laffer and Kemp extol Kennedy as a forerunner of the supply-side movement. They quoted the Democratic president's contention that "a rising tide lifts all boats" and his challenge that "our practical choice" is between a "chronic deficit of inertia, as the unwanted result of inadequate revenues and a restricted economy—or a temporary deficit of transition, resulting from a tax cut designed to boost the economy, increase tax revenue and achieve a future budget surplus."

That might evoke echoes of Coolidge and Mellon and a preview of Reagan and Kemp, but such comparisons mislead. "He was unquestionably the first Keynesian president," said his aide and biographer, Arthur Schlesinger, Jr.[18] The Kennedy tax cut was based on Keynesian theory as an intentional effort to enlarge a supposedly stimulative deficit; tax cuts were preferred over spending increases only because they were more politically feasible. Writing in 1978, Wanniski argued that "the only successful 'Keynesian' economic event of the past forty years was the Kennedy-Johnson tax cut of 1962–64, coincident with the Kennedy Round tariff negotiations of 1964. . . ."[19] While the tax cuts were pursued within a Keynesian framework by Kennedy's Council of Economic Advisers, their motivation at the Treasury was even further removed from supply-side economic expansion: as a supposed sweetener to facilitate removal of tax advantages for business and upper-income taxpayers ("reforms" which in fact were rejected by Congress and abandoned by Kennedy).

This mixed and fuzzy ideological parentage for the Kennedy tax cuts was to undermine their future. Lacking the doctrinal base of Coolidge's tax cuts, the Kennedy cuts could not survive. Although Lyndon B. Johnson promptly gained passage of the stalled tax bill as a "monument" to his assassinated predecessor, he became a tax *increaser* as the Vietnam War lengthened and broadened. By the time he left office in 1969, Johnson's surtax had put the top marginal rate back up to 77 percent.

"We are all Keynesians," Richard Nixon declared in explaining his economic program. Breaking his 1968 campaign commitment to end the surtax, President Nixon extended it for a year in his 1969 tax "reform" bill. That measure raised taxes in other, more permanent ways, most notably in tightening treatment of capital gains. Charls Walker, masterminding Nixon Administration tax strategy as undersecretary of the Treasury, pushed through a "maximum" tax lowering the top marginal rate to 50 percent but at a cost that negated any beneficial effect: the top marginal rate on income from dividends and interest (now called "unearned" income) was to be kept at 70 percent, not only creating two classes of income for the first time but ensuring that funds of the rich would go to tax shelters rather than productive enterprises.

The worldwide economic shocks of 1973, the advent of chronic inflation amid the decline of the dollar and continuous economic stagnation, brought no change from the successive administrations of Republican Gerald Ford or Democrat Jimmy Carter, both of whom emulated Herbert Hoover in trying to balance the budget with tax increases, as impossible then as it was fifty years earlier. Carter especially was the victim of Keynesian inability to cope with the economy, his efforts to fine-tune it confounded both by forecasting error and by the prospensity of ever-higher tax rates (through inflationary progression of taxpayers to higher marginal rates) to aggravate both inflation and stagnation. To the end Carter was true to his Keynesian mentors, threatening as a lame duck to veto any tax reduction measure passed following his defeat by Reagan.

The reason for talk about a lame duck tax veto stemmed from the election night tax statements of November 4, 1980, by Senator Robert Dole of Kansas. Unexpected Republican control of the Senate would soon elevate him to chairmanship of the Finance Committee, and an exuberant Dole impulsively proposed passage of tax reduction during the lame duck session of Congress. The bill he had in mind, approved by near unanimous vote of the Finance Committee during the election year summer, adopted liberalized depreciation allowances but cut individual tax income rates only an average of 4 percent and just 1 percent in the top marginal rate for all incomes over $50,000. It was grossly inadequate by supply-side standards but had been endorsed in the summer of 1980 by all Republicans, Reagan included, as an election-year goad to Carter and the congressional Democratic leadership, who had no intention of letting even so inadequate a measure pass.

On November 6 at his first postelection press conference in Los Angeles, President-elect Reagan was asked about Dole's suggested lame duck tax passage. "It'll be fine with me," was the breezy reply. Three days later, his chief of staff, Edwin Meese, hardened that into policy by specifically endorsing lame duck passage of the tax bill. Kemp and the other supply-siders were desolated. Passage of the inadequate tax bill in 1980 would blight their expansive plans for 1981. Hurried strategy sessions were called to discuss sending a delegation to Reagan at his Santa Barbara ranch to dissuade him, but Jimmy Carter saved them the trouble. True to the last to Keynesian doctrine that tax cuts fuel inflation, Carter threatened a veto and House Democratic leaders suppressed any tax activity.

That confirmed suspicions not about Reagan's commitment to tax reduction but about his understanding of supply-side doctrine. Those suspicions were raised during the final week of the campaign when his persistent calls for Kemp-Roth-style tax reduction were justified with the argument that the nation's capacity was "underutilized"—a Keynesian, not a supply-side, justification that implied tax rate reduction would *not* be justified if the economy were prosperous. That formulation had been hurriedly prepared by a speechwriter unversed in economic doctrine working in the confusion of a campaign plane, but the fact is that Reagan read the words without flinching. His November 6 acceptance of the Senate Finance Committee tax bill suggested to the supply-siders that the new president badly needed counselors by his side.

Their principal objective was not the Treasury, where tax policy was made, but the Office of Management and Budget. For much of the past twenty years, budget directors had been in the vanguard of those opposing tax cuts. The supply-siders wanted an OMB director who, if budget cuts were not deep enough to meet Reagan's specifications, would still not only support tax reduction but would insist on it. Their man was David Stockman, the young congressman from Michigan who had been a Vietnam War dissenter in college, attended divinity school at Harvard (where he was a live-in student in the home of Professor Daniel Patrick Moynihan, now Democratic senator from New York) and was John Anderson's aide in Congress. Innovative, aggressive and sometimes abrasive, Stockman did not meet the specifications being set for Reagan's Cabinet. He was certainly not on the list of recommendations by the Kitchen Cabinet, Reagan's millionaire friends who were advising him on Cabinet selections. Nor did Meese, who preferred mature and colorless figures out of the establishment, want Stockman. Indeed, Stockman would not have been named to OMB had he not so impressed Reagan impersonating his old boss, Anderson, in the debate rehearsals; that performance, in turn, won Stockman the job of impersonating Carter in rehearsals for the second debate. After the election, Reagan told Stockman that although he believed he had taken the measure of John Anderson in debates, he had never defeated David Stockman. Consequently, Reagan was more than receptive when Kemp pressed hard for Stockman at OMB.

The supply-siders never truly had a viable candidate for Treasury, where Meese and the Kitchen Cabinet wanted a substantial captain of industry and finally chose Donald T. Regan, chairman of the Merrill Lynch brokerage house. Regan's views on taxes as on all economic questions were unknown and, as it soon became clear, unformed. Kemp moved quickly to insert supply-siders as Regan's lieutenants. His success was spectacular. Dr. Norman Ture, a Washington-based consulting economist who had helped draft the original Kemp-Roth bill, was named undersecretary for taxation. Dr. Paul Craig Roberts, Kemp's sometime aide and pioneer supply-sider, was named assistant secretary for economic policy. Roberts' deputy assistant secretary was Dr. Steve Entin, one of the bright young supply-side economists on Capitol Hill. Why did Don Regan, the sober Wall Streeter of presumably conventional views, fill his Treasury with such heretics? His candid answer: "I read what President Reagan said during the campaign, and he made clear he was in favor of what is called supply-side tax cuts. I tried to find the best men with those views."

The supply-siders now tried to grab the third seat in the economic troika: chairman of the Council of Economic Advisers. Their candidate was New Yorker Lewis Lehrman, a Yale- and Harvard-educated theorist and scholar who built his family's drugstore chain into a highly profitable enterprise. Kemp and Stockman had been pushing him, without success, for a declining succession of offices: secretary of the Treasury, deputy secretary of the Treasury, undersecretary of the Treasury for monetary affairs. But Lehrman, unlike Stockman, never had met Reagan, and his interview with Meese did not win over the president's chief aide. Now Martin Anderson, Reagan's long-time aide who had been named domestic policy chief under Meese, relayed the opposition of the economic fraternity to putting a supply-side businessman in the post long held by academic Keynesians. Anderson's recommendation, Dr. Murray Weidenbaum of Washington University in St. Louis, not long before would have aroused outrage from that fraternity. No Keynesian macroeconomist, he was a microeconomist specializing in government regulation and deregulation. But he was no supply-sider, and that was enough for the traditionalists—indeed, as it soon turned out, enough also to slow down the supply-side express.

From the beginning, the concept of an ardent supply-sider as budget chief had limitations. Beginning his sixteen-hour days immediately after being named while many of his Cabinet colleagues were whiling away the transition in leisurely vacations, Stockman was transfixed by the enormity of the prospective budget deficits. What worried him was the retroactive January 1, 1981, effective date for the first 10 percent tax cut. Since the bill would not be passed in time to change tax withholding before July 1 at the very earliest, taxpayers would be seeking tax refunds in early 1982 covering the first half of 1981 just as Kemp-Roth's second 10 percent annual tax cut came into effect. Stockman envisioned a $100 billion deficit with horrendous consequences.

A major problem for Stockman was his inability to dent the encrusted practice of revenue forecasting by Keynesian models. He had quickly dislodged the OMB bureaucrats and brought in outside economists who forecast greater revenue, based not on econometric models that had been hideously inaccurate through the 1970s but on a scenario of therapeutic effects from supply-side tax cuts. However, Alan Greenspan, exerting substantial influence on the White House as an outside adviser, fought hard against what was immediately labeled the work of Miss Rosy Scenario. The downgraded budget estimates compounded Stockman's difficulties and threatened to prevent the deep tax cuts the supply-siders considered necessary for economic expansion.

But Kemp also argued that Stockman had forgotten what had transformed his economic philosophy when he had read the galley proofs of Wanniski's *The Way the World Works* late in 1977: how merely the announcement of tax reduction can cause expansionary business currents that increase, not decrease, revenue. Supply-side domination at the Treasury produced a draft tax program keeping the retroactive January 1 tax deadline, and Reagan tended to agree instinctively. But Stockman insisted on moving the effective date forward to July 1, and was supported by traditionalist economists advising the new president from outside the administration. Arthur Burns would have preferred no tax cut at all, but since Reagan had to fulfill his campaign promise he suggested an October 1 effective date, advice echoed by Greenspan and Charls Walker. In that sense, Reagan's decision for a July 1 effective date was a compromise. Nevertheless, Stockman's desire to minimize budget deficits by delaying tax reduction was all too reminiscent of disastrous efforts by presidents from Hoover to Carter to balance the budget by raising tax rates. In addition, by requesting a July 1 effective date, Reagan guaranteed that Congress would delay it still more—to no earlier than October 1.

Any despondency in that quarter, however, was more than compensated by elation over what seemed an imminent triumph. In December, Kemp and Stockman agreed that the basic Kemp-Roth tax package should be given enhanced economic velocity by a major addition: immediate lowering of the 70 percent top marginal rate on "unearned" income to 50 percent. The effect on not only the stock market but the dangerously moribund bond market would be galvanic. Savings to finance the big budget deficit would expand as money flowed out of tax shelters. The Treasury supply-siders bought it, and Don Regan was enthusiastic. It went into the draft tax program.

So did a practically untouched version of Charls Walker's fast tax depreciation, usually called 10-5-3 (depreciation of buildings in ten years, equipment in five years, cars and light trucks in three years). Kemp and the supply-side purists did not like it, viewing it as just another tax shelter for established big corporations that would be little or no help to up-and-coming entrepreneurs, the future hope of the capitalist system who above all wanted a quick drop in taxation of "unearned" income.

As the week of February 9 began, this was the shape of the tax bill that Reagan would present to Congress February 18: Kemp-Roth, plus 10-5-3 and an immediate end to the distinction between "earned" (wages and salaries) and "unearned" income (interest and dividends). But the events of the next few days were to cast a long shadow and temporarily dilute this aspect of the Reagan Revolution.

After serving as chief strategist for the Reagan campaign, pollster Richard Wirthlin had not entered government but instead chose to be an outside adviser to Reagan. In that role, Wirthlin strenuously opposed the drop in taxes on "unearned" income. His Ph.D. was in macroeconomics (Keynesian variety) from the University of California at Berkeley, but that was not the source of his opposition. Functioning as a pollster, Wirthlin told the president the drop in rates on "unearned" income unnecessarily risked his blue-collar support and played into the hands of Democrats who would label him the rich man's president. Most Reagan noneconomic advisers agreed, on political not ideological grounds. That included James Baker, who had entered the White House as Cabinet-level chief of staff, and, surprisingly, Lyn Nofziger, the political aide charged with maintaining the administration's conservative purity.

But Reagan understood better than his advisers the dramatic impact of the "unearned" tax proposal. In fact, it excited him. He was unworried by warnings from Wirthlin, Baker and Nofziger. "I can sell it to the American people," he told an aide on February 9.

On the next day, distinguished outside economic advisers assembled at Blair House across the street from the White House for lunch. This was the idea of Marty Anderson, to provide Reagan with an alternative and more traditional source of economic opinion apart from the supply-siders at Treasury and OMB and microeconomist Weidenbaum at CEA. The lunch was viewed with trepidation at Treasury as an end run, trepidation soon to be justified.

Burns delivered a denunciation of the drop in taxation on "unearned" income. He was supported by Dr. Herbert Stein, the conservative Keynesian who had been architect of Nixon and Ford fiscal policies, and by almost everybody there, including Walker. George Shultz, OMB head and Treasury secretary under Nixon, interjected that he thought it an excellent idea economically but was not prepared to offer a political judgment. That left real defense of the idea to the only two supply-siders present at the luncheon table, Kemp and Laffer. But they too opposed the drop in "unearned" tax rates.

The two supply-siders thought they had a trade-off, correcting a defect in the original Kemp-Roth bill as drafted four years earlier. While purporting to cut individual tax rates 10 percent across the board, Kemp-Roth left unchanged the top marginal rate on "earned" income of 50 percent—a condition left intact by the Treasury draft of Reagan's tax proposal. Kemp and Laffer proposed that this too be reduced until it reached a top marginal rate of 37 percent after three years. The consensus around the luncheon table was that it was a good idea.

When the outside economic advisers met later that afternoon with Reagan, the deal seemed firm: no immediate drop in the rate on "unearned" income, but *all* rates, including the top marginal rate on "earned" income, to drop 10 percent a year. Reagan specifically asked Laffer if he had in his campaign promised a quick drop in the "unearned" rate; Laffer replied he had not. Later, when defending the decision, Meese (who originally seemed to support the lower "unearned" rate) cited the backing from Laffer and Kemp. But the two supply-siders were euphoric about a 37 percent rate in sight.

Other supply-siders, including the Treasury policy-makers, were not. They were furious over the Kemp-Laffer defection on "unearned" income. Nor was there any trade-off. When Anderson went to the Treasury to find out the revenue loss from cutting the top marginal rate on "earned" income down to 37 percent over three years, he was told such estimates were impossible. Anderson later gave that as the main reason for rejecting the idea.

In fact, the revenue loss was easily calculated, and it was relatively modest: $200 million for the first year, rising to $1.2 billion in the third year (though this was a static analysis that probably overemphasized the loss). The real reason was that Ture resented Kemp and Laffer coming in at the eleventh hour and dumping the "unearned" tax provision in favor of the lowered rate on "earned" income, which he viewed as irrelevant in economic impact; he contended there were all too few persons who had so neglected tax shelters that they had $215,000 in taxable salaries.

It had been a bad week for the supply-siders. They had lost the "unearned" tax rate drop, viewed as the most dramatic aspect of the program and an invaluable financing tool for the budget deficits. They had lost the proposed 37 percent rate on "earned" income, which would approach the magic 25 percent figure of the golden Coolidge-Mellon era. Contentions by administration spokesmen of substantial overall tax reductions for "earned" income even in the highest bracket, even though the marginal rate would not go below 50 percent, had failed to take into account an underlying precept of supply-side economics: the marginal, not the average, tax rate induces greater production and greater investment.

After the market closed on the afternoon of Friday, February

13, Press Secretary Brady announced the death of the lowered rate on "unearned" income. He took pains to announce that Reagan had rejected the recommendations of Treasury and OMB, an unusual announcement viewed at the Treasury as an attempt to reduce the effectiveness of the supply-siders there. But the 10-5-3 depreciation schedule remained intact, and unlike individual tax rate cuts, retroactive to early 1981.

The following Monday was the Washington Birthday holiday. Not until Tuesday, February 17, the day before Reagan's speech, did the markets reopen. The result confirmed the views of those who believe the stock market is a rational barometer of the public mood and a rational reactor to public events. The Dow-Jones average, reflecting stocks of older companies in need of tax shelters to survive, rose 8.11. The American Stock Exchange index, reflecting the stocks of newer companies seeking entrepreneurial venture capital, fell 2.41.

The fall of the entrepreneurial stock on February 17 occurred without full knowledge of backstage developments the preceding Friday the thirteenth. While Brady was publicly savaging the Treasury and OMB supply-siders, their work was being privately savaged by the White House staff.

Stockman, heading the president's economic task force, had brought to Washington the best writers he could locate to help prepare the president's report to Congress—including George Gilder and Lewis Lehrman. Written under forced draft Tuesday and Wednesday, February 10 and 11, their work reached the White House on Friday. An explosion resulted. "Why, this is just a supply-side primer," complained Weidenbaum, as he read Gilder's eloquent introduction. David Gergen, who had been virulently antitax-cut as a speechwriter and adviser in George Bush's presidential campaign and was now a deputy to Baker in the White House, was put to work. Not a word of Gilder, Lehrman and the other supply-siders survived. Indeed, even the words "supply side" were struck. Reagan's revolutionary tax program was deliberately being described in most unrevolutionary language.

Efforts were even made to describe it in Keynesian terms. While the Keynesian career economists had been largely removed from authoritative positions at OMB and Treasury, they still flourished at Weidenbaum's CEA. The result was CEA-written sections of the president's reports, provoking this marginal note from a Treasury supply-sider: "Jesus Christ! Did Keynes write this report?" When the report talked about economic factors being "underutilized, as is currently the case," the marginal note-writer scrawled: "Underutilization or excess capacity is a Keynesian concept. It implies the need for stimulative *demand* policies. Get these concepts out of Reagan's Economic Report!!!"

They were removed, leaving the report neither Keynesian nor supply-side. It was less than satisfying for the supply-siders. Kemp was well aware of what had happened to the report, along with the collapse of his compromise promising the 37 percent top marginal rate, when he spouted over to the *New York Times* reporter that he was breaking with Reagan. The next day's call from the president reassured Kemp that he too wanted to get those rates down to Coolidge-Mellon levels and intended to keep at it through his term.

Kemp was back on the reservation, but the question of whether supply-side tax cuts could survive without supply-side ideology remained, as pointed out by one internal government memo, presumably written by a supply-sider:

> The Reagan Administration claims "No Business as Usual," but the economic report belies the claim. There is no economic analysis provided as justification for turning from "business as usual." Indeed, there is just the usual business of deploring too much government spending, too much inflation, too much regulation and too high a tax burden. Carter did the same. The economics underlying the report do not differ markedly from the Carter Administration. . . .

Another unsigned memo was in the same vein:

> I think it is extraordinary that the first Reagan economic report . . . by the first explicitly supply-side president ever elected to office provides no explanation whatsoever of the new policy that he is the carrier of and for which he has made so many claims.

The internal debate over the language reflected the fact that although the supply-siders in general terms had won the battle for tax policy, they by no means dominated the Reagan Administration's policymakers. This is how the major economic actors in the administration shaped up:

David Stockman, OMB director: Despite his occasional lapses and preoccupation with expenditure reduction, he was an authentic supply-sider counted on to press for a free market solution to the nation's problems.

Donald T. Regan, secretary of the Treasury: Having come to the Treasury as an economic agnostic, he was soon a converted supply-sider (thanks to Undersecretary Ture and Assistant Secretary Roberts). By spring of 1981, he was an effective tax cut salesman.

Dr. Murray Weidenbaum, CEA chairman: As a specialist in microeconomics, he had no macroeconomic ideology. As an assistant secretary of the Treasury in the Nixon Administration, he had been a leading force in successfully pressing for wage-price controls but now confessed error and promised it would not happen again. He backed the tax cuts and free market but seemed leery of supply-side philosophy.

Dr. Martin Anderson, assistant to the president for domestic policy: While staunchly backing the letter of Reagan's campaign promises, he was skeptical of supply-side doctrine. He was instrumental in establishing the council of outside advisers, many hostile to supply-side doctrine.

The White House staff: Not much enthusiasm for supply-side doctrine here. Meese, as usual, kept his cards face down. Baker, the former Bush campaign manager, was openly skeptical of tax reduction. The clearest antitax figure in the White House was Gergen, another ex-Bush supporter. But by early spring of 1981, they had stopped fighting the program. As loyal term players, they would fight for what the president wanted.

Outside advisers: They ran the full gamut from supply-side purist Arthur Laffer to conservative Keynesian Herbert Stein. The overall tone, however, was skepticism toward the tax cut program. Arthur Burns was particularly vociferous in telling everybody that the tax reductions were too deep and might have to be abandoned. Milton Friedman, the most famous of the outsiders, supported tax cuts as a necessary step toward dismantling government while continuing to downgrade supply-side doctrine.

In sum, even if the supply-siders were not totally in control, there was no robust alternative in contention to either their overall philosophical thrust or their tax theory. Ronald Reagan's own determination guaranteed that. But monetary policy was another matter. There Professor Friedman ruled.

When Lehrman arrived at the OMB from New York on February 13 to help write the economic report, he was given one order by Stockman: "Avoid that four-letter emotive word."
The word was no obscenity; it was *gold*. Inherent in supply-side doctrine was reforging the link between gold and the dollar, finally severed by Richard Nixon's New Economic Policy of 1971 which coupled wage-price controls with floating currency rates. Once before, during the Civil War and continuing for some years afterward (1862–1879), U.S. currency had been totally divorced from gold. That period, like the years following 1971, brought painful and chronic inflation. Kemp wrote in 1979:

> Over thousands of years we have learned that when a government guarantees the value of its currency, by promising to redeem it any time in the future with something of value in a fixed amount, there is no inflation. Whatever the international monetary system or standard of value—usually silver, gold or some other precious metal— periods of stable prices have always depended on such a guarantee. If government indeed acts on its guarantee, there is no decline in the value of its currency, no inflation.[20]

In the Republican platform proceedings at Detroit in 1980, Kemp and Stockman collaborated to adopt a draft calling for a "monetary standard"—presumably based on gold, not green onions—without objection from Reagan. Still, this was one part of supply-side doctrine that was not quite part of the Reagan Revolution.

As a member of the conservative movement, Reagan long had been intrigued by gold and over the years now and then made casual comments about undoing Nixon's policy of 1971. But most political aides advised him that the reaction from the financial establishment would be negative. Probably more convincing was the counsel of Milton Friedman, an impassioned foe of the gold standard.

When Reagan arrived at the Hollywood studio on January 27, 1980, following his loss to Bush in Iowa, to cut the tapes that would save his campaign, he was taken aback to find that one of those prepared by Jeff Bell (an ardent "gold bug") advocated a gold standard. Bell's script probably did not offend Reagan's own political sensibilities, but it surely ran counter to Friedman's advice. Reagan told Bell he would go ahead and cut the tape but would decide what to do with it later. Based on a report from Wirthlin that the gold spot fared poorly in tests with voter panels, it was left on the cutting room floor. There was talk of Bell preparing a new gold spot with more punch, but the sacking of Sears on February 26 removed Bell—and any further talk of a gold spot—from the campaign. Even after the adoption of the Kemp-Stockman "monetary standard" at Detroit, Reagan was evasive on the rare instances when a reporter asked him about gold.

Accordingly, the supply-siders played it cautiously on gold. Lehrman, the most outspoken gold advocate of all the supply-siders, did not once mention the "four-letter emotive word" in a confidential memo to the Reagan transition team written two days after the election. Instead, he limited himself to radical reform of the Federal Reserve system, the nation's central bank. "Monetary policy has been guided for almost twenty years by a seasonally adjusted computer model—not by the disciplined decisions of men subject to rules determined according to market considerations—such as a stable price level," Lehrman wrote. "Such a Fed computer model has failed to account for the complexity of money and credit market phenomena, and as a result, monetary policy has been systematically expansive and volatile—and therefore restrictive of spontaneous market tendencies which might otherwise help to produce reasonable price level stability."

Kemp and Stockman pushed Lehrman as undersecretary for monetary affairs to put these views into effect. But his "gold bug" reputation disqualified him in the eyes of both Meese and Donald Regan. The post instead went to Chicago banker Beryl Sprinkel, a follower of Friedman's monetarist economic school (concentrating on control of the money supply). While not a gold advocate, Sprinkel agreed with Lehrman and the other supply-siders that the central banking system needed basic reform.

The same view was taken by Lawrence Kudlow, a brilliant young Wall Street economist recruited by Stockman as OMB's chief economist. A monetarist with supply-side views on taxation and gold, Kudlow directed a chapter of the presidential economic report on February 18 to include sharp criticism of the Federal

Reserve (though not a word about gold). That died in the White House as surely as Gilder's supply-side rhetoric. Burns (a former Federal Reserve chairman), Greenspan and Weidenbaum had persuaded Reagan not to pick a fight with the Federal Reserve. That was changing by the end of Reagan's first hundred days. At a meeting of Cabinet-level officials on April 30, Kudlow and Sprinkel presented harshly critical reports on Federal Reserve practices, contending that its intervention in financial markets was combining the twin evils of rising interest rates and an inflated money supply that, if persisted in, could bring a financial collapse amid inflationary ruin.

When word of this got into print, officials and friends of the Fed went into action. Arthur Burns, who during his tenure as Federal Reserve chairman had succeeded in elevating the central bank's status to political inviolability on the scale of the Supreme Court, was on the telephone to key administration officials insisting that such talk only further disturbed financial markets and had to be stopped. Paul Volcker, the Carter-appointed Federal Reserve chairman inherited by Reagan, was in contact with the same officials suggesting a verbal nonaggression pact. Volcker would cease his public criticism of Reagan's tax program, which he labeled inflationary; Stockman at OMB and Donald Regan at Treasury would order an end to criticism of Fed operations.

Fearful that public contention within the government (even though the Federal Reserve, by law, is independent from the administration) would upset markets, Meese and Baker at the White House wanted the dispute ended. The president agreed. The deal was sealed at a May 18 meeting at the White House, when Volcker delivered a long lecture to Reagan on problems faced by the central bank. Treasury and OMB chafed under this nonaggression pact. They felt the Federal Reserve was the only arm of government still conducting an interventionist, fine-tuning policy along Keynesian lines. Sooner or later, they thought, it would be necessary to confront the Fed; sooner or later, it would be necessary for the president to ask for Volcker's resignation.

All this did not immediately enhance prospects for gold. Anderson and Weidenbaum had kept not only Lehrman but any pro-gold supply-sider off the three-member Council of Economic Advisers. Instead, the seat went to banker-economist Jerry Jordan, an anti-gold monetarist.

There was an entente between supply-siders and monetarists inside the administration. Monetarists Kudlow, Sprinkel and Jordan supported the supply-side tax cuts. Supply-siders Stockman, Ture and Roberts supported monetarist restraint of the money supply. Gold was not mentioned.

Kemp had agreed not to introduce a gold bill or even talk about gold until the tax program had passed Congress (a retreat opposed by an outraged Wanniski). Gold was to remain a forbidden word until it became clear where the economy was going.

It would seem that the triumph of Milton Friedman was complete. Or was it? While accepting a monetarist program in the arcane regions of monetary policy comprehended by few if any politicians, Reagan did not embrace it as he did a supply-side program in the more politically understandable area of fiscal policy. Reagan was in truth a supply-sider who would insist on giving his tax policy a fair trial against all adversity. He was no such committed monetarist, much less a committed Friedmanite who would fight the specter of gold.

Gold was not the dead issue it seemed. Stockman and Kudlow remained committed to it. So did Kemp and much of the militant right on Capitol Hill, typified by Jesse Helms. And there was informed speculation within the administration that the president himself was a closet gold bug.

Gold could become policy only in the event of opposite economic extremes—a magnificently recovered economy that made radical experimentation permissible or, contrariwise, a financial collapse when extreme remedies would be sought in desperation. In any event, nothing was likely much before two years.

But the return to the gold standard, inherent in supply-side doctrine, had not been expunged finally from the Reagan Revolution.

On the evening of February 18, 1981, Reagan's acceptance of supply-side tax policy became official presidential policy. Members of Congress who that night lustily cheered the new president's call for budget cuts grew silent as he demanded tax reductions. The reason for the silence partly stemmed from Reagan's prosaic rhetoric to describe a radical and exciting new departure (endorsing "incentives to increase productivity for both workers and industry"). But it also reflected the decision by the Democrats and not a few Republicans to oppose the Reagan Revolution on this ground, not on budget cuts.

Two generations of statesmen drenched in Keynesian logic had not been entirely moved by the economic system's increasing failure to function over the last decade. Even such Republicans as Finance Committee Chairman Dole persisted in viewing tax reductions in terms of static revenue losses. They would not or could not understand that supply-side incentives would affect not merely business but the ordinary worker.

"I sometimes wish we had never invented the term *supply-side*," Wanniski mused early in 1981. It had been expropriated by conservatives who claimed that only business-oriented tax cuts or taxes specifically "targeted" to savings constituted "true" supply-side tax cuts. This was the position privately taken by many Republicans and publicly by the conservative Democratic caucuses in both House and Senate and by Representative James Jones of Oklahoma, the moderately conservative chairman of the House Budget Committee. Rejecting the primacy of marginal tax rate reduction, they embraced as the heart of "supply-side" tax cuts the rapid depreciation viewed as the least effective tax reduction by the men who had given the movement its name.

But on the left, the passion against Reagan's tax program had deeper roots. That was demonstrated as the Reagan Administration began by a perceptive freshman congressman from Massachusetts. Rep. Barney Frank was new to Washington but not to politics; he long had been a resourceful and often ferocious liberal activist in Boston, most recently as a state legislator. Now he had braved the conservative tide and come to Washington at the same time as Ronald Reagan. Frank acknowledged claims about the Reagan tax cut that "it will more than pay for itself," then added: "But I don't think they really believe that. I think the purpose of Kemp-Roth is to reduce the revenue of the federal government so that it simply isn't possible to have very many constructive, directed programs."[21]

Here indeed was the crucial explanation of why Democrats concentrated their fire against the tax cuts, not the budget cuts. Budget-cutting had been tried before with mixed results; the federal leviathan grew ever larger and more powerful. But tax reduction was a true threat to a half century of centralized government steadily widening and deepening its power. Poorly explained though it was, suspect in its own house though it was, supply-side was the cutting edge of the Reagan Revolution.

That cutting edge was honed on March 10, 1981, when a bill to end the distinction between "earned" and "unearned" income was introduced by Representative William Brodhead of Michigan. This was the quick drop in the top marginal tax rate on dividends and interest from 70 percent to 50 percent recommended by Stockman and the Treasury but reluctantly rejected by Reagan, on advice of his political aides and outside economic consultants, because it seemed to favor the rich.

Democrat Bill Brodhead had no such fears. He represented a blue-collar Detroit district and he had been endorsed as suitably liberal by the United Auto Workers. No mere rank-and-file liberal, he was chairman of the Democratic Study Group, the House liberal caucus, and was a key liberal on the tax-writing House Ways and Means Committee.

Brodhead was not acting alone. His fellow liberals on Ways and Means endorsed his bill. The committee chairman, Representative Dan Rostenkowski of Illinois, gave his blessing. The new chairman of the Democratic National Committee, Charles T. Manatt, endorsed it in a speech to the National Press Club.

Democratic motives were obvious: to make veto-proof any tax bill passed by the Democratic-controlled House even if it did not contain across-the-board tax rate reduction on the Reagan-Kemp-Roth model. But that strategy was defective. While delighted by the Brodhead bill as giving him something he would have had trouble pushing through the House on his own, Reagan was still insisting on multiyear, across-the-board individual tax cuts—no unreasonable goal in the climate of soaring presidential popularity following the assassination attempt.

Yet, the Brodhead bill connoted something more than just a defective Democratic ploy. While hastening to make clear he was no supply-sider, Brodhead also asserted that the rich as well as the poor needed tax reduction and talked about his proposal increasing rather than decreasing ultimate federal revenue (the Laffer Curve?). Wanniski wrote Brodhead congratulating him as his day's Arthur Vandenberg (the isolationist Republican senator from Michigan who after World War II collaborated with President Truman in a bipartisan internationalist policy).

However exaggerated Wanniski's appraisal was, it could be said that the advent of the Brodhead bill was the sign that the intellectual struggle for supply-side tax reduction was over. Ronald Reagan, Jack Kemp and the rest of the supply-siders had won. The rest was detail.

From the moment Reagan took power, an overriding fear had haunted supply-siders: Thatcherization. Hopes for economic regeneration in Great Britain aroused when Conservative Margaret Thatcher became prime minister in May 1979 quickly turned to ashes. Unemployment rose, inflation persisted and economic growth remained stagnant. Kemp, Laffer and Wanniski all had predicted these results from doctrinaire reliance on monetary policy pursued by Friedman's disciples in the Thatcher government while not enough was done to reduce government spending—her government actually *increased* the effective marginal tax rate on most Britons.

As the New York bond market fell in the spring of 1981, Wanniski feared that monetarist policies in Washington had brought Reagan to the brink of Thatcherization. The protection against that was the element Margaret Thatcher had neglected: a supply-side tax cut, combining elements of Kemp-Roth with Brodhead. It was essential to the survival of the Reagan Revolution.

6

Avoiding an Economic "Dunkirk"

On November 16, 1980, President-elect Reagan summoned a collection of famous economic experts to Los Angeles to confer on the troubled economy and recommend cures to the new administration. They were an all-star team of orthodox Republican thought: Dr. Arthur Burns, Dr. Alan Greenspan, Dr. Milton Friedman, Dr. George Shultz, Dr. Charls Walker. These were learned doctors of economics, all (with the exception of Friedman) veterans of the Nixon-Ford administrations and therefore responsible for the policies during those eight years of deepening economic difficulty for the nation. These were not revolutionaries. None had been an enthusiastic supporter of Reagan prior to his nomination. None was an advocate and most were foes of supply-side economics. Also present at the Federal Building in Los Angeles was William Simon, then the leading prospect to be secretary of the Treasury and an early Reagan backer. His attitude toward supply-side economics was ambivalent, and toward some of the ardent supply-siders, especially Jude Wanniski, downright hostile.

Only one Reaganite supply-sider was invited to the Los Angeles conference. He was not a Ph.D., not an economist and not a veteran of high finance. His academic degree was a Bachelor of Science in physical education from Occidental College, and his lack of formal economic training was matched by an absence of business experience. Supply-sider Jack Kemp was all alone. It would seem superficially that the supply-side was badly outgunned around the table in Los Angeles.

But unlike the distinguished economists, Kemp was a practicing politician. While his learned colleagues came to the meeting without written papers or proposals, Kemp brought a document: a thirty-page monograph titled: "Avoiding a GOP Economic Dunkirk." Had it not been for Kemp and his paper, the conference in Los Angeles would have been no more memorable and no less sterile than scores of other meetings during the transition.

But Kemp and the paper he brought to Los Angeles set the agenda for the early days of the Reagan Administration: the most concerted effort since the coming of FDR's New Deal to bring the growth of federal spending under control.

Thus the most emphasized and most publicized aspect of the Reagan Revolution in its early days was one of its least radical and (in Republican terms) most orthodox elements. It was, ironically, an aspect given only glancing notice in Reagan's campaign oratory when compared with his intensity on national security, tax reduction and regulatory relaxation. It was an aspect of Reagan policy that disturbed some supply-side advocates—including Kemp himself, the man who had done most to position budget reform on top of Reagan's priority list. Almost from the moment he raised the imperative of budget reform in Los Angeles, Kemp was uneasy about it. Indeed, the enemies of Reagan's overall revolutionary design of reducing the governmental "wedge" were plotting to seize on budget reform as the means of blunting tax reduction, the sharpest point of Reagan's radical efforts to transform the economy.

Reagan, to be sure, always had talked about cutting the cost of government—especially the California state government fourteen years before he became president. Taking the oath of office as governor in Sacramento on January 1, 1967, Reagan declared: "We are going to squeeze and cut and trim, until we reduce the cost of government. It won't be easy, nor will it be pleasant, and it will involve every department of government." But while such promises never disappeared from Reagan's basic political oratory in the coming years, they were subordinated to other issues—particularly in the campaign of 1980.

As presidential nominee, Reagan said no more about budget-cutting than had the Republican Party's previous candidates of the past fifty years—and not much more than the Democratic Party's nominees over the same period. The pattern was familiar: candidates preaching vague budgetary restraint and ignoring those preachments once in the Oval Office—a pattern initiated in 1932 by Franklin D. Roosevelt. Having campaigned against Hoover's allegedly excessive spending, FDR launched the New Deal to begin an uninterrupted half century of ever bigger government and ever higher federal spending.

Throughout the 1920s, with Coolidge and Mellon steadily cutting tax rates, the federal government had maintained a constant spending level of around $3 billion a year, with ten consecutive budget surpluses averaging about $850 million each. The Great Depression and the New Deal ended that. Roosevelt's first budget, for the fiscal year beginning July 1, 1933, resulted in government outlays of $6.6 billion and a deficit of $3.6 billion.

Not once in the Roosevelt Administration was there a budget surplus. The last full budget before World War II produced outlays of $13.3 billion and a $7.1 billion deficit. World War II spending grew to an eventual peak of $98.3 billion in outlays with a $53.9 billion deficit. War's end reduced spending to $33 billion in fiscal year 1948 with an $8.4 billion surplus, resulting from the economies of the Republican Eightieth Congress. But by the 1952 election, after four years with both executive and legislative branches under Democratic control, spending had soared back to $65.3 billion with a $4 billion deficit.

The election that year of General Eisenhower as the first Republican president since Hoover, enjoying the first wholly Republican Congress since 1930, failed to produce any radical change in these trends. The great Republican split that opened in 1912 when Theodore Roosevelt challenged President William Howard Taft had never healed. The Taft wing of the party (led in 1952 by Taft's son, Senate majority leader Robert A. Taft) wanted a return to Coolidge-Mellon economic policies with radical tax and budget reduction. But the party's progressive wing (led by President Eisenhower) had a different agenda—moderate change, yes; radical change, no. During his eight years, Eisenhower managed budget surpluses on only three occasions and suffered through the 1958 recession. By the time Eisenhower left office, federal spend-

ing had surpassed the $80 billion annual level, inexorably climbing
to the $100 billion mark never reached in World War II.
It reached $87.8 billion in fiscal year 1962, the first budget for
which President John F. Kennedy was fully responsible. Social
welfare programs, blocked by the eight Eisenhower years, blossomed under the New Frontier label and meant a $6.4 billion
deficit. Truly dramatic growth in government activity that expanded the New Deal came not with Kennedy but with his successor. Lyndon Johnson, desperate to convince the Democratic Party's liberal wing of his true credentials, enacted—amid prosecu-
tion of the Vietnam War—the Great Society spending programs
that extended a widened federal wedge throughout the society.
The $100 billion spending level was pierced in fiscal 1966. Two
years later, in LBJ's last full year, outlays had reached $153.1
billion with a stunning deficit of $28.4 billion—this in a period of
relatively low inflation. Yet the full impact of the back-loaded
Great Society programs—far more spending in future years than
present years—would not be felt until the 1970s.

In his successful campaign of 1968, Richard M. Nixon had
made the Republican politician's perfunctory obeisance to smaller
government. But that stood low on his list of priorities, if it
belonged there at all. The tip-off came immediately after the 1968
election when Nixon induced Professor Daniel Patrick Moynihan
of Harvard, a liberal Democrat who had supported Robert F.
Kennedy for president that year, to join his administration as
senior presidential adviser on domestic affairs. Although he
served as a middle-level official under both Kennedy and Johnson,
Moynihan's criticism of Great Society spending programs had
excited Nixon's interest. Moynihan's acceptance of Nixon's bid
had lasting consequences. Moynihan felt that the legitimacy of
government itself had been undermined by the Vietnam-spawned
turbulence of the 1960s, and that a wholesale dismantling of the
Great Society by Nixon would only widen those divisions. Knowing Nixon's Anglophilia, Moynihan instructed him that the British
Conservative Party had made a practice when regaining power of
not undoing the social reforms of the preceding Labour Government. Specifically, Moynihan convinced Nixon to keep alive
Johnson's overballyhooed "war on poverty," even though its expense dwarfed its value. The Job Corps, a much-criticized pro-

gram that established camps to train unemployed youth, had been marked for extinction by campaigner Nixon but was retained by President Nixon. He even continued the Model Cities program of federal aid to selected municipal governments; Moynihan advised Nixon that, worthless though the program was, it was a symbol of the federal commitment to saving America's cities and therefore should not be stopped.[1]

In accepting Moynihan's advice, Nixon rejected the pleas of Arthur Burns (serving as a Cabinet-level "counselor" during 1969 before becoming head of the Federal Reserve system the next year) to conduct a serious assault on spending. Inflation combined with the stagnant economy reduced revenues while devaluing the dollar, pushing Nixon's budget numbers to staggering levels. After eight years of Nixon-Ford budgeting, outlays were $269 billion with a $68.8 billion deficit; including Social Security under the new accounting system instituted in 1973 put spending at $366.4 billion and the deficit at $66.4 billion.

No Democratic presidential nominee since Roosevelt in 1932 had given such a clear signal as did Jimmy Carter in 1976 of budgetary restraint. But voters who thought they were choosing reduced federal spending did not read Carter's fine print: while promising a balanced budget and more efficient government, Carter never once promised a *smaller* government.

He certainly did not produce one. The governmental wedge widened under Carter, old programs growing and new programs added. The heavily publicized political warfare between president and Congress over Carter's attack on selected water projects obscured the overall rise in federal spending. In Carter's last year, the figures (under the new accounting system) were $579.6 billion in outlays with a $59.6 billion deficit.

Reagan mentioned these runaway figures only in passing during his 1980 campaign partly because he was too skilled an orator to anesthetize audiences with green eyeshade speeches that sounded like Bob Taft. But apart from practical political considerations, there were no doctrinal arguments for ardent budget-cutting in the supply-side economic philosophy newly embraced by Reagan.

The pure supply-side doctrine preached by Arthur Laffer held that the economy, as it traveled down the tax reduction side of the Laffer Curve, would generate so much additional revenue that spending restraint would not be necessary. On the contrary, Laffer was opposed to severe spending restraint; in May 1978 he told a reporter he would end support for the statewide referendum cutting California's property taxes (overwhelmingly passed the next month) if he thought it would reduce government services. Jude Wanniski did not go quite so far but wrote at the same time that some of those who supported the California referendum because it would cut government spending were doing the right thing for the wrong reason.[2]

Wanniski's brilliant treatise *The Way the World Works*, which in 1978 popularized supply-side economics, completely ignored what should be done about government spending. But by the time George Gilder's *Wealth and Poverty* was published three years later, the question had to be considered. As the Kemp-Roth bill became the center of political contention, its liberal opponents displayed newfound concern for fiscal integrity by arguing that the tax cuts would bloat the budget deficit. "It is always best to cut government spending wherever its yield or benefit is less than private spending," said Gilder.[3] But having conceded that, he abruptly left the subject of spending for tax reduction and launched an impassioned supply-side argument against seeking a chimerical balanced budget by raising taxes.

Practicing politicians could not be so cavalier as either Wanniski or Gilder. To support Kemp-Roth, many Republican candidates felt they must come over strongly in favor of reduced spending. So dedicated a supply-sider as Jeff Bell had no trouble in his New Jersey Senate campaign of 1978 coupling budget reduction and tax reduction. Jack Kemp was slightly more hesitant. In *An American Renaissance*, published in 1979, Kemp devoted thirteen pages to defending himself against the "misplaced accusation" of "not wanting to reduce excessive government expenditures . . . because I do not advocate ripping away the safety net of government support services." Kemp hastened to assert that "I take a back seat to no one" in contending that "spending restraint is desirable."[4] But he went on to suggest that "tax incentives" should be given emphasis and priority above "spending restraints" because "significant spending reductions require both a strong economy and some fundamental long-term plans in order to sustain the required public support."[5]

Yet there was one supply-side politician, more scholarly but far less well known than Kemp, who disagreed fundamentally with Kemp's lower emphasis and priority on spending restraint—a disagreement that was to start a chain reaction of far-reaching impact.

Businessman-scholar Lewis Lehrman was the unsuccessful supply-side candidate for secretary of the Treasury. But he disagreed fundamentally with his friends Laffer and Wanniski on the budgetary question. Lehrman believed dramatic and drastic expenditures reduction was no less imperative than tax reduction, rejecting Kemp's notion of greater priority for the latter.

In New York City on November 6, 1980, two days after the election, Lehrman completed a fourteen-page memorandum with the deceptively dry and academic title "The Struggle for Financial Order at the Onset of the Reagan Presidency." It was deceptive because nothing written by Lehrman's lucid economic pen was dry and because its impact was anything but academic.

Like many other Republican faithful, Lehrman had been asked by E. Pendelton James, personnel chief of the Reagan transition, to present his views. He did so by defining inflation as "a *monetary* and a *financial* disorder, engendered by the federal government" (emphasis in original). His remedy: "(a) Reduce as rapidly as possible the federal budget deficit. . . . (b) Simultaneously encourage the Federal Reserve system to moderate creation of new money and credit. . . . (c) At the same time, one must reform the tax structure. . . ."

Lehrman painted a picture of chaos in the financial markets caused by the borrowing needs of a federal government whose spending was rising at a quarterly rate of 18.6 percent before the election. "The previous administration sowed chaos, and, I regret to say, President-elect Reagan may very well reap the whirlwind. If he is not ready, if he does not understand what is happening, he could easily be swept away by its hurricane velocity." To prevent that, he declared that the Reagan Administration "must move much more rapidly than originally planned to establish budgetary equilibrium in the federal government." Lehrman gave Reagan a mere six months, dating from the election, to avert "an ongoing financial crisis" with high unemployment, permanently high interest rates, double-digit inflation, bankruptcy, wage and price controls and "the humiliation of our new winning coalition at the polls in 1982."

Although Lehrman stamped his memorandum CONFIDENTIAL in large block letters, he sent it to many Republican politicians. Most of them, however, only received the first nine pages. James and a handful of others received a five-page addendum, containing an action plan for the new administration.

The primacy of budget reduction was dramatized by Lehrman's epigraph to the action plan, a quote from Marcus Tullius Cicero in the first century B.C. "The budget should be balanced, the treasury should be refilled, public debt should be reduced, the arrogance of officialdom should be tempered and controlled, and assistance to foreign lands should be reduced lest the state become bankrupt. The people should . . . work and not depend on government for subsistence."

Lehrman then declared that the president-elect must act "*discreetly but immediately* . . . to undertake an emergency plan for economic stabilization and renewal at the onset of his presidency" (emphasis in original). He described in detail a proposed task force on the economic crisis that "would assemble every direct, contingent and scheduled federal expenditure and liability which might be deferred or rescinded during the next six months."

The imperative for speed was stressed by Lehrman, who wanted the economic plan in Reagan's hands three weeks before the inauguration so that it could be implemented fully in the first hundred days. That was not the only evocation of Franklin Roosevelt. "It may be necessary for the president, by executive order, to declare a national economic emergency," Lehrman warned.

It is doubtful whether this call for action survived the jungle of paper that had sprung up in Reagan's transition headquarters in Washington. But it was closely read by one of the few outsiders to whom the full fourteen-page version was sent: Representative David Stockman of Michigan.

Awed by the prospect of representing supply-side philosophy amid the professors of orthodoxy in Los Angeles November 16, Kemp asked his friend Stockman for a memo to present there. Stockman had been deeply impressed by Lehrman's arguments and used them as the inspiration for his own more specific paper.

Borrowing from Lehrman's memo, budgetary statistics thrown together by his congressional staff and his own knowledge of the federal government, Stockman over a three-day span personally drafted a document that would alter the course of the Reagan Administration: "Avoiding a GOP Economic Dunkirk." At the beginning, Stockman broke from the supply-side purists in maintaining that tax reduction was not enough:

> The preeminent danger is that an initial economic policy package that includes tax cuts but does not contain *decisive, credible elements* on matters of outlay control, future budget authority reduction and a believable plan for curtailing the federal government's massive direct and indirect credit absorption will generate expectation of a continuing Reagan inflation [emphasis in original].

The danger was outlined by Stockman in rhetoric that would soon become widely quoted. Because of new federal aid programs automatically triggered by recessionary dips, the federal budget had now become an automatic "coast-to-coast soup line." The resulting hemorrhaging of federal spending could cause "deferral or temporary abandonment of the tax [reduction] program" and a resultant "erosion of our capacity to govern." Hence the "GOP Economic Dunkirk."

Not only had federal outlays grown $157 billion since the end of the 1979 fiscal year on October 1 and $73 billion since fiscal year 1980 ended, but also $25 billion in the less than four months since the last congressional budget resolution was passed in August 1980. Stockman's analysis pointed to the staggering $100 billion in new federal financing needs if this spending continued unchecked. Like Lehrman, Stockman demanded speed. "If bold policies are not swiftly, deftly and courageously implemented in the first six months of the Reagan Administration, Washington will quickly become engulfed in political disorder commensurate with the surrounding economic disarray." Picking up Lehrman's idea, Stockman recommended that "President Reagan should declare a national emergency soon after inauguration."

That would make it easier to demand congressional action on an economic package including budget cutting beyond anything envisioned by Reagan's transition budget task force under Caspar Weinberger, who had been federal budget director under Nixon; Weinberger was talking about a cut of no more than $25 billion in the fiscal 1982 budget (for the year beginning October 1, 1981). Stockman wanted much more: a $50 billion reduction in the current fiscal year 1981 budget and a $30 billion to $50 billion annual cut for future years. He spelled out a few areas for wholesale cuts in his paper; many more he kept in his mind.

Kemp endorsed Stockman's proposals and carried them to Los Angeles. Two days later, the first of a flood of leaked accounts of what variously came to be known as the Stockman Manifesto or the Stockman-Kemp Manifesto appeared in print, linked with intense efforts by Kemp to win Stockman's appointment of director of the Office of Management and Budget. Indeed, the "Dunkirk" memo was not only a battle plan, it was a major self-advertisement for Dave Stockman.

When the old Budget Bureau was expanded into the Office of Management and Budget as part of the Nixon Administration's attempts to modernize the federal government, it was thought that OMB's director would serve as general manager of the government. The highly regarded George P. Shultz, the first holder of the new post, moved in that direction. But after his transfer to the Treasury, Shultz's successors at OMB tended to wield no more influence than old-fashioned budget directors. Reagan's Kitchen Cabinet, in making the first list of Cabinet possibilities, did not regard OMB as a major post. Having caught Reagan's eye as the Anderson-Carter stand-in in the debate rehearsals, Stockman was definitely Cabinet timber but was listed as a possible secretary of energy—a job he did not want.

As a member of the House Budget Committee, Stockman for some time had been pondering the aggrandizement of OMB as a lever for overall control of the federal government. The man he had in mind for the job under Reagan was William Agee, dynamic young chief executive officer of the Bendix Corporation. Stockman had raised the idea with Kemp, a friend of Agee; Kemp enthusiastically agreed. But widely publicized gossip about Agee and Bendix Vice President Mary Cunningham ruled him out. Besides, the kind of budgetary campaign envisioned by Stockman and Lehrman could not be conducted by an outsider from the corporate world who would first need a time-consuming cram course in the federal government. Stockman needed no such course.

As Stockman wrote his Dunkirk memo, Republican staffers on the Senate Budget Committee were preparing a memorandum for the conservative Heritage Foundation to be given Reagan proposing that OMB be given enlarged authority as a policy fulcrum of the administration. The report also urged Reagan to ask Congress for additional powers to delay and eliminate congressional appropriations—a partial return of the powers to impound funds withdrawn by Congress in its Watergate Era attack on the powers of the presidency. The authors of the Heritage report clearly had Stockman in mind.

On Thanksgiving Day, Reagan telephoned Stockman to offer him the OMB post. In reference to his frequent claim that Stockman had badly beaten him in the debate rehearsals, the President-elect told him: "David, I've been looking for a way to get even. I think I'll send you to OMB." While others designated to the new Cabinet embarked on vacations to ready themselves for the ordeal of power, Stockman immediately launched into preparation of the radical budget revision he had proposed in the Dunkirk memo. He was head of the transition economic task force that had been suggested by Lehrman (but that now excluded Lehrman from membership). The Reagan Revolution had started down a road from which there was no turning back.

In a Cabinet dominated by millionaire businessmen in their sixties, Stockman was a thirty-four-year-old congressman with a net worth of less than $500,000 who had never met a payroll or even been on a private payroll himself. While most of his Cabinet colleagues had to familiarize themselves with the basic outlines of their departments, Stockman was delving into the entire government's most intimate details. Other Cabinet members were told what policy they would execute; Stockman was making the policy.

Other than the president himself, Stockman was the sole convert in the administration's senior levels. When Governor Reagan was taking a hard line against student radicals at the University of California's Berkeley branch during the Vietnam War, Stockman was a student radical himself as an undergraduate at Michigan State University—agitating against the draft, signing newspaper advertisements placed by the radical leftist Students for a Democratic Society, participating in the antiwar Vietnam Summer project. Intellectually, he had spurned the Republican conservatism of his rural Michigan upbringing and was studying the liberal theology of Reinhold Niebuhr at the antiwar, socially activist Evergreen United Church of Christ in Lansing, Michigan. It was to further his study of Niebuhr rather than pursue a life in the ministry that Stockman enrolled in the Harvard Divinity School in 1968, which automatically exempted him from the draft. At Harvard, he became a live-in baby-sitter for Professor Moynihan, who that single year had gone from Bobby Kennedy supporter to Nixon staffer. While still at Michigan State, Stockman had begun to question the left-wing conventional wisdom prevailing there. If he were in ideological transit, so was Pat Moynihan, who along with fellow professors Nathan Glazer and James Q. Wilson was now labeled "neoconservative." They influenced young Stockman a great deal more than his theology professors.

Stockman was calling himself a Republican in 1970 when he enrolled in a course taught by *Washington Post* columnist David Broder, on a fellowship at Harvard's Kennedy Institute of Politics. Broder recommended Stockman to liberal Representative John Anderson, who had just been elected chairman of the House Republican Conference and was seeking policy advisers. Stockman got the job and soon became one of Anderson's key aides. How quickly Stockman's rightward course back to his Republican roots progressed as an Anderson staffer has become the subject of controversy, with Anderson loyalists describing Stockman as a Keynesian in economics. Stockman did influence Anderson toward conservative positions on labor-management relations as an effort to repair his shaky base for reelection as conference chairman. By 1975, he had clearly reached a position on the budget close to what it would become six years later as an instrument for shaping national policy. What makes this indisputably clear is his first public exposure to the greater political world: "The Social Pork Barrel," his writing debut in the spring 1975 issue of *The Public Interest* (a memorable edition that also contained contributions from two of Stockman's neoconservative Harvard mentors, James Q. Wilson and Nathan Glazer, plus the trailblazing first attempt by Jude Wanniski to sell the yet unnamed supply-side doctrine to the world).

In describing a "crisis of the budget," Stockman displayed neoconservative roots in blaming the social pork barrel on both "conservative duplicity and liberal ideology"—a formulation he would soon drop. By and large, however, the essay accurately

previews the Reagan Administration six years later. Passages
such as the following do not reflect John Anderson at all and Pat
Moynihan only a little; they showed a distinctive Stockman outlook:

> While national health and welfare reform have been time and again
> artfully deferred, Congress has not been loathe to add a billion here
> for black lung compensation, when the costs should properly be borne
> by the coal industry or a billion extra there for disaster relief, when
> losses from building on a floodplain or raising crops in drought-prone
> areas should be the responsibility of the risk-takers. Like clockwork,
> it raises each year's appropriations request for the National Cancer
> Institute, although the therapeutic preoccupation of the medical
> guild which operates the program has produced no noticeable
> improvement in cancer survival rates during the last fifteen years of
> multibillion-dollar research efforts. Although medical school sub-
> sidies and graduate traineeships basically represent a reverse redis-
> tribution of income, OMB-initiated effort to reduce these outlays are
> rejected as mean-spirited attempts to shortchange "human needs."
> And so it goes. With revenues fully committed for years in advance,
> the federal budget process, potentially the basic forum for serious
> policy choices, has been reduced to a mere annual ritual of accounts
> juggling.[6]

Praised by *Public Interest* editor Irving Kristol in the *Wall
Street Journal*, "The Social Pork Barrel" was Stockman's unusual
entrée into elective politics. It helped arouse interest in his rural
conservative Michigan district, where he had not lived since
high school days, to enable him to run for Congress, force the
veteran Republican incumbent out of the race and be elected in
1976 at age thirty.

Considering Stockman's rapid ideological journey from left to
right, opponents wondered if he might be deflected from the
policies of the Reagan Revolution. But Stockman held these views
with the tenacity of a convert. Indeed, his intent to revolutionize
budget policy went far beyond what Jack Kemp had in mind when
he promoted him for the post.

Almost from the beginning, Kemp experienced misgivings
about what he had wrought. "I fear that there would be blood on
the floor," he said publicly in response to ambitious budget-cutting

projections. But Reagan loved it. In Stockman, he had the government finance officer he had never found during eight years in Sacramento: expert in the intricacies of government and committed to cutting it back. Reagan exuberantly backed Stockman's plans for a radical restructuring of the federal government.

So vigorous was Stockman in his quest to reduce the budget, however, that he momentarily stepped into a trap set by OMB bureaucrats: to cut down the deficit by reducing "tax expenditures," the bureaucratic nomenclature for money lost through tax deductions. That term presumes that all money belongs to the federal government unless specifically granted to the taxpayer. Some reductions of "tax expenditures" reached as high as Cabinet level before Reagan himself objected. When Stockman brought in a proposal to gain revenue by repealing what was left of the oil depletion allowance, Reagan brought the Cabinet meeting up short by saying softly: "Wait a minute. This is not the last administration." But on reduction of actual government expenditures, Reagan almost never restrained his budget director.

Actually, the area where Kemp was most worried about "blood on the floor"—reducing expenditures for fiscal year 1981, which had begun October 1, 1980—was abandoned. Much to the consternation of Lehrman, it was determined that deferral and recision of existing appropriations was too much trouble considering the difficulty of prodding Congress into action so early in the new session of Congress. The request for partial restoration of the president's power to block congressional spending would come later.

The economic emergency first suggested by Lehrman, seconded by Stockman and enthusiastically embraced by Kemp was rejected by Reagan, heeding the advice of his new Cabinet-level presidential counselor, Ed Meese. Reagan's unwillingness to risk dislocation of nervous financial markets, which might react in panic to a presidentially declared emergency, sacrificed lightning-fast action in the new Congress on his economic package. There would be no Hundred Days duplicating the FDR model.

Thus, Reagan's $655.2 billion in outlays for fiscal 1981 was not much below President Carter's proposed $662.7 billion and was well short of the $635 billion target first mentioned in Stockman's Dunkirk memo. It was for future years that Reagan was proposing reduction in the rate of spending increases previously thought unrealistic in view of the federal system's built-in entitlement programs for the poor and disadvantaged. Outlays for fiscal 1982 were set at $695.5 billion, $48.6 billion below Carter's proposal. Because of reduced authorizations now, federal spending in future years would decline steadily. By fiscal year 1986, spending estimated by the last Carter budget at $1,050 billion (the first trillion-dollar budget) would be nearly $100 billion lower at $912 billion, according to the Reagan budget.

The inherent rationale for the budget first advanced by Lehrman and Stockman had subtly changed. Instead of a short-term feverish effort to reduce the government's financing needs, Reagan was starting a long-term grind that would change the shape of the U.S. government.

On December 18, 1980, Kemp escorted the newly designated OMB director on a tour of the great Wall Street financial houses. The visit was designed mainly to introduce Stockman to the captains of finance but also to reassure them that the proposed "national emergency" (not yet rejected by Reagan) was in no way related to Roosevelt's bank-closing emergency of 1933 and in no way a prelude to wage-price controls.

Stockman and Kemp found that once they were reassured about the proposed "emergency," the financiers were exuberant about budget-cutting. Too exuberant. They were eager to cut back on Social Security recipients by downward adjustment of cost-of-living allowances. In Kemp's phase, that would balance the budget "by throwing widows and orphans into the snow."

That illuminated the political pitfalls in the Reagan budget. If Reagan were perceived as a plutocrat shrinking welfare payments to the poor while promoting tax breaks for the rich, his program was doomed. On December 18 in Wall Street, Stockman told the financiers privately what he would declare publicly once the Reagan Administration took power: general Social Security payments would *not* be reduced.

Stockman's tactic, as he privately described it, was not to shear flocks of sheep, as would be inevitable with broad Social Security cuts, but to cull goats from the herd—goats whose shearing would be more politically acceptable. The goats in the case of Social Security were college students, who as dependents of Social Security beneficiaries would receive $700 million for fiscal 1982. Reagan proposed that all be eliminated.

As part of the strategy of sparing the "flocks of sheep," the White House on February 10 listed seven programs immune from cuts: Social Security basic retirement (32 million beneficiaries); Medicare (28.6 million beneficiaries); veterans benefits(2.8 million beneficiaries); Social Security supplemental income aid to the blind, disabled and elderly poor (4.2 million beneficiaries; free school lunches and breakfasts (9.5 million beneficiaries); Head Start preschool (374,000 beneficiaries); youth summer jobs (665,000 beneficiaries). Listing these sacred cows triggered some grumbles on the right, but it kept Reagan from assault by angered recipients of popular mass programs.

Stockman also was eager to find "corporate welfare" recipients ready for shearing along with social welfare "goats." He was none too successful. His best candidate was the Export-Import Bank, whose loans to U.S. companies to promote trade ballooned 400 percent during the Carter Administration but helped only a small fraction of exporters. By cutting the budget authorization one third, $6 billion would be saved over the next five years. Nearly $3 billion in government funds for the new Synthetic Fuels Corporation would be saved over three years by requiring a 40 percent contribution by any participating private firm; Gulf Oil would be unable to get $2 billion from the federal government by making only a $50 million contribution.

Most of the "goats," however, were not subsidies for corporate business. The recipients of the federal government's ever-broadening largesse tended to be individual citizens, subdivisions of government, quasi-governmental corporations and nonprofit activities. In his fourteen- to sixteen-hour days and seven-day weeks, Stockman cut them all.

A representative selection of ten targets, large and small, shows not only how the Stockman ax missed nothing but how varied had become the scope of governmental activity:

Legal services for the poor: The program, budgeted by Carter to rise by $37.7 million to $328.3 million in fiscal 1982, was to be eliminated. On no budget cut was Reagan more enthusiastic, harking back to his days as governor when he battled President Nixon over what he considered federal aid to leftist revolutionaries in the guise of legal help to the poor.

Black lung trust fund: Financing of the fund to aid coal miners afflicted with black lung disease, a disabling malady caused by inhalation of coal dust, would be switched from the federal Treasury to a levy on the coal industry and limited to persons who were "truly medically disabled." Federal spending of $483 million would drop to $105 million in fiscal 1982.

Solar subsidies: Subsidies to encourage solar technology, set for $149 million in fiscal 1982, would be entirely eliminated.

CETA jobs: Temporary government jobs under the Comprehensive Employment and Training Act would be phased out entirely by fiscal 1984, for which the Carter Administration had budgeted $4.4 billion. The fiscal 1982 figure of $3.8 billion would drop to $20 million.

Mass transit: Federal operating subsidies for urban mass transit would be phased out by fiscal 1985, when otherwise the present $750 million budget would grow to $1.3 billion. The official Reagan OMB rationale: "There is no reason for someone in Sioux Falls to pay federal taxes so that someone in Los Angeles can get to work on time by public transportation."

National endowments for the arts and humanities: On the theory that private philanthropy should support these grants to encourage the arts and scholarship, the fiscal 1982 budgets of $163 million for the arts and $167 for the humanities would be cut in half.

HUD planning assistance: This aid from the Department of Housing and Urban Development for planning by cities would be cut from $35 million to $9 million in fiscal 1982 and ended entirely the next year.

Dairy subsidies: This infamous source of politicking and corruption in the past would drop quickly, with $1.1 billion cut out of the previously budgeted $1.7 billion for fiscal 1982.

Guaranteed student loans: This is a typical program of "off-budget" spending by one of Stockman's favorite targets: the Federal Financing Bank. In point of fact, the bank was a few Treasury officials doling out funds to buy financial paper. By eliminating this government purchase of guaranteed student loans, $1.9 billion would be saved in fiscal 1982 and $15 billion over five years.

Amtrak: The basic financing for the passenger train service would shift from the federal Treasury to passenger fares (which as Reagan took office paid for only 40 percent of the costs). That meant a projected drop in federal outlays from $964 million to $649 million in fiscal 1982 and from $1.4 billion to $350 million within five years.

No matter how much talk there was of a "safety net" for the poor, (a concept more closely associated with Kemp than Reagan), the principal social thrust of Reagan's revolutionary budget was a shrinking of welfare aid. While the supply-side purists generally were unenthusiastic about massive budget reduction, they provided Stockman with considerable theoretical backup on this point. Laffer's governmental wedge included disincentives to work—that is, incentives not to work—through welfare payments. Wanniski put it this way: "Governments increasingly spend the tax receipts of the expanding wedge on payments to individuals on the condition that they do not trade their labor in the central marketplace. Americans get welfare benefits, food stamps, unemployment insurance, government housing and, to a greater degree, retirement benefits explicitly on the condition that they be unemployed."[7] Gilder argued that welfare subsidies in general "pose very grave moral hazards, such as work force withdrawal, familial breakdown, and other adjustments to the term of the grants."[8] All this provided theoretical justification for what Reagan had felt intuitively for most of his adult life.

The logical extension of supply-side theory was to cut the rewards of nonwork so sharply that the incentive for compliance with the terms of welfare—including the broken family—would diminish. Without going that far and without saying so in precise language, this was the true thrust of the Reagan budget.

One major proposed change, for the costly Aid for Dependent Children (AFDC), would bring no immediate cost savings but would seemingly reduce the attractiveness of welfare: a requirement that physically capable recipients work twenty hours a week to receive benefits. But other provisions in the Reagan budget would indeed save federal money while attempting to remove work disincentives. A ceiling would be put on Medicaid—medical benefits to the poor—that would save $1 billion in fiscal 1982 and $5 billion in fiscal 1985. Aid for workers thrown out of work by competition from foreign imports would decrease from $1.5 billion to $250 million in fiscal 1982. The $2.5 billion budgeted for fiscal 1982 payments to states with high unemployment to pay extended jobless benefits would be cut by $1.3 billion.

The built-in dilemma here was that attempts to cut welfare costs by strictly enforcing income eligibility would tend to create a means test and the means test itself would then become a disincentive for work; if you *don't* work, you get food stamps. Nevertheless, the Reagan budget concentrated heavily on the food stamps program.

This program had grown phenomenally from its start in 1965 when half a million people were receiving $2.5 million in aid, to 1980 when 21.1 million people were receiving benefits costing $8.6 billion. More than the poor were receiving such aid, and its disruptive effect on incentives to work, to produce and to save could not be calculated, in the view of the supply-siders. Reagan would begin by cutting the $12.5 billion fiscal 1982 budget by $1.8 billion, through limiting food stamps to families whose annual salaries are less than 130 percent of the official poverty level.

Inherent in the Reagan budget's attempt to shrink the accumulated benefits that constituted an alternative to work was a basic philosophical point that was fairly stated by a Democratic critic of the administration, Senator John Glenn of Ohio, during the Senate debate on Stockman's confirmation as OMB director:

> In Mr. Stockman's view, any means-tested welfare system is counterproductive because it offers a strong disincentive to recipient employment and outside earnings, leads to the dissolution of families, creates large incentives for the concealing of assets and other fraud, and wastes resources by requiring a massive administrative bureaucracy.

> Well, how about all those other folks who can only marginally make it in our very complex society? Are we just to ignore them and say they do not count?

> I know very few people who would defend our present welfare system in the United States. It does indeed suffer from some of the things which Mr. Stockman accuses it of. But are we a nation of compassionate people? Do we believe in the preservation of human dignity? Have we been willing to back up that philosophical commitment with our nation's resources? The answer, of course, is that we have.

But Reagan and Stockman also were saying that the cost of that compassion had been a weakening of the nation's economic system. It was no small part of the Reagan Revolution, imbedded in his prepolitical oratory and dominating his days as governor of California. It preceded the unexpected radical assault on the budget and transcended any dollar savings that might be realized there.

A microcosm of all that was involved in Reagan's budgetary policy was the Women's Infants and Children program—WIC— under which the Agriculture Department distributed food supplements to pregnant and breastfeeding women and to their children. This little-known program typifies the runaway growth of government.

As governmental services to the poor continued to expand in the late sixties and early seventies, several cities—Detroit, New Orleans, Denver and Washington—set up demonstration programs in 1968 to distribute basic foodstuffs to pregnant and nursing women and their infants. The next year, the White House Conference on Food, which the Nixon Administration believed had been taken over by liberals, recommended against this program on grounds it would prove to be impossible to limit the benefits to mothers and children, who would naturally distribute the food to other family members. Nevertheless, the WIC program was created as a pilot project in 1972 when the Senate hurriedly enacted an unprinted amendment offered by Senator Hubert Humphrey; there had been no hearings or other committee consideration, typifying the careless stampede toward the welfare state. It was enacted permanently in 1974.

WIC's growth mirrored the ballooning of the social welfare system: 37 percent annually in excess of inflation. Spending, beginning at $11.2 million in fiscal 1974, rose to $953 million in fiscal 1981 and a requested $994 million in fiscal 1982. Participation had grown from 300,000 in fiscal 1975 to over 2.2 million in fiscal 1981.

As the 1969 White House Conference had predicted, WIC food naturally benefited members of the family other than the mother and nursing infant. A 1979 study by the Urban Institute found that more than 80 percent of the households receiving WIC aid distributed it around the family table so that it became what Reagan's OMB called "a second food stamp program." Far from attempting the impossible task of policing the distribution of food so that it reached only mother and infant, WIC clinics encouraged sharing it throughout the family. The OMB report said some clinics "have offered recipes on how to use infant formula to make fudge or cookies" that would be eaten by other family members.

Not until June 1980, in the sixth year of WIC's operation, did the program establish income eligibility guidelines—for families with net salaries no more than double the poverty limit. As Reagan took office, this meant an upper income level of $17,800 for a family of four. In fact, however, almost all WIC clinics passing out food were operating with no guidelines at all. A mother would walk in off the street and obtain food without in any way proving her need. At least one third but probably many more WIC recipients were above the poverty line.

Chances are that was not the mother's only help from the government. OMB guessed that as Reagan became president, 40 percent to 50 percent of WIC recipients also received food stamps. About one third were on welfare. Here was a classic case of the multiple benefits for the nonworking poor that the supply-siders and Reagan considered an intolerable disincentive to work.

An OMB memorandum in March 1982 concluded that "the program is totally out of control." Reagan's budget recommendation was to cut the Carter WIC spending estimate down to $724 million, a reduction of $270 million.

This was a program which liberal Democrats in Congress could defend unequivocally and spontaneously. Infant mortality had dropped from 16.1 per thousand in 1975 to 12.5 in 1980. But this followed a long-term trend starting in 1920, when the death rate was 80 per thousand. OMB concluded there was no evidence that WIC had contributed to the progress.

But was it the infants or the bureaucrats that were being defended on Capitol Hill? In the last full fiscal year before Reagan, nearly 20 percent of all program funds—$180 million—was spent on "administration," which meant the cost of hiring dieticians and nutritionists. In this as in other social welfare programs, curtailment would immediately hit hardest against the bureaucracy, not the poor.

The Reagan Revolution was a direct assault on this new governing class—the bureaucracy and its auxiliaries. The struggle to curtail WIC was one skirmish in that war.

Congressional members of the governing class did not immediately recognize the seriousness of Reagan's budget assault, confusing it with the superficial efforts of the past. Understanding the public desire for less government spending, even liberal Democrats endorsed budget cutting. So enthusiastic was their newfound passion for economy in government that they insisted on getting expenditure cuts through Congress before tax reduction could even be considered. As so often in the past, tax reduction was being held hostage for budget reduction.

The motive was obvious. Tax cuts were the cutting edge of the Reagan revolution, as Representative Barney Frank had perceived. Even if they did not fulfill the expectations of the supply-siders and make the governmental welfare state superfluous, the liberals feared the loss of revenue would make the welfare state inoperable. Thus, the Reagan Administration's unexpected emphasis on budget cuts played into their hands of delaying tax action until the budget had been cut. The general assumption on Capitol Hill was that the budget was essentially uncuttable in 1981, as it had been for the past generation.

The ploy did delay tax reduction far beyond the time that the supply-siders and Reagan himself preferred. But to the amazement of official Washington, it soon became clear that the budget exercise was very serious indeed. While the ploy delayed tax reduction, it would not kill it.

That the Reagan budget-cutting was not just another perfunctory bow toward fiscal restraint became known early in 1981 even before the budget details were determined. The normal battle of Cabinet members, defending every last dime of their departments' budgets against the ax-wielding OMB, was not played out this time. Most Cabinet-level department heads *urged* Stockman to cut their budgets, and Reagan could be depended on to back Stockman nearly every time in the rare instances of a Cabinet officer defending his budget.

One such instance was Secretary of State Haig, who insisted on strenuously defending increased foreign aid spending inherited from Carter. He lost most of the increases, with Reagan backing Stockman.

Another instance was Secretary of Energy James Edwards seeking government funds to buy a privately constructed, economically unfeasible nuclear reprocessing plant in Barnswell, South Carolina. Stockman called this "corporate welfare," bailing a company out of an uneconomic business decision. Reagan backed Stockman.

Reagan's only constant adversary was Samuel Pierce, a New York lawyer who as secretary of housing and urban development was the Cabinet's only black and only bona fide liberal Republican. Pierce defended the costly HUD programs that had been growing since the days of LBJ's Great Society, and repeatedly lost out to Stockman—with one notable exception.

Stockman wanted to phase out urban development action grants, a new and growing source of federal largesse to cities that could find private money to accompany it. This time Pierce had a powerful ally: Ed Meese, who had been convinced by real estate developers in California that "leveraging" federal funds was a good idea. Stockman insisted that such temptations are what had brought about the present financial disorder of the federal government, but Reagan followed Meese's advice. UDAG did not die. Instead, Carter's $610 million estimate for fiscal 1982 was raised by $17 million in the Reagan budget. It is an exception worth noting only because exceptions were so rare.

The size of Reagan's budget reductions was not the only surprise. Even more unexpected was their nature. However insignificant a $50 billion cut might seem to be to a trillion-dollar economy, there was no doubt that Reagan and Stockman were doing more than reducing federal outlays. They were changing the nature of the federal government. By eliminating and phasing out whole programs, by exempting the "sheep" and going for the "goats," they had a tactical strategy of maintaining public support behind them.

The hard truth came home to congressional Democrats on Sunday afternoon, March 22, 1981, when Stockman, by now a ubiquitous figure on television screens and magazine covers, was finishing a half-hour interview over ABC's *Issues and Answers*. The last question was asked by ABC's Barry Serafin:

MR. SERAFIN: Do you stand by your statement that the right to a lawyer is not a basic right of citizens? And, if so, doesn't cutting back on legal services disenfranchise a lot of people from legal help?

MR. STOCKMAN: I don't believe that there is any entitlement, any basic right to legal services or any other kinds of services, and the idea that's been established over the last ten years that almost every service that someone might need in life ought to be provided, financed by the government as a matter of basic right, is wrong. We challenge that. We reject that notion.

Stockman went on to add that states might want to use block grant funds to fund their own legal services for the poor. But that constituted a wholly different federal role, and thoughtful liberals such as Barry Frank thought block grants might merely be "a way station" toward even more radically reduced federal spending.

The budget figures only hinted at the breadth of Reagan's strategy. The intended impact on public policy was to be greater than the sum of the parts: to reduce the scope of government, to reduce the governmental interference on the economy, to reduce reliance of individuals on the government.

The pressure would not relent after a hundred days. Disappointed by the failure of the bond market to respond favorably to the budget cuts, Stockman admitted that Lehrman was right in pressing for greater reductions in fiscal 1981 and pushed for an additional $5 billion in cuts there. He also had come to believe the markets demanded proof of intent for deeper expenditure reductions in future years, requiring a cut in Social Security entitlements—defiling one of the seven sacred cows and perhaps scrapping Kemp's safety net.

Not even the adoption by Congress of a budget resolution approving Reagan's figures, by a surprisingly comfortable margin in the Democratic-controlled House on May 7, convinced the battle-weary bond traders in Wall Street that Reagan and Stockman meant business. Alan Greenspan warned from New York that stronger medicine was needed to convince the bond boys. On May 8, a Social Security reform imposing a penalty against early retirement, drafted under Stockman's guidance, was routinely approved at the White House by Meese. On the following Monday, May 11, Reagan himself, presiding over a cabinet-level meeting, enthusiastically endorsed a reform of the kind that over the years he had prophesied was necessary, often to his political misfortune.

It again proved politically poisonous. Not only was part of the safety net removed, but the early retirement provisions affected so many millions of Americans that, under Stockman's formula, this was a matter of shearing sheep rather than culling goats. Democratic leaders in Congress, licking their wounds after a succession of losses to Reagan on the budget, attacked ferociously on grounds he had violated his campaign promises. The administration retreated in disorder from the political firestorm, admitting a major tactical blunder. Nor did the bond traders seem the slightest bit impressed.

Yet, Reagan had given warning that Congress would have to do something soon about the insolvency of the Social Security system. Similarly, it soon became clear that Reagan's fight for block grants would not be won in his first year but would require prolonged combat against education and other social welfare lobbies. Finally, triumphant passage of the budget resolution did not guarantee a final budget victory; individual appropriations bills would have to be battled over, again with social welfare lobbies surrendering ground grudgingly. The same fight would have to be repeated each year of Ronald Reagan's presidency. On the budgetary front, the Reagan Revolution had just begun.

7

Not on Our Backs

At 10:48 A.M. on his third full day as president, Ronald Reagan called reporters into the Oval Office to unveil Professor Murray Weidenbaum of Washington University, St. Louis, Missouri, as his selection for chairman of the president's Council of Economic Advisers. Since Weidenbaum was being named weeks after Stockman and Donald Regan were in place making economic policy, he looked like a second-class policymaker in the new administration. Possibly to compensate for this, Reagan himself, not Jim Brady, announced the appointment and embellished it with a personal note: "He [Weidenbaum] has advised me economically for over five years. Now, a good share of that time he didn't know he was advising me, but I was following his writings and his utterances and many times referred to them and referred to him in my own weekly radio broadcasts."

Those "utterances" came from Weidenbaum's Center for the Study of American Business at Washington University, where the adverse impact of government regulation was the subject of critical scrutiny. Reagan loved it. For years, he had been clipping newspapers and underlining reports to accumulate evidence of absurd, even comic excesses of big government oppressing little business. That evidence was part of The Speech from the beginning and continued there in his triumphant drive for the presidency.

This was particularly true in the spring of 1979 when campaign manager John Sears decreed a low profile for front-running candidate Reagan: no new material, nothing controversial. Forced to fall back on his own resources as he traveled across the country to appear before Republican and business groups, Reagan dredged up 5 × 8 index cards recording governmental excesses. One of his favorites concerned OSHA, the mild-sounding acronym for Occupational Safety and Health Administration in the Department of Labor that carried a dread note of bureaucratic tyranny in businessmen's ears. In inimitable prose, OSHA had defined an exit as "that portion of a means of egress which is separated from all other spaces of the building or structure by construction or equipment as required in the subpart to provide a protected way of travel to the exit discharge." Based on that regulation, Reagan told audiences, OSHA had ordered the owner of a small business in Indiana to place exit signs over the twelve-foot doors at the back and front of his seven-person shop, "so, in case of a fire, a newly hired employee could tell where the door was." When Reagan told the story with an actor's sense of superb timing, it evoked titters but not all that much laughter, not even from business audiences.

It was a little too old hat, particularly for the newsmen accompanying Reagan. They even doubted the accuracy of the governmental horror stories, including the Indiana OSHA tale (which, in fact, was all too true). Accurate or not, Reagan worked hard to milk applause and laughter from business audiences while waiting for his staff to prepare newer, more exciting material. His aides, Sears included, admitted as much.

But all these—aides, newsmen and most of his listeners—missed the vital ingredient these anecdotes held for Reagan's revolutionary prescription for America. An assault on government regulation was an essential component of the Reagan Revolution, its importance not diminished because Reagan's pursuit of this course happened to be so instinctive. It was more widely accepted than tax reduction, more important than budget reduction and easier to put into effect than either. Inherent in Reagan's scheme to remake the face of the American government was taking the pressure off that small businessman in Indiana. On January 20, 1981, Reagan made his intention clear in his Inaugural Address:

> Now, so there will be no misunderstanding, it's not my intention to do away with government. It is rather to make it work—work with us,

not over us; to stand by our side, *not ride on our back.* Government can and must provide opportunity, not smother it; foster productivity, not stifle it [emphasis added].

Federal regulation was mild for the first 150 years of the republic, the light hand of the government coinciding with mild taxation and restrained government spending for a climate conducive to sustained economic growth. That ended with the Great Depression, when the stock market crash brought in the Securities & Exchange Commission as a regulatory watchdog. The New Deal meant, along with higher taxes and higher government spending, a proliferation of regulatory agencies to prevent economic abuses and control the communications, airline, energy and other industries. Much as businessmen wailed, however, the tyranny was more psychological than fiscal. While increasingly curbing the businessman's freedom, the New Deal and attendant regulation did not seriously reduce his profits.

Change began in the 1960s, accelerating into runaway in the 1970s. The starting point can be traced to 1965 with publication by an unknown lawyer named Ralph Nader of *Unsafe at Any Speed,* an exposé of alleged safety hazards in American cars. No single book had a deeper impact on the nation's history. It spawned the consumerist-environmentalist movement as a major force on the American scene, with Nader himself rising to become its founder and chief arbiter.

What previously had been government regulation for economic purposes became regulation for social purposes. Whereas previous regulation was aimed principally at preventing monopolistic combinations and conspiratorial price-fixing, broader objectives were involved in the emergence of OSHA and the Environmental Protection Administration, the Clean Air and Clean Water acts and a tougher new breed of regulators at old-line agencies such as the Department of the Interior and the Federal Trade Commission. The aims were to protect the consumer, to protect the worker, but mainly to protect the environment. That mandated a policy of limited growth at best. Among the environmental regulators, it was not clear which took precedence: Was low growth necessary for environmental protection? Or was environmental protection merely a pretext for a philosophy of low growth, with the ultimate goal of changing the American lifestyle?

What was beyond doubt, however, was that costs to business were secondary, if not irrelevant. The prevailing Naderite philosophy, which pervaded Capitol Hill and the bureaucracy in the seventies, was this: We cannot talk about red ink on a business ledger when it comes to saving lives and protecting the nation's environment.

The cost to American business was immense, probably immeasurable, the burden of paperwork multiplying geometrically. When established in 1970, OSHA required nearly all employers to complete, for each employee, OSHA forms 100, 101 and 102: a log of occupational injuries and illnesses, a supplementary record of each occupational injury or illness, and a summary sheet of injuries and illnesses, respectively. OSHA was only a part of the burden. In 1973, the Graymills Corporation, employing 120 persons, submitted to Congress a list of forty forms it had to fill out, some of them several times a year, some of them for each of its employees.

Beyond paperwork were capital costs required to meet everrising environmental standards. That meant, Weidenbaum wrote in 1979, "a larger share of company investment—about one tenth at the present time—is being devoted to the required social responsibilities rather than to increasing the capacity to produce a higher quantity or quality of material output." The result was "a smaller productive capacity in the American economy."[1]

Lack of productivity added its own inflationary impact to other regulatory causes of inflation. By 1968, federal requirements (then only seat and shoulder belts and exhaust emission standards) had raised the retail price of the average American automobile by $47.84. Just ten years later, in 1978, the figure was $665.87 ($146.66 of that total coming in 1975 when the catalytic converter was required).

The capital costs profile of American business was transformed. In 1976, the share of total capital expenditures by the Bethlehem Steel Company that went *solely* for environmental control equipment mandated by government regulation was 15 percent. But the real costs of environmental control went far beyond that: the rusting, vacant steel mills of Youngstown, Ohio, closed because of inability to conform to EPA requirements. Those ghost steel mills, visited by Reagan in the 1980 campaign, typified hundreds of foundries that closed their doors beginning in 1968, financially unable to comply with OSHA and EPA requirements.

The companion of old plant closures was inability to get new plants opened. In 1976, Dow Chemical Company spent $186 million to comply with federal regulations, an increase of 27 percent over the previous year. More important than the gross figures was $4 million spent by Dow in 1975 and 1976 in an attempt to gain environmental clearance for a $300 million petrochemical complex in California to meet West Coast demand for the company's products. In January 1977, Dow gave up; it cancelled the project, wiping out its investment and sacrificing thousands of jobs. Out of sixty-five governmental clearances necessary to build the petrochemical complex, Dow had obtained only four.

The strangulation of business by government was becoming evident in the 1970s. John Dunlop, who as secretary of labor was the Ford Cabinet's most liberal member, said in 1975: "The country needs to acquire a more realistic understanding of the limits to which social change can be brought through legal compulson. . . . Government has more regulation on its plate than it can handle."

At about the same time, Weidenbaum published a landmark monograph: "Government-Mandated Price Increases: A Neglected Aspect of Inflation." Weidenbaum's thesis was that the proliferating government regulations "would increase the cost of doing business and would inevitably lead to higher prices for consumers or to lower wages for employees. If the trend continues unchecked, the resulting loss in productivity could lead to stagnation in real living standards."[2]

Nevertheless, the Ford Administration did little more to diminish this danger than the Nixon Administration, which entirely neglected it. On the contrary, President Ford's signature on the 1975 Energy Act spawned a vast new bureaucracy with widening regulatory powers. The Carter Administration did partly eliminate what OSHA bureaucrats themselves called Mickey Mouse regulations, but the appointment of ardent environmentalists and regulators by Carter measurably lengthened the regulatory reach of Washington during his administration. Lawyers and activists who had been filing environmental and consumerist lawsuits against the federal government suddenly were on the other side of the desk in Washington. Their feeble defenses against suits by their erstwhile activist colleagues aroused some suspicion of collusion. While "deregulation" was becoming more popular as a political catchword even to such liberals as Senator Edward M. Kennedy, it was applied to economic regulation of specific industries—radio-television, trucking, airlines; the broad regulatory thrust of environmental and health protection was left untouched by Carter and Kennedy.

Thus, as Reagan took office, his plans for regulatory reform departed from established governmental policy of the last generation, under both Democratic and Republican administrations, no less radically than his proposals for tax and budgetary change. But unlike those proposals, there was no dissent on the regulatory front. All were in agreement on this issue: Herb Stein and other conservative Keynesians, Milton Friedman and his monetarist school—and the supply-siders. Laffer's theory of the governmental wedge equated the disruptive effects on the free economy resulting from both taxation and regulation. Indeed, Laffer said that regulation *is* taxation, so that regulatory relaxation *is* a tax cut. Gilder wrote: "The most serious damage inflicted by excessive controls is the discouragement of innovation and entrepreneurship and the perpetuation of slightly laundered and government-approved obsolescence."[3]

Reagan himself had been excoriating government regulation at countless banquet tables and lecture halls while other politicians ignored the issue. He had, indeed, gotten himself into some political trouble during the 1980 campaign by citing environmental regulation as a major cause of what ailed the American economy.

He did so on October 9 in Youngstown, where he blamed empty steel mills and long lines of unemployed on EPA zeal. Speaking to workers there, Reagan attacked EPA's use of 1970 data in setting its regulatory standards: "Since then, new evidence has become available and air pollution has been substantially controlled. But these 1970 rules have helped force factories to shut down and cost workers their jobs." EPA officials have gone beyond guidelines for protecting the environment, said Reagan. "In reality, what they believe in is no growth."

That was good political medicine in Youngstown, but drew retorts elsewhere—including Reagan's home base of Los Angeles, then undergoing its tenth consecutive day of pea-soup smog. EPA bureaucrats in Washington denounced Reagan's claim that air pollution had been "substantially controlled," and Reagan on the campaign trail was led to plead: "I am an environmentalist." The uproar reflected the fact, proved in the polls, that environmentalism enjoyed substantial popular support. When asked by pollsters, people tended to say government should do more to clean up the air and water.

The answer to the political problem for Reagan was a largely ignored comment in his Youngstown speech. As president, he would require a cost-benefit analysis of any environmental regulation. While people wanted Washington to do more about the environment, the polls showed they also overwhelmingly agreed on a cost-benefit test that would require a showing that regulations produce more in tangible value than they cost.

Weidenbaum, as chairman of Reagan's campaign task force on regulation, refined this point in his report to the candidate: "For each new rule they proposed, the regulatory agencies should be required to demonstrate at least a reasonable relationship between the costs imposed and the benefits proposed—and to demonstrate further that they have chosen the most efficient (least costly) method of achieving those benefits."[4]

Still, there was a trade-off inherent here: accepting less clean air and water in exchange for more economic growth. Similarly, Reagan and Weidenbaum offered another trade-off: less stringent safety regulations in exchange for more productivity. If there was an implication of possible life-threatening illness, the people would not accept the trade-off. But if all that was threatened was the quest for pristine purity of the environment or absolute safety in the workplace and of products bought in the marketplace, Reagan and his advisers felt the American people would accept their trade-offs.

Any doubt that Reagan was deadly serious about radical deregulation was dispelled with the selection of James Watt, a forty-four-year-old Denver lawyer who, as founder and president of the Mountain States Legal Foundation, had been battling the environmental movement in the courts the past four years. Weidenbaum's task force report had listed "appointment power" as Reagan's first line of offense in easing government regulation. Stockman had privately urged a ruthless purge of "environmentalist zealots" in government departments, getting rid of them if possible, at the least transferring them to innocuous positions. But presidential appointments were the key, and secretary of the interior was foremost among them.

For much of the century, that post had been held by ardent

conservationists. After his election in 1968, Nixon sought and found an exception in Governor Walter Hickel of Alaska, who held a memorable press conference attacking conservationists for wanting to "lock up lands for no reason. . . . If we set standards too high, we might even hinder industrial development." But the Senate Interior Committee forced Hickel to swallow each and every such statement before confirming him, and in the process produced a genuine environmental convert. Carter selected an avowed environmentalist in Governor Cecil Andrus of Idaho, an outdoorsman who shared the view of Interior Department bureaucrats that industrial development was a defacement of nature.

Reagan accepted the recommendation of his Kitchen Cabinet and other advisers to name former Senator Clifford Hansen of Wyoming. But Hansen did not want to return to government service because of painful financial divestiture and disclosure. He recommended Jim Watt to Senator Paul Laxalt, Reagan's emissary. Laxalt was enthusiastic. Watt also received ardent backing from Joseph Coors, conservative activist and president of Adolph Coors brewery in Golden, Colorado, a substantial contributor to Watt's foundation. Hansen's views were antithetical to Andrus's, but they were both easygoing Western politicians with the outdoors in their faces. Watt was different from Andrus not only in ideology but also in style. While born and raised in Wyoming, he had spent his adult life as a big-city lawyer who considered being on horseback "too much like work." Watt was a teetotaler and a religious fundamentalist, his thick rimless glasses magnifying his intensity. He was raring to follow Stockman's plea to clear the zealots out of the department.

That also set him apart from most other Reagan Cabinet members, who entered office without a clear idea of what they wanted to do. In a Cabinet dominated by centrist millionaires, he was a radical activist. Watt was one of only three Cabinet members with a declared net worth under $500,000 (the other two were Stockman and Secretary of Education Terrel Bell). Watt knew the capital from the inside out, giving him an insider's view in a Cabinet studded with newcomers to Washington. After getting his law degree in 1962, he spent the next sixteen years in the capital as senatorial aide, U.S. Chamber of Commerce lobbyist and middle-level bureaucrat in the Interior Department and the

Federal Power Commission. It was the last four years at the Mountain States Legal Foundation that had made Watt a bogeyman for the environmental movement.

Watt filled the Interior Department with like-minded Westerners. Named to head the Bureau of Land Management was the speaker of the Colorado House of Representatives, Robert F. Buford, a cattle rancher holding grazing rights on U.S. public lands. The new director of the Office of Surface Mining was Indiana State Senator James R. Harris, who pushed state lawsuits challenging the federal strip-mining law and was closely associated with the mining industry. Appointed as Interior Department solicitor was William H. Coldiron, vice chairman of the Montana Power Company.

Outside the Interior Department, the pattern was similar. Just as Carter had reached into the ranks of environmental activists for his regulators, Reagan recruited antienvironmentalists who were hostile to regulation.

The new head of EPA was Anne Gorsuch, a Republican member of the Colorado legislature and lawyer for the Mountain Bell Telephone Company, Denver. Another recommendation of Joe Coors, she had publicly urged restraint in environmental regulation. She was chosen over Professor John Hernandez of New Mexico State University, the early choice, who was vetoed by Watt, Coors and others as excessively moderate on environmental questions.

Thorne G. Auchter, head of his family's building contracting firm in Jacksonville, Florida, was named head of OSHA, which he said symbolized governmental overregulation.

Raymond A. Peck, vice president for regulatory affairs of the National Coal Association and a longtime advocate of deregulation, was named administrator of the National Highway Traffic Safety Administration. He replaced the zealous Joan Claybrook, whose conduct of the agency during the Carter Administration led the automotive industry to call her the Dragon Lady.

On December 22, 1980, when Dave Stockman learned of the appointment of James Watt as secretary of the interior, he telephoned Watt in Denver to offer his congratulations and a suggestion: Why not reconsider the decision of Andrus to exclude from possible oil exploration four areas off the California coast? As a congressman, Stockman had specialized in energy and felt Andrus's decision was unwise. Besides, the federal Treasury needed the money. Offshore oil leasing was a profitable activity helpful to an OMB director-designate facing a budget deeply in deficit. No more receptive ears could have received Stockman's plea. Watt was the only Cabinet member other than Stockman to call himself a supply-sider at the time he was nominated, and he gave economic growth priority over environmentalist objections to new drilling along the California coastline. Watt brought the matter up at a February 8 staff meeting at Interior. Scenting the new atmosphere, many of the bureaucrats quickly made themselves appear enthusiastic. He was urged to reopen the excluded areas by Heather Ross, a civil servant serving as deputy assistant secretary for policy, budget and administration. There were few if any dissents. On February 11, Watt announced his decision to include the four areas in possible offshore leasing. California Democrats, led by Governor Edmund G. Brown, Jr., protested strenuously against defilement of their coastlines, but in vain (save possibly later in the year for one area suspected of containing no oil or gas anyway).

For Brown in California and other environmentalist politicians elsewhere, there would be hard times ahead in Washington. Energy conservation with stringent federal controls over production and pricing had ended. Watt's decisions on the California oil leases meant that federal policy would no longer use environmental restraint to impede energy production.

On January 28, Reagan removed all remaining price controls on gasoline and domestic crude oil prices, effective immediately. That ended federal control over allocations of gasoline, which had resulted in angry gasoline lines across the country in 1979, and ended the entitlements program that had propped up small refiners to keep them in business. All that was left under federal price control was natural gas, and Reagan wanted to move on that too when the time was ripe.

So Reagan's campaign promises of a new deal for energy had been quickly translated into action: a free market, setting higher prices to discourage consumption, and the easing of production restrictions to expand the supply.

The final days of the Carter Administration were filled with intense activity that showed how much power the bureaucracy had seized from the people's elected representatives in regulating the nation. Throughout the Carter Administration, departments and agencies of the government had been issuing regulations without asking the president's leave. The election acted as a trip wire, unleashing a flood of new regulations without the lame-duck president's permission or even his knowledge. The process, reaching its climax as January 20 neared, produced so many new regulations that on January 16, 1981, two additional volumes of the *Federal Register* (the daily record of all new regulations) had to be published. It continued through January 19 when, bemused but also angry, Reagan called the 119 new governmental edicts the Midnight Regulations and the name stuck.

But not the regulations. On January 29, the president put a sixty-day freeze on those new regulations, a period for study by the new presidential Task Force on Regulatory Relief. Nominally headed by Vice President Bush, it was actually run by James C. Miller III, a new OMB associate director. Miller, an economist, had spent the last few years at the American Enterprise Institute, a conservative think tank, analyzing the impact of federal regulation. Now he was able to transfer analysis into action. The staff of the Council on Wage and Price Stability, which under Carter had attempted "voluntary" control of wages and prices and was quickly abolished by President Reagan, was assigned to Miller. On February 17, Reagan signed an executive order officially establishing the cost-benefit yardstick.

By the time the sixty days had expired, the work of the Miller task force was well underway. While the budget was slowly making its way through Congress and the tax program was not nearly ready for action, the Reagan Administration had killed or at least suspended thirty-six new regulations. A sample shows the pervasiveness of governmental interest. The regulations would have:

▼ Required schools to provide catheterization services to handicapped students during the school day (Education Department regulation).
▼ Tightened restrictions on toxic wastes that industries send into municipal sewage treatment plants (EPA regulation).
▼ Listed the Hawaiian tree snail under the Endangered Species Act (Interior Department regulation).
▼ Prohibited government contractors from paying membership

fees for their employees in private clubs that practice discrimination (Labor Department regulation).

▼ Set eligibility criteria for federally funded car pools (Transportation Department regulation).

▼ Banned oil and gas exploration in California's Point Reves–Farrallon Island sanctuary for gray whales and nesting seabirds (Commerce Department regulation).

That was only the beginning. On the regulatory front, the Reagan Revolution was a fact.

On January 19, 1981, while the last of the Midnight Regulations were emerging on the Carter Administration's final day, Dr. Eula Bingham made a decision that climaxed the decade-long career of OSHA as the hairshirt of America's businesses.

As OSHA director, Dr. Bingham, a physician, was more attentive to the complaints of workers relayed by labor leaders than to the regulatory wedge and its affect on the American economy. As much as OSHA had been hated by businessmen during its first eight years, she raised it to a high plateau of emotion in November 1979 with OSHA's new standard limiting a worker's daily exposure to lead—affecting at least 800,000 American workers. The United Steelworkers argued that the respirators worn by workers were not only uncomfortable but for workers with breathing difficulties constituted a severe problem. OSHA agreed, requiring instead that companies install large air filters and make other engineering changes at immense expense. OSHA also ordered companies to take workers off the job when medical tests showed abnormally high levels of lead content in the blood until those levels dropped to the agency's standard. During that time, the workers would receive full pay and benefits and seniority protection. Nothing exemplified better the agency's lack of interest in a cost-benefit standard for regulation.

The industry went to court, and in August 1980 the U.S. Court of Appeals in Washington upheld OSHA but ordered it to review the decision over a six-month period to determine whether its lead standard was too severe. In six months, however, Jimmy Carter and Eula Bingham would be gone from Washington. So on January 19, 1981, Dr. Bingham joined the other Midnight Regulation writers and reaffirmed her 1979 decision.

That lasted less than a week. Even before a new OSHA director had been named and a new secretary in the parent Labor Department had been confirmed by the Senate, middle-level officials met with industry lawyers (union officials were not invited) and reversed Dr. Bingham. On February 4, the Labor Department asked the U.S. Court of Appeals to set aside the regulation at least temporarily. It was a symbol of change at OSHA that could scarcely be measured.

When building contractor Thorne Auchter was named OSHA director on March 17, he moved quickly in ways that antagonized organized labor. He immediately ordered destruction of 100,000 booklets about cotton dust, the cause of "brown lung" disease in textile workers, because of its cover—a photograph of a diseased worker that Auchter found "offensive" and "obviously favorable" to labor. At the same time, he withheld distribution of films and slide shows about workers' safety rights.

The change in tone was reflected in Auchter's answer when Philip Shabecoff of the *New York Times* asked him whether he agreed with Eula Bingham that "uncomfortable" respirators are ineffective as a safety device because workers will not wear them. Calling respirators "absolutely appropriate" safety devices, Auchter added: "As to whether devices are comfortable for employees, well, employers are asked to do things under the government's Safety and Health Act and under OSHA regulations that are not always comfortable for them. Both employers and employees have a responsibility to comply."[5]

That interview was published March 29, two days after Auchter made a radical departure from the practice of past OSHA directors. He announced his agency would review all existing regulations from a cost-benefit standard, in conformity with Reagan's direction. Furthermore, he asked the Supreme Court not to rule on the cost-benefit issue on regulations protecting textile workers from cotton dust, leaving OSHA to apply that test to the regulation. Ralph Nader, who had first referred to the affliction caused by cotton dust as "brown lung disease," said the Reagan Administration was "knowingly jeopardizing the lives of 75,000 textile workers." It was a clear sign that the Reagan Revolution was deadly serious about deregulation.

Reagan kept his sense of humor, though, even about OSHA. After a brief talk with leading editorial page editors in the East

Room just before he sent his economic message to Congress February 10, he turned from the podium and started to leave, tripping and almost falling over the edge of the low platform on which he had been standing. Stockman caught him before the stumble became a fall. Reagan turned back to the editors and said: "We must get OSHA to look into this—" drawing an appreciation chuckle with a one-liner about the agency he had just upbraided.

In its report to the Reagan campaign, the Weidenbaum task force urged "greater attention in the congressional budgetary process to the managing of regulation."[6] Before taking over OMB, Stockman had urged a 17.5 percent across-the-board cut in federal funding of regulation. In his first weeks in office, Stockman moved quickly to reduce money for two highly visible regulatory agencies.

The first was the Consumer Products Safety Commission, one of the new breed of regulatory agencies that had in the previous decade contributed so much to the regulatory wedge. Created in 1972, during the supposedly conservative Nixon Administration, to protect the consumer, the CPSC set out to scourge business and hang the cost. "If a company violates our statute . . ." said Chairman Richard O. Simpson in 1973, "we will put the chief executive in jail. Once we do put a top executive behind bars, I am sure that we will get a much higher degree of compliance from other companies." At the same time, Commissioner R. David Pittle said: "Any time consumer safety is threatened, we're going to go for the company's throat. . . . When it involves a product that is unsafe, I don't care how much it costs the company to correct the problem."

The tone was set by an early CPSC decision in January 1974 on 1,494 containers of windshield-washer solvent without childproof caps or labels warning of poison. The commission ruled that each of the containers must be *destroyed*. It practiced what Weidenbaum called Big Motherism—offering tips for skiers and skaters and pleading with consumers to "choose all toys carefully." In its first ruling, the CPSC ordered every manufacturer, distributor or retailer of any product that "creates a substantial risk of injury" to provide what Weidenbaum called "a staggering array of information."[7]

Stockman's response was a meat-ax slash of 30 percent in the CPSC budget. The White House backed him, despite pleas from Naderites and the commissioners themselves. Later, he proposed that the commission be abolished entirely.

But there was a different outcome in efforts to cut the other agency targeted for a quick slash by Stockman: the Federal Trade Commission. One of the oldest of regulatory agencies, the FTC was created in 1914 to enforce the newly enacted Clayton Antitrust Act—that was all. It had been so lethargic in performing those duties that it was widely known as the Old Lady of Pennsylvania Avenue.

In 1967, Congress substantially increased the FTC's powers. The dynamic force behind the new legislation was Michael Pertschuk, longtime staff director of the Senate Commerce Committee. Two years later in 1977, President Carter named him FTC chairman. The commission abruptly woke from its long sleep and hurtled itself into the regulatory land rush with an astonishing array of pursuits. Pertschuk's investigators hunted monopolistic tendencies in the automotive and energy industries. It probed funeral parlors and accused the industry of charging too much. It flayed the life insurance business for skimping on interest rates. Among the defendants of Pertschuk's legal onslaughts were Exxon, General Motors, I.T.T., Kellogg, Levi Strauss and Sears, Roebuck. Using its new powers, the FTC took on the task of policing the nation's advertising. Geritol was accused of "nonverbal" implications that made the tonic seem something it was not. False claims in restaurant menus became a federal sin. To justify a protracted investigation of food advertising, chief presiding officer William D. Dixon said: "People often eat for the wrong reasons." The Old Lady of Pennsylvania Avenue had turned into Big Mother.

Stockman wanted not only to cut FTC's fiscal 1981 budget by 13 percent and its fiscal 1982 budget by 25 percent but proposed that it phase out antitrust functions that were its original reason for being. But the sixty-seven-year-old FTC had more political supporters than the nine-year-old CPSC—including Vice President Bush. He joined with influential Republicans in Congress, small business groups and the National Association of Attorneys General to block Stockman's phasing out of antitrust activities for the FTC. The White House also forced Stockman to cut down his

FTC budget reductions for the two years to 5 percent and 11 percent. That was the first sign of Bush rising to blunt the Reagan Revolution and the first check to the administration's anti-regulatory wave.

Contrary to expectations excited by Stockman and Weidenbaum about severe budget slashing in the regulatory agencies, most cuts for fiscal 1982 were relatively modest. Overall Carter budget figures of $7.8 billion for regulation would be reduced by only $395 million. But the point was not size, it was direction. The movement was all downward.

Nor could the radical nature of what Reagan was doing be measured solely in dollars. Just as consumer advocates were congratulating themselves for averting disaster at the FTC, the commission's bureaucrats gave a sign that they, too, had their fingers in the wind. That was clear when the staff recommended dropping Mike Pertschuk's pet project: regulation of television commercials aimed at children.

But the power of government breeds a tendency to regulate even among those intellectually disposed in the opposite direction. That included one of the most impressive members of Reagan's new Cabinet: Drew Lewis, a millionaire businessman-politician who had the political standing to request and get the post of secretary of transportation. After holding Pennsylvania for Gerald Ford against Reagan in 1976, he was conscripted by John Sears for Reagan's 1980 campaign and ended up as national deputy political campaign director. Besides this political due bill, he had the qualifications. A Philadelphia-based management consultant, he was a court-appointed trustee for the bankrupt Reading Railroad, which he reorganized and folded into the federally supported Conrail system. He specialized in revitalizing businesses or, as Lewis himself put it, "I'm an expert in troubled industries."

That was to lead him unwittingly down a path toward government regulation. It was not that Lewis obstructed the basic intent of the Reagan Revolution. On the contrary, he was among the Cabinet's most enthusiastic supporters of Reagan's budget; far from resisting it, he wholeheartedly embraced Stockman's scheme to get the federal government out of rail transportation by dismantling the Conrail and Amtrak systems. By the end of March, he was calling himself a supply-sider and had convinced no less a supply-sider than Wanniski that he really meant it.

Lewis's problem was the series of events that followed his selection to head a task force for the ailing auto industry. Lewis had in his hands a Transportation Department report from the previous administration drafted by Dr. Charles Swinburn, a hold-over career civil servant who was continuing as deputy assistant secretary for policy and international affairs. On three occasions during the first five weeks of his presidency, Reagan exhorted his Cabinet to remove civil servants from policy-making posts on grounds that "you can't trust" the permanent government. Nevertheless, Lewis embraced the Swinburn report that called for limiting Japanese auto imports, which were running at 1.8 million a year. Lewis enlisted the aid of two other millionaire businessmen in the Cabinet, Secretary of Commerce Malcolm Baldridge and Secretary of Labor Raymond Donovan. The dynamic Lewis very nearly convinced Reagan that he might have to set aside his free trade and free market scruples to save a dying industry whose troubles stemmed partly from the governmental wedge (overlooking the industry's own blindness to the small-car trend).

More than free trade was at stake. As the enthusiastic Lewis described it, the quota was the lever for a bounty of benefits. The United Auto Workers would moderate their future demands and even scale down their present contracts if imports were reduced. That labor restraint in turn would modify auto industry pricing. Sitting at the table with auto labor and auto management would be the federal government (perhaps in the person of Drew Lewis) as conciliator.

"Why, that's an incomes policy!" responded Murray Weidenbaum when he heard Lewis's views at the Cabinet table. Guilty of helping persuade the Nixon Administration to adopt an incomes policy (wage and price controls) a decade earlier, Weidenbaum was a converted sinner immune to further temptation. With powerful help through Don Regan and Stockman, he waged a spirited campaign to convince the president that Lewis's grand design was government more on the scale of Benito Mussolini or at least John Connally than of Ronald Reagan. Martin Anderson's council of outside economic advisers was brought in to help. Milton Friedman provided a convincing argument.

The choice was between two alternatives: try to save the automotive industry by reducing imports, along with fine-tuning prices and wages in the industry; or let the free market function, hoping it would adjust prices and wages and, eventually, that Reagan's economic program would increase the consumption of automobiles. If it did not work out that way—the free market included the right to fail as well as to succeed—Detroit would have to live with its past mistakes, by both management and labor. Reagan ended up sliding between the two alternatives. While not openly calling for quotas, the president did not adopt the pure free market policy that would result from pledging to veto any quota bill. Instead, back-door negotiating pressure nudged Japan into a "voluntary" restraint on imports negotiated in Tokyo at the end of April. That was a defeat for Don Regan, Stockman and Weidenbaum, who warned inside the Cabinet that the Japanese import agreement would be a signal to other depressed industries to seek help from Washington. It was a victory for Baldridge, no foe of protection, and for Special Trade Representative William Brock, who negotiated the Tokyo agreement. And for Drew Lewis.

By the end of March, Lewis had removed himself from the trade question and concentrated on help for Detroit more faithful to Adam Smith than Mussolini. Lewis announced the Reagan program of help to the auto industry on April 5, 1981. He said not a word about import protection. Instead, thirty-four environmental and safety regulations for cars and trucks were ordered ended or deferred. Savings to the consumer and industry: over $9 billion. That was the first reversal of ever more stringent federal regulation of the auto industry of the past decade.

The cost-benefit standard ordered by Reagan was used to justify elimination of rear bumpers and to reduce the strength of front bumpers to a level protecting the car on impact up to 2.5 miles per hour. According to the government's new analysis, the *old* standards—rear and front bumpers—would save $18 a year in damages over the ten-year life of the car, or $180. The analysts estimated annual benefits of the reduced bumper protection at $53 in cheaper cost of the car and $30 in reduced fuel because of the lighter weight—$830 over ten years. That amounted to a $65 one-year net saving or $650 for the life of the car. Based on 10 million cars sold in any one year, that saved $650 million.

The changes also eliminated a requirement that all 1984 passenger cars be equipped with "high altitude" emission standards. In addition, the carbon monoxide emission standard set for 1982 model year cars was postponed to 1983, one of the proposals in Stockman's Dunkirk memo.

Another Stockman-Dunkirk proposal announced by the administration April 6 dramatized the change in direction. The requirement that by September 1, 1981, new large cars must have air bags or other "passive" safety devices that require no action by passengers was postponed for one year, during which it would be studied—and quite likely junked. That saved the auto buyer $105 a car and the industry $30 million in capital investment. The air bags proposal was so closely identified with the regulatory philosophy of Ralph Nader that its defeat was the clearest sign of the Reagan Revolution's turn off the road mapped out in *Unsafe at Any Speed* sixteen years earlier.

In *The Future of Business Regulation*, written before he left academic life to enter government again in the Reagan Administration, Murray Weidenbaum argued for a more restrained policy of regulation. But he cautioned "it would be futile to return to the status quo ante. Public concern with environmental safety, equity and similar matters remains strong."[8]

Weidenbaum received a little ribbing from colleagues in the Reagan Administration for that caution. On March 12, 1981, addressing the Woodrow Wilson International Center for Scholars at the Smithsonian Institution in Washington, Weidenbaum refined his position:

Like government as a whole, regulation is not about to wither away. Nevertheless, it is not written in the stars that the historical trend of expanding regulation is unstoppable. . . . Fundamental to this administration's thinking about business-government relations is the notion that the private sector is the central engine of economic growth and progress. The role of the federal government is key—the watchdog for the public interest. But that role must be exercised with full knowledge that the forces of competition in the marketplace, more often than not, are the most effective mechanism for achieving the high level of economic well-being that is the true end product of the business system.

This was not how Jim Watt or David Stockman or Ronald Reagan would have put it. But coming from the economist often labeled the most moderate member of the Reagan team, it described in cautious, academic, nonhyperbolic language the radical change envisioned by the new president.

It had begun far more quickly but also more quietly than the dramatic tax and budget proposals. It would continue with basic changes in the Clean Air Act to be sought from Congress. It was the quietest but perhaps the most radical battlefront of the Reagan Revolution.

8

Reagan versus the Kremlin

As Ronald Reagan took office, the competitive position of the United States against the Soviet Union was in worse disarray than the economy. The new president's first task was to restore U.S. confidence, lost in the fiasco of Vietnam just when the Soviets went on the march worldwide.

The Kremlin had penetrated the African continent, intervened in Afghanistan, established a new political and military foothold in South Yemen on the tip of the Arabian peninsula, intruded into the Caribbean and Central America with a subversive campaign, bullied Western Europe in an effort to split the NATO alliance. Never before had Moscow so clearly led Washington in the competition over who would most influence the rest of the world.

The restraints placed on a president's freedom of action by Congress during its days of deepest suspicion after Vietnam and the CIA scandals contributed to the Soviet lead. Ford had been blocked from countering Soviet subversion with its Cuban surrogates in Angola. Carter had been inhibited by congressional restraint from sending arms to shore up vulnerable Pakistan. This weakening of presidental powers was part of America's diminished position in the world inherited from Carter by Reagan.

Jimmy Carter surely did not start the relative decline of the United States and the elevation of the Soviet Union. He was a midshipman at the U.S. Naval Academy when the Soviet drive for equality and ultimate superiority over the Americans began. That was the day World War II ended. Following Stalin's masterful diplomacy in gaining the West's consent for hegemony over all of Eastern Europe, the Soviet leader sought to establish Soviet influence in the Far East with last-minute pretensions that Soviet power had turned the tide against Japan. General Douglas MacArthur's refusal to grant Moscow any hand in Japan's postwar political arrangements there stopped Stalin at the starting line, but the Soviet intent had been clearly revealed.

That intent did not show signs of being realized until the Soviet humiliation caused by U.S. superiority in strategic weapons during the Cuban missile crisis of October 1962. When Khrushchev was deposed two years later, the Kremlin began an arms buildup unprecedented in peacetime. It took a decade for that drive to erase the U.S. superiority that had humbled Khrushchev. Not until Carter's presidency did this become obvious.

Yet, until nearly the end of his term, Carter insisted on putting the best possible face on Soviet moves across the world chessboard, not because he wanted to hide the facts but because he and his advisers refused to believe the East-West struggle depended on force of arms or could be won in an arms race.

Following this passivity, the world that Reagan glimpsed on the day after he took the presidential oath was one in which the dominant Soviet role could not be denied. The Russians had increased their military posture in three main categories: first, guns, tanks and other conventional weapons on the ground in Central Europe, along with a new navy capable of patrolling all the world's oceans; second, long-range nuclear missiles that for the first time could threaten in a single, first strike to destroy U.S. land-based missiles; third, a shorter-range nuclear missile deployment aimed at Western Europe that could be used as a terror-propaganda weapon to frighten vulnerable U.S. allies. Thus did the military potency of the Soviet Union reinforce its growing political potency.

What made this political power particularly dangerous was relative Soviet proximity to the two regions of the world containing the wealth essential to Western economic health: the oil of the Persian Gulf and the minerals of southern Africa—both white-controlled South Africa and the black-controlled states above it. Geographic proximity enabled the Soviets to invade Afghanistan, gave Moscow direct access to southeasterly Iran (Iran is one of the world's richest oil areas) and permitted Moscow-directed terror operations against Turkey.

The balance sheet of U.S.-Soviet competition in the four years preceding Reagan was almost all red ink. The single exception was Poland where, through no effort of the West, forces of nationalism were demanding political freedoms in the guise of free labor unions.

Carter had not appealed to his country's combative will to reverse this balance. Reagan's reaction was the opposite. He was convinced that the American people would compete if only their leaders let them. He was contemptuous of those leaders.

"They know too little, not too much of history," Reagan told the Conservative Political Action Conference in Washington on March 17, 1978. "They have lost faith in their own country's past and tradition."

"They," of course, were the Carter Administration's foreign policy and national security handlers, starting with Jimmy Carter himself. Reagan's mind set never had changed from the early 1960s: The Soviet Union was the enemy. He shocked the foreign policy establishment in his first press conference as president by saying that he knew of "no leader of the Soviet Union since the Revolution who did not pursue the goal of world revolution. . . . The only morality they recognize is what will further their cause, meaning they reserve unto themselves the right to commit any crime, to lie, to cheat."

It was true enough that presidents did not talk that way, but this one did—and had without variation for a long time. The bedrock foreign policy in the Reagan Revolution was expressed in Reagan's speech to the Chicago Council on Foreign Relations in March 1980 when he gave vent to his shame over what was happening to his country. "We all have been dishonored and our credibility as a great nation has been compromised, to say the least. Our shield has been tarnished . . . pride in our country seems to be out of fashion" in the era of "vacillation, appeasement and aimlessness."

This contrasted with the conviction of American presidents dating back at least to Richard Nixon in 1969 that if the United States only played its cards right, it could have security on the cheap through a marvelous phenomenon called détente. It was a conviction that Reagan himself deeply believed was born not out of reality but one of political pathology at home: defeatism, pessimism and appeasement. Explaining his decision to run against President Ford in 1976, Reagan came closest to revealing his bitterness at the Nixon-Ford Administrations' refusal to confront reality. "Ford should have taken his case to the people," he said on August 4, 1978. "He should not have accepted what Congress did [in cutting his defense budgets] without more of a fight."[1]

Therein lay the heart of the matter when it came to Ronald Reagan's anger over America's course in the world during his own career as a working politician. He had shuddered during Henry Kissinger's celebrated stewardship; Reagan was convinced that Kissinger's two bosses, Nixon and Ford, had pursued détente so assiduously not because they were sure of its rectitude, but because they assumed—incorrectly, Reagan thought—that the American people were psychically and economically unable to bear the burden of outright competition with Moscow. Reagan's scorn for the Nixon-Ford brand of Republican foreign policy, emphasizing close relations with the Soviet Union, had its origin in his conviction that Nixon and Ford had sold their country short by refusing to test their countrymen's backbone, by not asking them to spend more for national defense. The nation's ability to compete with Moscow, therefore, was not yet measured.

Lamenting President Carter's flawed record in negotiating the second Strategic Arms Limitation Treaty, Reagan spelled out his thesis during the 1980 campaign. It was, he said, quite impossible to obtain an arms control agreement that would actually slow down the alarming pace of Soviet weapons building as long as the Russians remained confident that their lead would keep on increasing. The only way to relieve the Kremlin of that comforting conclusion, Reagan said, was to "clearly demonstrate to the Soviet leadership that we are determined to compete."

In contrast were Carter's mistakes about how politics in the Kremlin and Washington operate: ignorance of Soviet horror at being taken by surprise, as they were when Carter proposed scrapping the negotiating record under Ford; ignorance of the reaction of U.S. military leaders when he proposed to them a radical reduction in long-range missiles for each side; ignorance— or at least lack of appreciation—of the political disdain in Congress regarding the SALT II agreement he finally did negotiate with the Russians.

One explanation was Carter's passion, perhaps affected by his deep religious convictions, against all nuclear power based on the fission or fusion of the atom. Reagan entertained no such fear. What he feared was Soviet use of the atom to build an arsenal of land- and submarine-based nuclear missiles that, in explosive power, already exceeded the U.S. arsenal. What he feared most was that the United States was no longer competing, but was relying on the old doctrine of Mutual Assured Destruction, which held that Soviet fear of U.S. retaliation guaranteed no Soviet first strike.

Reagan wanted to compete not only in building nuclear weapons but across the board in foreign policy. Competition would start early, with Reagan and Secretary of State Alexander Meigs Haig, himself a hard-line product of Kissinger's stewardship, sharing in sending signals to the Soviets. Those signals, or "markers" in Haig's idiom, were calculated to leave no doubt that times had changed in the United States and that, as Reagan had once said, the new administration would test the theory that "America will remain great and act responsibly only so long as it exercises power."

To "exercise power" compelled its acquisition; to acquire it meant convincing the American people that they could once again learn to compete; to convince the people meant taking his case to them. As Reagan entered the White House, the process began at once.

Reagan had summoned Al Haig to California on two separate occasions in the campaign spring and summer of 1980. The future president had no firm idea then that Haig was the man he wanted as the leading member of his Cabinet. George Shultz was far above Haig in speculation about the Reagan Cabinet. Shultz served in several Cabinet posts in the Nixon-Ford Administration and was now a Bechtel Corporation official, widely respected for his competence if not his imagination. Haig, on the other hand, had two classes of enemies: first, conservatives who distrusted his rise from colonel to four-star general in four years as Dr. Kissinger's deputy on the National Security Council staff, and who complained that he had not come out in forthright opposition to SALT II after resigning as NATO supreme commander in 1978; second, liberals who claimed (without basis of fact) that Haig, as Nixon's White House deputy in 1973–1974, was more villain than hero of the Watergate tragedy.

In fact, Reagan had fixed on nobody, including Shultz. He might have picked Schultz's colleague at Bechtel, Caspar Weinberger, another Nixon-Ford Cabinet veteran who had been one of Reagan's favorite advisers as state finance director in California, and was widely billed for any one of four key Cabinet posts under President Reagan. Haig's prospects seemed to be fading in November with senior Reagan political advisers cautioning the president-elect that Haig carried too much Watergate baggage.

But that was changed by the Democratic leader of the Senate, Robert Byrd of West Virginia, at one of his regular Saturday morning press conferences. Senator Byrd declared that if Reagan picked Haig as secretary of state, he might have to oppose the nomination because of alleged Watergate complications. That did it. Haig's supporters in the Reagan camp knew that the new president could not let Bob Byrd (soon to become leader of the minority, instead of majority, as a result of the Republican Senate takeover) pick his Cabinet. Reagan agreed.

Here was no petty case of pique by the president-elect, deciding to use Al Haig to teach Senator Byrd a lesson. A political principle of some importance was at stake the moment Byrd raised the question about Haig's competence: whether the new president was so unsure of himself that a whispered warning on Capitol Hill could influence his choice for the most significant post in his government. In addition, to have bypassed Haig in reaction to Byrd's threats would also have enhanced Byrd's thesis that poison from Watergate was still capable of infecting contemporary politics, a thesis thoroughly rejected by Reagan.

His two long talks with Haig in California, one alone and one with Reagan's close aide Michael Deaver sitting in, defined the broad outlines of Reagan's foreign and national security policies. Reagan and Haig found themselves in remarkable agreement on most of the issues, with only two possible areas of potentially mild contention: Israel and Communist China (Reagan was friendlier to Israel, less friendly to Communist China than was Haig). Haig came away from those two sessions convinced that he knew what he needed to know about Reagan's views; Reagan, for his part, decided then that Haig could fill the post of secretary of state as well as anyone else. He had read most of Haig's writings, some of his congressional testimony and many of his speeches, both when Haig was at NATO and during Haig's short-lived, unannounced presidential candidacy in 1979. He liked what he read.

It was, then, a relatively easy matter for Haig in January 1981 to reply to Soviet foreign minister Andrei Gromyko's congratulatory note on his confirmation as secretary without checking every word with Reagan. Haig wanted to send Gromyko a "marker" that would leave no doubt as to the new president's reservations about Soviet conduct around the globe—invading Afghanistan, encouraging Iran's hostage policy and threatening armed intervention in Poland. Reagan had defined that concern during the second of his 1980 conversations with Haig. The Soviets, Reagan and Haig agreed, had a two-stage scenario that guided their intervention in foreign states, starting with so-called wars of liberation often fought with proxies—usually Cubans but sometimes Libyans or even East Germans—and ending with direct Soviet involvement. The pretext of intervention was to cure "social injustice." The Soviet tools were local subversion, followed or accompanied by heavy control of the media for propaganda purposes, selective terrorism and massive "disinformation" for consumption by the outside world. The drama worked all too well, leaving the Soviets in control either directly or by proxies. Angola, Ethiopia, South Yemen, Afghanistan, to one degree or another, showed how the drama was played out, with the Soviets dominating the stage.

Having received Gromyko's note of congratulations on his appointment, Haig decided to educate the Soviet foreign minister, well known to Haig from the Nixon days, about the president's concerns over these patterns of Soviet aggression. His letter was to the point, sharp and unambiguous. Gromyko's response was an unprecedented public letter to Haig that raised the decibel level considerably in what was proving to be the noisiest verbal battle ever between the Kremlin and a new U.S. administration. In his letter, Gromyko rewrote contemporary history, claiming that Soviet behavior toward the affair of the American hostages in Iran was impeccable; that Poland "cannot be a subject of discussion" between the United States and the Soviet Union; that if only the United States would persuade Pakistan to recognize the Soviet-imposed government in Afghanistan, all would be well.

Nothing could have played more cleanly into Reagan's hands. His Soviet policy—indeed, the success of the Reagan Revolution abroad—would depend on persuading the American people and U.S. allies, particularly in Europe, that détente had been bent out of shape by the Soviets, and that from now on the United States would be labeling Soviet imperialism for what it was. Gromyko's decision to publish his letter in the U.S. press drove home the point that under Reagan, U.S. policy toward the Soviet Union had radically changed—hardened in a way the new president hoped would rally his country toward a new nationalism, a higher patriotism, a realization that the world was indeed a place of danger demanding sacrifice: much larger defense spending; "guns" instead of "butter." Reagan was "taking his case to the people" in one-syllable words anyone could understand, and old Soviet functionary Gromyko was helping him.

Since the final days of the Ford Administration, the Russians had made substantial territorial gains. More ominous for the West, they had been able to do so without much more than a whine and a whimper from their superpower adversary. The world whose Western command post Reagan inherited from Carter was ripe for one of two things: either remorseless lengthening of the Soviet strategic grasp of control over Mideastern oil, a monopoly over African minerals, a larger base in America's Caribbean backyard and sea-lane choke points everywhere, a process likely to frighten even the best American allies into neutrality; or an American response, painful, costly and perhaps unsuccessful, to turn back the challenge even at the risk of major war. Reagan was committed to the latter course. When Haig testified before an often hostile Senate Foreign Relations Committee during his tendentious confirmation hearing, he made no effort to underplay either the challenge or the risk.

The "central strategic phenomenon" of the post-World War II era was the change of Soviet military power from "a continental and largely defensive land army to a global offensive army, navy and air force fully capable of supporting an imperial foreign policy." This transformation, added Reagan's chief diplomat, had produced what was "perhaps the most complete reversal of global power relationships ever seen in a period of relative peace," making international civility almost impossible and threatening to "paralyze Western policy altogether."

Such language had not been heard on Capitol Hill for more than thirty years, not since the Berlin Airlift and, two years later, the Korean War. Was it shocking that Haig spoke thus, or was it cleansing and refreshing? The consensus of senators seemed to say the latter. As Jimmy Carter had acknowledged after the Soviet invasion of Afghanistan in December 1979, the Soviets were on the move in most unpleasant ways. But whether Haig's trenchant words shocked or refreshed the country, there could be no doubt that they were revolutionary judged against normal discourse by recent secretaries of state.

As Reagan began to settle into the high-backed, polished-leather armchair at his Oval Office desk, the designs of "imperial policy" were on Central America. It was here, in the Caribbean back door of the United States, that Reagan decided to call a halt. There was nothing novel about Soviet designs on the Western Hemisphere. Cuba had entered the Soviet empire more than twenty years earlier: some of the new island nations in the Caribbean Sea were high-priority targets of the Soviet Union. The first foreign visitor honored with an invitation to Washington by Reagan was the new prime minister of Jamaica, Edward Seaga, whose surprisingly large win over Marxist prime minister Michael Manley had elevated a pro-American politician to power in a key Caribbean state that had been moving toward the Soviet orbit.

But the mainland nations occupying the ribbon of Central America were not so fortunate. Reagan wanted an immediate plan of action to prevent the disastrous unraveling of central authority in El Salvador from leading to a Marxist government. It was not, to be sure, that Reagan and Haig had any fondness for terror from the right. But they viewed right-wing terror, as practiced in Guatemala when Reagan took office, as indigenous, localized and not an extension of a foreign superpower. Leftist terror had as its target the Western democracies and most particularly the United States; the rightists in Guatemala did not.

Haig drafted a four-point plan for National Security Council consideration at one of its first meetings, with Reagan presiding and his national security assistant, Richard V. Allen, playing a supporting role. Reagan moved fast into his first crash operation of crisis-avoidance to draw a line. Such a line could not be drawn in Poland, surrounded for months by twenty-seven Soviet divisions waiting to pounce once the Communist government showed itself unable to keep control. Nor in Afghanistan, thousands of miles from American military power. The Caribbean was the focus of those first NSC meetings. With Reagan and Haig taking the lead, the NSC came to several conclusions on a policy not only to prevent a Marxist takeover in El Salvador but to send an unmistakable message to Cuba's Fidel Castro and his Soviet arms suppliers in Moscow.

Cuba, not the Soviet Union, became the immediate target for American action. Reagan ordered Haig and Weinberger to prepare means for stopping the flow of arms from Cuba into Central America. He dispatched several emissaries to Europe and Latin America seeking backing for his new hard-line policy against Cuban interventionism and his new support for right-wing governments friendly to the United States.

Reagan knew what he thought about Fidel Castro and about Soviet control of the island ninety miles off the coast of Florida. He hated the Cuban mercenaries doing Moscow's dirty work thousands of miles away in Africa. Nearly five years earlier, he had expressed his views forcefully in the famous televised speech before the 1976 North Carolina primary that salvaged him as a national political figure:

> Ninety miles off our shore there is a hostile Marxist dictator who expresses his hatred and contempt for us. He exports revolution to Puerto Rico, he grants landing and refueling rights to the Soviet military, and he airlifts thousands of his own military forces to Angola. And all the while, our State Department proposes that we restore trade and diplomatic relations with him. Why? May I suggest that there be a considerable change in Fidel Castro's attitude and policies before he can expect a smile from us, let alone a resumption of trade and normal relations. And I think that we should be careful enough to insist that he prove by deed, not word, that his change is more than skin deep.

There had been no change since 1976. Pressure on the government of El Salvador from Cuban-armed and Cuban-trained guerrillas had reached a peak when Reagan moved into the White House. Reagan decided naval force would have to be used if necessary to quarantine Cuban aggression in the Caribbean. That policy was approved in the second week of February, and Reagan's emissaries strove, with only partial success, to win agreement from U.S. allies. Particularly wanted was the approval of left-wing socialist regimes that were sympathetic to the Salvadoran "insurgents." The first departure from four years of passive U.S. policy under President Carter would test Reagan's credibility with U.S. allies. However it would finally work out, one thing seemed certain at the outset: Just as Gromyko's published note to Haig showed that the Kremlin had gotten the message of the revolution in Washington, so had Castro on his island ninety miles off the coast of Florida.

Operating stealthily and out of public view, one of Castro's first reactions to the hardened policy line coming out of Washington was to return about one thousand of his mercenary troops from Ethiopia to Cuba, the first major reverse flow without new replacements that U.S. intelligence officials had noted in several years. There was more. Castro refused to give in to demands of would-be Cuban emigrants who had seized an embassy in Havana to pressure Castro for permission to come to the United States, as so many of their fellows had come in the tortured Cuban year of 1980. Quietly warned by the new administration that any more unwanted emigrants could provoke the United States into declaring a state of war with Cuba, Castro exhibited a hardness against the would-be emigrants he had not shown during the great exodus of 1980.

Castro was having no difficulty reading the new handwriting on the White House wall. The contradiction to 1977 could not have been more vivid. Then, even before taking the oath of office, Carter let it be known to the chief of naval operations that he would be displeased if a long-planned navy and marine training exercise at the U.S. base at Guantanamo took place. It was discreetly cancelled. The all-important political gestures four years later were as different as Reagan and Carter. Just before he moved into the ornate secretary's office on the seventh floor of the State Department, Haig laid out the predicament. "It would be very difficult for me to support efforts toward the normalization of relationships with Cuba just so long as they are spawning, instigating, manning and conducting terrorist activities in this hemisphere designed to change, by force, legitimate governments," Haig told the Senate Foreign Relations Committee. Castro knew that both the president and Haig meant every word of it.

Haig was aware that the national news media would quickly

seek to make El Salvador another Vietnam. Bracing himself for what would follow, he ordered a thorough search of post-Vietnam laws designed to restrain executive power before announcing his decision to dispatch noncombat military attachés and technical advisers to El Salvador. Congressional leaders were briefed by Haig himself or his principal aides before each step was taken. He was fearful of violating some forgotten statute from the early seventies that might suddenly appear to indict him for usurping authority.

While continuing the pretense that Reagan was shooting from the hip without knowing whether he had a real target, the Soviets, too, were in fact well informed of the change in Washington. What disturbed them most in those early days of the Reagan Revolution was not the president's scolding words or scalding tone ("They don't believe in an afterlife, they don't believe in a God or religion"). What chastened them was a little-noticed remark by Haig at his first press conference in which the secretary, answering questions about the crisis in Poland, said that "the problem involves internal reform in the Polish state" before economic stability could be reimposed.

Within hours, Soviet diplomats in Washington asked for an explanation of what they regarded as inflammatory rhetoric of the sort carefully avoided by presidents Nixon, Ford and Carter—the latter despite his human rights crusade. Demanding that Haig explain, the Soviets were told only that the words spoke for themselves. There was no elucidation, only repetition of the long-standing American policy that Moscow's Eastern European empire was not regarded by Washington as a political hunting ground. The Russians were clearly upset. In private talks with Reagan Administration officials, they protested the reference to "internal reform"—a taboo within superpower dialogue for decades. Haig had struck at a vulnerable point. But in another confidential exchange, the Russians told the new administration something else that seemed to indicate much awareness and some respect for Reagan's hardened, no-nonsense approach to Soviet-style "imperial" activity. They hinted that if the United States wanted to press its charge of tons of arms moving into El Salvador, they should take it up with the Cubans but leave Moscow out of it. Translated, that was notice to Castro: When it comes to tangling with Reagan over third countries in the Caribbean, you are on your own.

As Reagan took office, there was no way to predict the course of Soviet relations with the hardest-line American administration since World War II. Richard Nixon, once regarded in the Kremlin as a devil, became a hero to the Soviet Union with his détente policy. The Soviets applauded SALT I, a series of trade and cultural agreements and, despite his opening the door to Communist China as a potential ally against the Russians, Nixon's clear acceptance of a U.S.-Soviet relationship bordering on arm's length partnership. But Jimmy Carter, with no anti-Soviet record at all to bring with him to the White House, started out badly with the Kremlin and ended worse. Carter failed to deliver the most important signal that one nation is capable of giving another, whether adversary or ally: consistency and credibility.

For Reagan, performance on those two attributes of national maturity started better. Reagan was credible when he promised to end the Carter Administration's fixation on human rights as a litmus test for continuing friendship with the United States. He was equally credible, at the start, when he preached caution and delay on strategic arms limitation talks with Moscow. He elevated the policy of linkage, abhorred by Carter, to high national doctrine. The policy revolution in Reagan's switch on human rights and SALT placed him on new high ground; whether he would stay there—or could stay there—would depend on unknown events, but he obviously intended to make the effort. The first challenge came fast: hard, rising political pressure from America's best friends in Europe to negotiate with the Soviets.

A principal problem for the Europeans as they examined the new president was their ignorance on two scores. First, they could not know whether the Reagan Revolution as it affected U.S. diplomacy would outlast Reagan; second, they had lingering doubts, despite Reagan's consistency over the past two decades, whether the president truly meant to conduct as tough a foreign policy as he said he would during the campaign. If the answer to the first question turned out to be no, the revolution would not survive Reagan and the Europeans would tend to embrace it more cautiously. Positioned up front against the awesome military power of the Soviets and their European satellites, America's allies would be gambling if they let Reagan lead them into risky confrontations with the Kremlin. At the end of Reagan's presidency, his successor might reverse American policy—just as Reagan was reversing it in 1981—sticking the Europeans with a vengeful Soviet Union.

All this would apply, only much sooner, if it turned out that Reagan himself, perhaps under congressional pressures or a sudden shift in public opinion, backed away from his promise to "compete" with Moscow. Consequently, the highest resolve of Reagan and his national security advisers in the first months of 1981 was to establish their credibility, claiming the right to Europe's confidence and retaining the support and goodwill of the American public (which would assure cooperation from Congress). That was why Reagan sent special emissaries to Europe to make his case against Cuba, Nicaragua and the Salvadoran "insurgents"; why he welcomed the French foreign minister, Jean François-Poncet, to Washington even before the British prime minister Margaret Thatcher; why elaborate attention was lavished on Chancellor Helmut Schmidt of West Germany, the keystone in the NATO arch. The arch was weak from more than twenty years of turbulence in American internal politics. It had been undercut by the comparative growth of Soviet power and was almost given the coup de grace during the Carter years.

The Europeans, too, wanted assurances that under Reagan a consistent American purpose in dealing with Moscow would assert itself. But the sudden change of mood and temperament in Washington left them unstable. The West Germans were concerned lest their own foundation of détente be weakened irreparably; The French (prior to the Socialist election victory in May) were less concerned about Soviet reactions, but worried about U.S. consistency; the British, led by a conservative government, were frightened at the prospect of being asked to do more than they could in support of more aggressive Western policies, even though they welcomed those policies. These hopes and fears were centered on the SALT II Treaty between the United States and the Soviet Union and the pledge by the Western powers in December 1979 to modernize NATO's theater (intermediate range) nuclear forces while conducting simultaneous talks with the Russians designed to limit these theater nuclear weapons.

But there was no prospect of quick SALT negotiations in

Reagan's program. Confusion over Reagan's intent to abide by or ignore the unratified SALT II Treaty divided the president's official family.

At his senior staff meeting on March 4, the president glanced at a headline in the morning papers and softly remarked: "Who in the world at State is saying that?" The "who in the world" was none other than Secretary of State Haig, who had taken immediate and angry exception to a comment the previous day by Secretary of the Navy John Lehman. Lehman, a former deputy director of the Arms Control and Disarmament Agency (ACDA), told reporters at a breakfast meeting on March 3 that there was no legal basis for the United States to continue adhering to either SALT I or SALT II. Haig promptly went to extraordinary lengths to put him down, without specific clearance from the president. The news stories reporting Haig's harsh rebuttal in the newspapers that morning provoked the president's very private reaction, revealing Reagan's instinctive adherence to the foreign policy tenets of his own revolution. What happened next also exposed Reagan's dilemma in placating his European allies without infuriating his own right wing at home.

Haig issued a public statement repudiating Lehman and repeating the refrain that the administration was "reviewing" its SALT policy and would do nothing to "undercut existing agreements so long as the Soviet Union exercises the same restraint." But to placate Reaganites both in and out of Congress, the statement in a studied ambiguity also said: "No decision has yet been taken on our adherence to existing SALT agreements."

In the cable he sent to U.S. allies in Europe, Haig deleted the "no decision" part of his statement, leaving a slender hope with pro-SALT détentists of West Germany that Reagan might not renounce SALT II after all. That would ease the growing political problem in West Germany, Belgium and the Netherlands, where pro-SALT sentiment was particularly warm.

The difficulty of framing a SALT policy that would not be torn to shreds either by the Europeans or Reagan's conservative domestic supporters paled against Reagan's peace-keeping problems within his own official family.

For the first four months of the administration, ACDA was staffed by leaders of the hard-line, anti-SALT faction, epitomized by David M. Sullivan. Sullivan was a brilliant CIA Soviet analyst whose classified study warning of Soviet nuclear gains had been suppressed within the CIA. Sullivan leaked it to arms control specialists in the Senate in 1978—and was forced to resign.

Sullivan's reputation as an anti-Soviet hard-liner made him a prime target of the arms control lobby. When he was named acting ACDA counselor early in the administration (the job that Jimmy Carter had given to Adam Yarmolinsky, a fervent pro-arms control liberal), the symbolic direction of the Reagan Revolution in arms control was established. The top post of ACDA director, vacant for the first four months of Reagan's presidency, was finally filled with another anti-Soviet hard-liner, but one who was a Democrat and an establishment foreign policy leader from an earlier era: Professor Eugene V. Debs Rostow of the Yale Law School, who had been undersecretary of state for political affairs under Lyndon Johnson.

It would take months before Reagan's SALT policy finally emerged as hard fact. Only one decision had been made: to go along with the worried Europeans and adhere to the December 1979 two-track decision on theater nuclear weapons for NATO—build and deploy the modern, intermediate range ballistic and cruise missiles while starting preliminary talks with the Russians by late 1981 on eventual reduction of those same weapons. That fit the Reagan thesis: the U.S. must arm and restore the military balance even while it agreed to what predictably would be long, drawn-out talks on arms control. As for SALT, Reagan was in no hurry. The prospects of serious SALT talks lay somewhere far in the future.

If Reagan and Haig could not sell this plan to America's truest allies, they would wind up in trouble. The trend toward neutralization had made rapid progress in West Germany, particularly in the left wing of the ruling Social Democratic Party. It had even attached a new name to itself, not Finlandization but Swedenization: neutralism with membership in no "blocs" but with clear preference for the West. If that movement was not brought under control during Reagan's first term, it could sweep far beyond the borders of West Germany, drive the United States out of Europe and transform the world balance of power.

In his television speech about peace shortly before the election, Reagan effectively buried the Carter human rights program with the words: "We have a story to tell about the differences between the two systems now competing for the hearts and minds of mankind. There is the poverty and despair in the emerging nations who adopt Marxist totalitarianism and, by contrast, the freedom and prosperity of free market countries like Taiwan, South Korea and Singapore."

Lip service to the cause of human rights would continue; the concept had the appearance of too much political appeal to be savaged. But in fact, Carter's human rights policies had found a target in all three of the Asian countries Reagan singled out for praise, particularly South Korea—long a world flash point. In one traditional American ally after another, with heavy concentration in Latin America and Asia, the United States had been striking blindly against human rights "abuses." Sometimes these abuses did indeed involve officially sanctioned government brutality. But the bottom line of the Carter policy was the alienation of a friendly ally in pursuit of a chimera: perfect domestic civility in cultures and political societies that never in history had enjoyed it. "They were looking for Utopia," said Georgetown University's Professor Jeane Kirkpatrick in December, shortly before Reagan named her U.S. ambassador to the United Nations.[2]

Gone with the Carter policy were the arrogance and superiority of those entrusted with carrying it out. Singapore prime minister Lee Kwan Yew, America's close friend for two decades, did not enjoy the long lecture thrown at him by Patricia Derian, the State Department's assistant secretary for human rights, on her first official visit there. Told beforehand that Lee hated cigarette smoke in his office, Derian insisted on smoking anyway and the president moved the proceedings out to a balcony. In the Reagan Revolution, friends were not treated that way. Reagan's view, conveyed to one trusted adviser, was that General Augusto Pinochet, who took power in Chile after the assassination of Marxist president Salvador Allende, might be a son of a gun, but "he's our son of a gun" (cleaning up the phrase once used by Franklin D. Roosevelt in the late 1930s when he called Dominican dictator Rafael Trujillo "our son of a bitch"). Reagan applied similar reasoning to other rightist leaders in traditionally friendly countries.

As for human rights in the one country where Reagan believed they did not exist in any form at all—the Soviet Union—he saw no prospect of improvement under American pressures. Rectifying human wrongs in Russia, Reagan believed, was impossible without changing the Communist system. So, human rights as practiced by Carter was abandoned by Reagan with the full cooperation of Dr. Ernest Lefever, the scholar and theologian Reagan installed in the State Department's statutory Bureau of Human Rights replacing Ms. Derian.

Lefever was to Carter's human rights program what a revenue agent is to an illegal whiskey still: the destroyer. Indeed, of all Reagan's appointments in his new administration none symbolized the Reagan Revolution so purely as Dr. Lefever, a sixty-one-year-old Yale Divinity School graduate who passionately believed in the ideals of American democracy and passionately hated Communism. Reagan found him in the Georgetown Ethics and Public Policy Center. Writing in the Winter 1978 issue of the Heritage Foundation's *Policy Review*, Lefever let his convictions hang out:

> The human rights activists tend to underestimate the totalitarian threat to the West and totalitarian temptation in the Third World. They neglect or trivialize the fundamental political and moral struggle of our time—the protracted conflict between forces of total government based on coercion and the proponents of limited government based on popular consent and humane law. In their preoccupation with the minor abridgement of certain rights in authoritarian states, they often overlook the massive threat to the liberty of millions. . . . In terms of political rights, moral freedom and culture vitality, there is a profound difference between authoritarian and totalitarian regimes.[3]

Lefever's theme was picked up more authoritatively by Haig himself in an off-the-record speech March 31 (that the *New York Times* obtained several weeks later) to the Trilateral Commission, an influential group of businessmen and politicians from North America, Europe and Japan. Drawing a distinction between countries under the heel of totalitarian regimes (the Soviet Union) and countries under control of authoritarian regimes (Argentina), Haig said:

> . . . we must be discriminating in our action with an eye to the source of the violation and the impact of our protest on the violator . . . the totalitarian model unfortunately draws upon the resources of modern

technology to impose its will on all aspects of a citizen's behavior. [It tends] to be intolerant at home and abroad, actively hostile to all we represent to political change.

The authoritarian regime . . . customarily reserves for itself absolute authority in only a few politically sensitive areas. I am not making a case for the authoritarian government; I am making the case that such regimes are more likely to change than their totalitarian counterparts. When dealing with the violation of individual rights, we must weigh not only the international repercussions—does the regime help or hinder international aggression—but also the domestic prospects . . . not only the records of those in power but the record of and program of these in opposition.[4]

Haig's message was simple and direct: the existence and spread of totalitarian communism was a threat to the noncommunist world; the existence or spread of authoritarian governments was not.

This distinction was central to the Reagan Revolution. Both the president and secretary of state felt that if the distinction were removed, human rights naturally would be focused on countries where U.S. influence could be most intensely applied. That would mean greater pressure on friends than adversaries, as was the case under Carter.

Accordingly, the human rights issue became a major battlefield over Reagan foreign policy, with Lefever's confirmation in the Senate the focus. The policy was Haig's and Reagan's, not Lefever's. But Lefever, excitable and abrasive during the confirmation hearings in May and June, was a far easier target, and was forced to withdraw after rejection by the Senate Foreign Relations Committee.

Apart from the rejection of Lefever, Reagan's policy was a direct contradiction of the Carter-Derian school of human rights. The Reagan Revolution would end the practice of hauling friendly governments into the pit for public whipping and other punishment, such as withholding American aid. One early and important beneficiary was South Korean president Chun Doo Hwan, whose early state visit to Washington dramatized the policy switch from Carter to Reagan on withdrawing U.S. troops from the Korean peninsula. The military implications of this full-scale reversal of policy were, of course, paramount. But the human rights implications were hardly less dramatic.

The joint communiqué following General Chun's February meeting with Reagan announced that the United States would "resume immediately" the full range of governmental consultations with South Korea, including those related to military security that Carter had postponed to pressure the military leadership of South Korea on human rights and democratization. The capstone was these words by an official American spokesman: "What happens internally [in South Korea] is an internal affair of the Republic of Korea."

Yet the subtle pressure of secret diplomacy showed that Reagan was prepared to play his cards where warranted to ease authoritarian policies abroad. In an elaborate series of cloaked moves by Richard Allen before President Chun's visit, Reagan found ways to have the death sentence of Kim Dae Jung, the celebrated dissident, commuted to life imprisonment. But this was done in secret, without public flogging.

There were, as Haig confided to friends in the early days in the secretary of state's office on the seventh floor of the State Department, only two major regions in the world where the president's strong ideological and historical convictions seemed to need toning down. Whether or not the Reagan Revolution, if powered by these convictions, might actually damage the president, the prospect was seen in Haig's office as a live one. The first place was the West Bank of the Jordan River, that sliver of territory with its immense implications for U.S. security in the Arab Middle East and the Persian Gulf; the second was the People's Republic of China and the island of Taiwan.

Reagan had long been imbued with powerful feelings of friendship and loyalty for the state of Israel, partly because of his strong friendships among the Jewish community of Beverly Hills, Hollywood and the Santa Monica hills. While Carter had been suspect in those same places, and with their Jewish counterparts in other big states, Reagan inspired confidence. But partly because of this background, Ronald Reagan never had learned that there was another side to the bloody West Bank conflict between Israel, which had occupied it in the 1967 Six Day War, and the Kingdom of Jordan.

All during the campaign, Reagan made statements about the West Bank that were unacceptable to Jordan—and, more important, to Saudi Arabia, Kuwait and other Arab oil states on the Persian Gulf. Reversing thirteen years of American policy, Reagan declared that Jewish settlements on the West Bank were not "illegal"—a provocative statement guaranteed to boomerang into the president's face if Arab leaders friendly to the United States came to believe that countermanding thirteen years of a formal U.S. legal opinion was indeed part of the Reagan Revolution.

These Arab leaders were charitable, as they always had been with a new president, and little was said publicly. But prominent members of the American Jewish community, hoping that Reagan meant what he said, read his remark about Jewish settlements as new American policy. They had given Reagan more votes on November 4 than any Republican nominee at least since the New Deal. Reagan's support for the small democratic outpost in the heart of the Soviet-coveted Middle East, these leading American Jews hoped, was partly a result of his well-known ideological commitment, partly in response to his Jewish support in the election. They hoped Reagan would stick by his guns.

This posed a problem for the president. No matter how ideologically committed he was to the Jewish state, there had always been a higher commitment in his world view: to stop Soviet aggression. To achieve that in the Middle East he needed the support of the very Arab states most upset by Reagan's new policy on the West Bank settlements. Reagan tried to treat Israel less as a special case needing delicate U.S. handling and more as a full-grown partner of the anti-Soviet alliance. That was a subtle change which he hoped would make Israel understand the necessity of building the military power of Saudi Arabia against future Communist threats, and thus quiet its demands on Washington from the incessant pace of the last decade.

His greatest ally in this endeavor was his record: could the leaders of Israel really question Ronald Reagan's loyalty to the Jewish state?

The test burst upon the president shortly after April 1, the day the National Security Council gave final approval to the sale of five AWACS (radar and surveillance aircraft) to Saudi Arabia. Reagan was in George Washington University Hospital recovering from his bullet wound, but his presence at the NSC meeting would not have altered the decision. Reagan put his personal imprimatur on the AWACS sale three weeks later when he declared it "essential to protect our interests."

But in Israel and throughout the American Jewish community, the reaction was hostile. Israel's faithful allies in Congress, including strong conservatives and Reaganites, joined the attack on the president's decision. For all his credentials as Israel's sturdy friend and his credibility on the defense issue so vital to Israel, Reagan found himself criticized by Israel and its many political friends as had his predecessors, including Jimmy Carter.

Reagan and his revolution in national security policy seemed immune, however, and there were some who felt that Israel might be overreaching itself when it challenged Reagan's authority to say and do what he thought best for America's interests even to the point of arming Saudi Arabia to help in the defense of Persian Gulf oil. Indeed, the break between Reagan and Israel revealed once again the president's faithfulness to his own convictions: not even a rupture with the American Jewish community would be allowed to deflect Reagan from shoring up anti-Soviet defenses in the Middle East.

But if the president could be so faithful to his convictions in the Persian Gulf, how was it that he could terminate the Soviet grain embargo without any Soviet concession in or outside Afghanistan, the source of Carter's decision to punish Russia by limiting U.S. grain exports? Reagan's handling of the grain embargo came down to resolving two conflicting themes: Theme No. 1 was his campaign pledge to end the embargo, a promise that could not be redeemed without compromising Theme No. 2 —his basic demand that the Soviets end their aggressive conduct around the world. The campaign promise carried the day because of its built-in political appeal at a time the president needed every vote he could get for his economic program and, to a lesser extent, because he doubted the embargo's effectiveness. As he had said during the campaign, the grain embargo was wrist-slapping and hardly deserved to be called punitive; any serious American riposte to the Soviets would have to be across the board, shared in by all Americans, not just the farmers.

There were immediate costs, not the least of which was the declining status of Al Haig. In canceling the embargo against Haig's public recommendation, Reagan once again downgraded the handsome former general whose early notices as the most powerful and influential Cabinet member had proved to be exaggerated.

Haig arrived with his key State Department officials already picked, glowing with confidence, and on January 28 described himself as Reagan's foreign policy "vicar." The glow faded quickly. The reason lay not so much in his performance as in a misunderstanding by Haig—and perhaps at the beginning by Reagan himself—of Haig's proper role. Haig believed his portfolio as chief diplomat would be similar to Dean Acheson's or John Foster Dulles' in those two earlier presidencies when Harry Truman and Dwight Eisenhower gave carte blanche to their secretaries of state. Reagan's White House staff thought differently, and Reagan soon agreed with them.

Refusing to accept the collegiality of the Reagan cabinet insisted on by Meese and Baker, Haig seized the initiative from Reagan to broadcast the administration's new hard line on the Soviet Union and particularly its decision to halt communist penetration of the Caribbean and Central America. The rhetorical blasts from Haig overrode the administration's primary economic objectives. On Inauguration Day, while still in formal morning coat, the habitually well-organized Haig submitted to the White House a presidential directive for Reagan's signature that would grant the secretary of state control over almost everything that happened beyond the nation's shores.

Meese and Baker moved quickly to curb the only Cabinet member intent on making policy without first checking with the White House. They convinced Reagan that he should not sign Haig's proposed presidential directive, and instead drafted a substitute that made him more a "parish priest" than "vicar" and forced him to share power with Weinberger, a considerably more "collegial" Cabinet member. The tension was exacerbated when Baker and Meese talked Reagan into placing Vice President Bush in charge of operations when they reached the crisis stage, and Haig made the error of publicly complaining about his defeat. When Haig gave a flawed performance over national television in the hours after the president was shot March 30, the White House failed to come to his rescue with public reassurances. All the while, Baker and other White House aides undercut Haig in off-the-record talks with prominent reporters ("We will bring that man under control," Baker told a reporter in mid-April).

The result was the partial destabilization of Al Haig. The general who had come to Washington with expectations of being virtual second president for foreign policy was shrunk to size. There was no place in the Reagan Revolution for any member of the administration to nurture delusions of grandeur even if the president had suggested just such a role for the man who had run the nation during the agony of Nixon's final year. Meese, trained to honor the staff system through long experience with Ronald Reagan, and Baker, guarding against any personality cult that might weaken George Bush as heir apparent, had their own reasons for cutting down Haig. Both knew that Reagan would back them up, as he did. The consequence was one of the most unexpected events of the early Reagan presidency: a secretary of state forced into a mold of subservience to the powerful White House staff.

But Haig's problems were not limited to contests for power with the White House staff. He was the target of a crossfire, the left assaulting what they considered his Cold War rhetoric and the right viewing him as a surrogate of his former chief, Henry Kissinger. That attack from the right was orchestrated by the second-ranking Republican on the Senate Foreign Relations Committee, Jesse Helms, who after fighting hard for Haig's confirmation proceeded to make life miserable for him.

The memory and specter of Kissinger haunted Helms and his colleagues, fearful that the fruits of ideological victory would be denied them after their long, hard march to power. They trembled when Kissinger was consulted during the campaign, rejoiced when he was shut out by Reagan after the election, were concerned when Haig was named secretary of state and outraged when he filled State Department slots with foreign policy establishment figures more closely associated with Kissinger than Reagan.

Typical of these choices was Lawrence Eagleburger, a foreign service officer who had been Kissinger's right-hand man and was Haig's choice to be assistant secretary for European affairs. His other nominations were held up for weeks by Helms, who relented in Eagleburger's case only after Eagleburger answered questions for one hour in the senator's office and pledged to follow the

Republican national platform. On foreign policy, Helms and other figures on the right believed, the Reagan Revolution had stalled.

Yet, to less passionate revolutionaries than Jesse Helms, the Reagan Revolution seemed to have permeated the country's foreign affairs—including such peripheral matters as the Law of the Sea Treaty. That treaty had been brought close to fruition during seven years of negotiations under a Republican (Nixon-Ford) and a Democratic (Carter) administration. But to Reagan, the new treaty threatened the United States and other developed nations with a loss of sovereignty that belied their power and rightful place. Here was a classic struggle between the internationalists and the free market; under Reagan, the decision to pull back from imminent agreement on a final treaty in favor of the free market was predictable, but when the announcement came in early March no one had stopped to think about it. It was a sledgehammer blow to the international community and might lead to the end of efforts by the rich industrialized countries to assure that untold wealth from the bottom of the seas would go to the poor Third World states.

The opposition stemmed from a consortium of U.S. mining concerns: Lockheed, Kennecott Copper, U.S. Steel and International Nickel. All had serious objections to the mining provisions of the proposed treaty that would limit their exploratory operations and deliver part of the profits to the undeveloped countries. These provisions collided with Reagan's nationalism, his impatience with the efforts of Third World countries to force concessions from the United States and his natural instincts for free enterprise and the free market. In deciding to postpone all further work on the treaty until the State Department had given it a full review, Reagan moved with characteristic speed and without concern for diplomatic niceties. He fired Ambassador George H. Aldrich, who was preparing for the tenth and possibly last drafting session at the United Nations, and asked for an indefinite delay. Reagan's antipathy for the treaty was reinforced by the Republican platform, which stated that American mining companies felt the treaty would inhibit "exploitation of the seabed for its abundant mineral resources." Potentially at stake were uncounted billions of seabed wealth; Reagan was not about to cede this to any other country, rich or poor, without close and lengthy study.

The China problem could have become, along with Moscow, Cuba, arms control and human rights, a showcase example of the Reagan Revolution at work. No greater ideological conviction did the new president ever have than his belief that the Carter Administration sold out Taiwan, the island stronghold of the anti-Communist Chinese Nationalists, when he normalized relations between the United States and Communist China on December 15, 1978.

Here again, as with Israel's claim to the right of settlements on the West Bank, Reagan's ideological commitment to Taiwan was insensibly diluted within the larger ideological framework of his commitment against Soviet Communism. He made both positions clear many times, as in this August 1978 exchange:

Q. Do you see any use in getting closer to the Peking regime to help keep the Russians off balance?
A. Yes, I think it [is] logical because Russia goes up the wall every time we say something about being nice to Peking. At the same time, the United States should maintain its treaties and its relationships with the Republic of China on Taiwan. We ought to tell the Red Chinese that their terms are unacceptable.[5]

Carter did the opposite, accepting the basic demands of Peking, and Congress went along, with many saving clauses and softening provisos. What might have happened had Reagan decided to open up this delicate question in the Republican Platform Committee at Detroit is anybody's guess. But Reagan's foreign policy adviser, Richard V. Allen, came to the convention armed with a private communication from the Taiwan government stating that the 1979 Taiwan Relations Act was acceptable as a basis for its long-range relations with what it hoped would be the new Reagan Administration. That was enough—but only barely enough—to bank the conservative fires and persuade Jesse Helms and his backers not to tamper with the fragile deal that Nixon and China started to create with "Ping-Pong diplomacy" in 1971.

Still, banked fires are live fires, and Reagan's emotional and ideological commitment to Taiwan was viewed in the State

Department as a probable problem for the future. If so, the banked fires would break out over the problems of "official" U.S. representation in Taiwan, the American obligation to arm the island and its 18 million people for defensive purposes and—most important—a demand that Peking renounce military action against it.

For America's other traditional allies—Japan, the countries of Western Europe, the contiguous neighbors, Canada and Mexico—the impact of the Reagan Revolution was more subtle and less pronounced. Consigning détente to the asterisks of history ("The policy of détente is, to a large extent, an illusion and not a reality of East-West relations") and demanding harder work to defend freedom by U.S. allies would affect U.S. allies worldwide.

Within weeks after taking office, Reagan was under attack from opposite directions.

From the right, Helms and his colleagues on Capitol Hill grumbled that Haig had not cleaned house sufficiently at the State Department, so that policy—African policy in particular—looked too much like Carter's.

From the left, the dialogue of a decade earlier was repeated both in congressional hearing rooms and in the streets as the dispatch of twenty-five technicians to El Salvador was heralded as the beginning of another Vietnam.

But beyond this crossfire, what did Reagan set as his goals in a revised superpower relationship? Whether or not he reached them would go far in determining the success of his presidency.

These were the immediate goals:

▼ A nation judged by the world as one to be trusted to keep its promises in foreign affairs and to be true to its allies.

▼ A halt to Soviet penetration of the nation's Caribbean and Central American backyard.

▼ A pause in new strategic arms agreement until the United States could repair its defenses.

On a long-range basis, Reagan wanted:

▼ Greater contribution by West Germany, Japan and other allies to the common defense.

▼ A halt to Soviet subversion, particularly in Africa and the Mideast.

▼ Severe inhibitions on Kremlin provocations, including its use of terrorists.

▼ A new SALT treaty actually requiring a dismantling of some existing strategic weapons, including the big Soviet missiles, and equality for the United States in matching missile size with the Soviets.

But before any of these ambitious goals could even be approached, the balance of power between the Soviet Union and the United States had to be restored.

9

Restoring the Balance

On January 25, 1980, talking informally to reporters covering his presidential campaign, Ronald Reagan accused President Carter of trying "systematically to diminish and dismantle what one of his predecessors called the great arsenal of democracy." Hyperbole is customary in the heat of campaigning, but the fact here was that Reagan believed what he was saying.

Therein lay the key needed to take the measure of the president and his sentiment about American power in a dangerous world. Accusing Reagan of courting nuclear holocaust, as Carter did during the campaign, or of willingness to sacrifice other national interests for the sake of defense, was like accusing a watchdog of barking at a stranger. No watchdog was more sincere in instinctively sounding an alarm than Reagan was in sounding his trumpet blasts against military weakness.

Reagan believed, as he told the Veterans of Foreign Wars just after winning the Republican nomination in the summer of 1980, that "our best hope of persuading [the Soviet Union] to live in peace is to convince them they can't win a war." He believed that Vietnam was "a noble cause," an indiscreet phrase that caused consternation within his own campaign. "We dishonor the memory of 50,000 young Americans who died in that cause when we give way to feelings of guilt as if we were doing something awful." He felt no guilt because he believed, wholeheartedly and certainly not self-consciously, what he was saying. That was an early lesson to be learned in 1981 by his countrymen and the Congress—and also by America's allies and the Soviet Union—about Ronald Reagan. Those convictions would lead to decisions that might transform the world. Certainly they would, at the outset, raise new dangers. Having consistently spent for military power at an annual rate at least 40 percent higher than the United States ever since 1970, the Soviets had performed a feat beyond the wildest nightmare of Western statesmen in the period after World War II. They had surpassed the United States in most categories of conventional weaponry, had converted a small coastal naval force into the world's second mightiest fleet with new ships coming faster than the United States could build them, and had achieved superiority in the world's most awesome weapon, the intercontinental ballistic missile, as well as its shorter-range counterparts.

Soviet military superiority was a new problem for the United States. As World War II ended, Soviet strength was superbly positioned in Central Europe but could not penetrate west of the Soviet zone in Germany for one reason: the American nuclear umbrella was more than sufficient to prevent any breakout into West Germany.

Awesome U.S. nuclear supremacy of thirty years earlier faded into parity by the mid-1970s and was accepted by the United States as a highly desirable standoff. President Carter slowed development and production of strategic arms—delaying the new Trident submarine missile, postponing the MX land-based missile and cancelling the "neutron" warhead and the B-1 bomber. In contrast, the Soviets used the standoff as a platform for achieving superiority.

Never before in U.S.-Soviet history had a responsible defense official made the admissions that came from Dr. William J. Perry, Carter's respected undersecretary of defense for research and development, in an interview with the *Washington Post's* George C. Wilson in mid-December 1980.[1]

"How did President Carter and his team at the Pentagon allow this missile gap to open up" after the Russians reached parity in the late seventies? Wilson asked Perry. "Were they guilty of malfeasance or nonfeasance in this crucial area of national security?" Perry "admitted" to Wilson that the Soviets had surprised him "by demonstrating in missile tests of 1977, 1978 and 1979 that they were improving the accuracy of their existing SS-18

and SS-19 missiles. . . . I have to admit I was quite surprised."
The indisputable intelligence on the new tests, he went on "gave us
a new sense of urgency, *told us we were caught short*" (emphasis
added).

This Soviet breakout from parity to strategic superiority
confronted Ronald Reagan with a frightening future. He faced a
Soviet Union that had used the four Carter years to engage in a
forced-draft development and production of long-range missiles
capable of knocking out all of America's 1,000 land-based Minute-
men and 52 Titans. Wilson's conclusion: "The Pentagon weapons
chiefs will have nothing to offer the new president to close this gap
between the U.S. and Soviet Doomsday offenses during his first
term."[2]

In addition, Reagan found shortages of all kinds of
weapons—conventional, nuclear, exotic (binary chemical and the
outlawed bacteriological) and space. The Soviet Union had doubled the percentage of its Gross National Product invested in
defense between 1960 and 1980, from 9 percent to 18 percent; the
United States dropped from almost 10 percent in 1960 to around 6
percent in 1980.

During the Carter years, ideological commitment to arms
control and unwillingness of the administration's defense and
foreign policy-makers to credit bad news from military skeptics
also took a toll. In an October 23, 1977, "Dear Harold" letter to
Secretary of Defense Harold Brown (classified secret), Secretary
of State Cyrus Vance exemplified these two trends that dominated
Carter thinking on how to handle the Soviet Union. The issue was
whether the United States, as the Pentagon wanted, should at
long last proceed with experimental production of binary chemical
munitions. Vance wrote Brown:

> I believe that if we were to forego plans for production we will have
> achieved a significant psychological advantage over the Soviets. This
> would force them into the position of having to respond to a U.S.
> initiative by taking a positive step toward reducing their own CW
> [chemical warfare] program. Additionally, such restraint would
> serve to demonstrate our sincere intent to limit offensive weapons,
> thereby improving the overall climate for our arms control efforts.

Vance simply did not credit intelligence information that the
Soviets were moving at full speed on chemical warfare and were

even experimenting with dread bacteriological weapons. But even if they were, Carter Administration policy-makers believed the United States could turn them around by its own example of uprightness. Such tendencies dominated Reagan's predecessor right up to the Soviet invasion of Afghanistan in December 1979. That at least partially explained these trends in conventional weapons: a 3-to-1 Soviet lead in combat navy vessels; 3-to-2 in cruisers; 3-to-1 in ballistic missile submarines, more than 2-to-1 in attack submarines. U.S. Air Force shortages in two important components—pilots and fuel—complemented each other: lack of gasoline, drastically rationed because of cost, restricted front-line combat pilots to dangerously short flying time (as a result, hundreds of them quit to enter lucrative airline work).

The marine corps had been compelled by budget cuts to reduce its strength and the army, groping through its painful experiment with an all-volunteer force, had reached the most critical shortage of noncommissioned officers in its history. With the economy caught in seemingly perpetual "stagflation," unemployed blacks flocked to the army in unprecedented proportions, causing concern over a racially unbalanced regular army. The army's size and its weapons were excelled by the Soviets in almost every category. Although he had been sounding the alarm back well before Carter's presidency, even Reagan was shocked at what he learned during postelection briefings from the Pentagon and the CIA.

How could the Kremlin respond when Reagan made clear to the world that, as president, he meant at least to catch up and possibly to surpass this formidable Soviet military, naval and space power? "Since when has it been wrong for the United States to be first in military strength?" he asked an applauding campaign audience in Massachusetts. "How is military superiority dangerous?" He had expressed it differently before. "I am not a warmonger, but war will result if the Soviets believe there is no place at which we would risk war to stop them."

This would have been politically unacceptable in the America of the 1970s, when the promise of détente blended with the guilt of Vietnam. Wars were a thing of the past. Had not Carter himself advised the American people that the time for "inordinate fear" of Communism was gone? Reagan's trumpet blasts struck a note that his countrymen had not heard since John F. Kennedy's Inaugural

Address twenty years earlier. Reagan promised military superiority, a war against terrorism, full speed ahead on exotic new
weapons cancelled or slowed by Carter, the use of American force
if needed and a sharper eye to halt American and Western
technological exports to the Russians.

He promised more than he could possibly deliver. But much of
what he promised he could and would deliver. There was an
applauding echo for his promises across America. By mid-spring
1981, Reagan held the high ground; whether he could keep it would
depend partly on himself, partly on events over which he had little
or no control.

The heart of the Reagan Revolution in national security was
to make the United States militarily strong again. He followed the
precept laid down throughout the campaign, that an arms race was
underway and had been for years but that "only the Soviets are
racing." The portent of change between a Reagan Administration
and what had preceded it was the contrast between the January
1980 and the January 1981 versions of the Joint Chiefs of Staff
"Military Posture" statement and the introductory overview by
General David C. Jones, the air force officer who was chairman of
the Joint Chiefs.

In his 1980 overview, General Jones seemed out of the customary military mold in listing the most important reasons for
what he termed the "widespread international turmoil and instability" in the year ahead. "The first springs primarily from
economic considerations and includes the great rise in appetites
and expectations accompanied by diminishing resources and di-
vergent patterns in the distribution of the world's wealth." The
second was the energy crisis. Not until he reached the third reason
did the general call attention to "the growing capability and inclination" of the Soviet Union "to project military power—its own or
proxy forces—to influence political outcomes." This was scarcely a
call to arms by the nation's first soldier.

When the general wrote that overview posture statement in
January 1980, President Carter's chances for reelection in
November were still good. The hostage crisis was still a plus, not a
minus, for Carter and the Republican opposition looked only so-so.
So Davy Jones played to his most important audience, Jimmy
Carter, emphasizing exactly what Carter himself had dwelled on

190 ▼ THE REAGAN REVOLUTION

so heavily for the preceding three years. Jones, who had approved
the Carter decision in 1977 to scrap the B-1 bomber, gave the issue
short shrift in his 1980 overview, saying only, "We must continue
with the development of a manned penetration aircraft to succeed
the B-52."

The Reagan Revolution burst into Jones's scheme of things
with a vengeance after November 4, 1980. His January 1981
posture statement showed its impact. The need merely to "de-
velop" a new manned bomber now ripened into the need for "de-
ploying a new, manned penetrator" as "a top priority among the
new strategic initiatives" for the immediate future.

While Jones's 1980 overview ignored alarming Soviet gains in
chemical warfare (he knew Carter did not want it), a year later he
discovered a "one-sided Soviet chemical warfare advantage" that
had produced "an even wider gap" between the Warsaw Pact and
NATO than existed in their respective nuclear arsenals. Many
other disparities showed how the impact of the Reagan Revolution
affected the general's reports, who until early February had
looked ripe for sacking by Reagan on grounds that he had been
politicized during the Carter years. True or not, General Jones
rode the leading edge of the new president's military buildup. He
did so with aplomb, clearly one of the reasons Reagan decided not
to fire him after all.

While David Stockman's long shears were chopping away
overtime on the rest of the budget, Reagan immediately added $7
billion to Carter's defense budget for the balance of fiscal year 1981
and $25 billion for fiscal year 1982, but that was only the bow wave.
For the next four years, Reagan military spending was plotted on
a rising graph showing annual increases in the amounts Carter had
planned of $21 billion, $27 billion, $50 billion and, for fiscal year
1986, $63.1 billion. For the first time in perhaps a decade, a
president speculated out loud on the dread ultimate reason for
these immense additions to military security: "Budget resources
must be devoted to national defense to improve and sustain the
readiness of U.S. forces and to increase their ability to deter and,
should deterrence fail, to prevail *in response to aggression* against
U.S. interests" (emphasis added).

Even with this radical change in emphasis between domestic
and defense spending (the reverse of the liberal cry during the
Vietnam War for a "reordering of priorities" away from defense),

Reagan's military spending as a percentage of the overall budget would not come near the ratio reached by Kennedy in 1962. By 1984, Reagan's defense budget would equal 32 percent of the overall budget; following the 1961 Berlin crisis and his mobilization of the reserves, Kennedy allocated 44 percent of the 1962 budget to defense.

The Reagan plan was forging ahead on modernizing conventional weapons, assuring readiness, raising volunteer army pay, pushing production of expensive weapons and superweapons delayed too long. But between election and inauguration, there had been a bitter struggle over who would be Reagan's men in the Pentagon, casting doubt over how far the revolution would go.

On December 20, 1980, William Van Cleave, perhaps the most knowledgeable and certainly the most self-confident defense hard-liner on how to catch up to the Russians, flew to San Francisco for a long-sought appointment with Secretary of Defense-designate Caspar Weinberger. Van Cleave, a Reagan campaign adviser and head of the president-elect's transition team on defense, had asked for an all-day session with Weinberger to explain his months-long study for Reagan of America's defense needs. For the forty-five-year-old ex-marine enlisted man, the mission to Weinberger's Bechtel Corporation office was steeped in gloom. Leaked reports had been published of Weinberger's decision to pick Frank Carlucci, a nonpolitical, nonideological career civil servant with no defense experience, as deputy secretary. That put two defense neophytes in the Pentagon's two top positions. Van Cleave was puzzled, demoralized and angry.

It was not only Van Cleave, on leave as professor of international relations at the University of Southern California, who had hoped the deputy job would be his. His supporters ranged widely through the ranks of the defense community, including key defense leaders in the Congress.

On that December 20, he had asked for a full day with Weinberger to go over his voluminous transition-team report. Instead, he got a couple of hours and they were unfriendly, bordering on hostile. In the background was a sequence of extraordinary events that revealed Reagan's failure to keep personal control of the defense issue. It started when campaign manager William J. Casey took a gratuitous poke at Van Cleave's proposed recommendation for a radical increase in Carter's defense budget. It escalated when Van Cleave's friend, San Francisco banker Laurence Silberman, quit as chief of the CIA transition team in disgust at being barred by Reagan's high command from a formal briefing of Reagan by Carter CIA officials. It climaxed when Reagan picked Cappy Weinberger for defense secretary and permitted him to choose Carlucci, then serving as the Carter Administration's CIA deputy director. Carlucci's credentials for deputy secretary of defense were based entirely on his personal relationship with Weinberger, with whom he had served as deputy in two domestic agencies during the Nixon Administration. Van Cleave needed no interpreter to know what was happening. He had been cast aside, his work along with him.

Reagan's hard-line defense advisers feared the worst, that Henry Kissinger would somehow return to power under his old enemy Reagan. Silberman had been an ideological critic of Kissinger during his tour as ambassador to Yugoslavia. Van Cleave was an antagonist of Kissinger across the board on U.S.-Soviet policy, particularly over Kissinger's SALT policies during the Nixon-Ford Administration. This went to the heart of the ideological struggle for Ronald Reagan's mind. On one side was Weinberger, Kissinger's friend and a moderate. On the other was Van Cleave, an unabashed, avowed hard-liner.

At Weinberger's plush office in the Bechtel Corporation, the atmosphere was cold. Van Cleave explained that he was not trying to "usurp" the secretary of defense-designate, but recalled Reagan's instructions to Van Cleave that he wanted "to hit the ground running" on January 20 with his new defense plan. Weinberger, smarting from the reports that Van Cleave was trying to force him to accept a new defense budget written by Van Cleave, was glacial. As of December 22, he told Van Cleave, you and your team are finished. Van Cleave could scarcely believe his ears. Three days before Christmas? You think I am going to fire all my transition people? Weinberger gave him one more week. On December 29, Van Cleave and the transition team were officially written out of the new Reagan Administration. For the nation's defense, the result would be hard to measure in the months ahead. How could one quantify Van Cleave's dynamism and strong convictions?

There were some compensations for his point of view. The intercession of Senator Jesse Helms, chief guardian of defense hard-liners on Capitol Hill, prevailed on Reagan to compel Weinberger to take Dr. Fred Ikle as undersecretary of defense for policy, the Pentagon's number 3 key post. Ikle, the cautious, Swiss-born head of the Arms Control Agency under Ford, then persuaded Richard Perle, who had been the SALT expert on the staff of Democratic Senator Henry M. Jackson, and other anti-détentists to come with him into the department. But the loss of Van Cleave cast an uncertain shadow into the future. The full year of work he did for candidate Reagan, topped by two months of postelection transition work in his temporary Pentagon office, produced a voluminous report with careful recommendations not only on new money for defense but on the strategic implications of how it should be spent. When the first Reagan defense budget went to Congress in early March, the figures were within Van Cleave's range, but on the low side. What was lacking was a guiding strategy.

For example, was the army right in demanding ninety days of reserve supplies in NATO storage depots? Was the navy correct in loading up with glamorous new fighting ships at the cost of precious sea lift for troops and weapons? Could the nation afford the change in naval strategy by the new secretary of the navy, Dr. John Lehman, to give the United States a fleet of 600 ships and three new aircraft carrier groups? Was the plan to take two battleships out of mothballs and arm them with medium-range cruise missiles a correct one? Would this decision help the United States in its insistence that Europe's nuclear weapons be upgraded *on land?* Van Cleave had careful but generally negative answers to such questions. He also worried about the U.S. Minuteman force and its growing vulnerability. He wondered: Should the U.S. not install an antimissile defense around its Minuteman force, disperse that force throughout dummy silos and perhaps give up the huge MX mobile missile plan?

Those questions were extraordinarily difficult, but Reagan went elsewhere for answers. He ignored experience and knowledge, embracing two men who, though clearly intelligent, had neither experience no knowledge of defense matters. The lesson was painful, even bitter, for Bill Van Cleave. But its more important implication was what it meant to Ronald Reagan and his pledge to make America strong again.

The Reagan Revolution in military spending was an attempt to make up overnight for years of neglect. It would buy hardware of all kinds, from armored troop carriers to aircraft carriers, and finance research on exotic electronic and energy-beam weapons that someday might fatally wound Soviet long-range missiles as they emerged from the atmosphere into space on the way to their targets. But essential to put flesh on the bones of these new weapons was a strategy for the eighties to make the United States once again a world power capable of exerting its strength quickly where needed. Developing such a strategy was not a matter of weeks or even months. Even the resolve of President Reagan by no means made certain that such a strategy could be devised. As Reagan made available more procurement money, the army, navy, air force and, to a much lesser extent, the marine corps resurrected their pet weapons projects buried during the austerity of the seventies. Having lived on the margin for so long, the services were greedily engaged in commandeering what they could of the Reagan Revolution's windfall. That was only natural. But the president would have to find ways to impose discipline, to compel inter-service cooperation and—by far the most difficult—to write new strategy for capitalizing, not wasting, higher taxpayer investments in weapons and the new global strategy. The process started only a few days after the swearing-in ceremony on Capitol Hill. It started with Alexander Haig at the State Department in his first press conference talking about world terrorism and Reagan's intention to control it.

By Reagan Administration definition, terrorism in all its forms had been a major contribution to the Soviet political and military offensive. Since retarding and then turning back that Soviet offensive was Reagan's target abroad, reduction of terrorism by U.S. actions became essential. But how to do it? Haig set the new American policy in his first meeting with Washington reporters. Although previous administrations back to Nixon in the early seventies had waged their own wars on terrorism, Haig raised the ante: "International terrorism will take the place of human rights [as] our concern, because it is the ultimate abuse of human rights and it's time that it be addressed with greater clarity and greater effectiveness by Western nations and the United States as well."

No single endeavor by the new president in carrying out his

revolution would be any more difficult to live up to than the promise of handling terrorist crises with "greater effectiveness." Reagan had put down the foundation stones early in his campaign and, to the applause of most Americans, he kept building the counterterror structure. Expectations grew accordingly. The policy was laid down in candidate Reagan's October 19 televised campaign speech:

> Let us turn now to the need for the United States to assume the leadership role in curbing the spread of international terrorism. In sharing the outrage against terrorism, I will direct the resources of my administration against this scourge of civilization and toward expansion of our cooperation with other nations combating terrorism in its many forms. We must restore the ability of the Central Intelligence Agency and other intelligence agencies to keep us informed and forewarned about terrorist activities, and we must take the lead in forging an international consensus that firmness and refusal to concede or to pay ransom are ultimately the only effective deterrents to terrorism.

To "restore the ability" of the CIA meant finding a way around some of the restrictions and limitations placed on its operations—and hence on the powers of the presidency—to prevent excesses charged against it during its heyday in the fifties and sixties. More energetic use of the CIA, including beefing up its "human intelligence" resources—meaning undercover agents —was a major part of the new president's intention to attack terrorism.

Over the previous thirteen years, 7,300 terrorist events were recorded on the world scene, more than one third of them directed at American citizens or property. These events cost the lives of 173 Americans and wounded 970. What distinguished the Reagan Revolution from the way his predecsssors had tried to counter terrorism was his promise of retribution—speedy, thorough, unannounced. Reagan's strong implication was that not under him would the United States ever again stoop to bargaining with terrorists.

After some anguishing hours he shared with Haig studying the settlement documents and the record of the Iranian hostage crisis, Reagan finally agreed to honor obligations made to Iran by the Carter Administration. But the State Department's statement of February 19, 1981, was blunt: "It should be well understood that the decision to faithfully implement the agreements does not represent a precedent for future actions by the United States Government. The present administration would not have negotiated with Iran for the release of the hostages. Future acts of state-sponsored terrorism against the United States will meet swift and sure punishment."

What punishment? Reagan did not tell. Nor did Haig hint. The hostage outrage in Iran clearly marked a quantum leap in terrorist operations against the United States, whether or not instigated by the Iranian government. That required a more positive response, certainly starkly different from Carter's. The tough State Department statement of February 18 provided it. By its words, Reagan made certain that international terrorism would sooner or later test his courage and wisdom in fulfilling that responsibility and that pledge. He was the first president publicly and directly to link terrorism and the Soviet world offensive.

Even before his confirmation by the Senate, Haig seemed almost obsessed with the subject, as least as much as Cyrus Vance, during the Carter Administration, had been obsessed with the human rights question. On Haig's desk in the temporary State Department office he occupied before moving up to the secretary's office on the seventh floor was a copy of the newest scholarly study of world terrorism by two specialists at Stanford University's Hoover Institution on War, Revolution and Peace. More topical was *The Terror Network* by Haig's friend Claire Sterling, an esteemed foreign correspondent based in Rome. Although the book would not be published for two months, Haig was already touting it to anyone who would listen as imperative reading. Its conclusion: "There is massive proof that the Soviet Union and its surrogates, over the last decade, have provided the weapons, training and sanctuary for the worldwide terror network aimed at destabilization of Western democratic society."[3]

The spectacular shift of American policy from Carter to Reagan on this shadowy problem of Soviet-inspired terror introduced a new side to American foreign policy that, for now at least, took some U.S. allies by surprise. Haig disdained diplomatic language in hurling a challenge at the Kremlin never heard there before from a top American official. The Soviet government, he told his first press conference, was consciously seeking to "foster, support and expand" worldwide terror and was instrumental in "training, funding and equipping" terrorists who kill for political profit.

Alleged use of terror in a planned, conscious policy to weaken the Western democracies was only one of the more sinister Soviet policies that Reagan quickly put under his spotlight. Another obscure strategy that Reagan intended to expose was the Soviet disinformation campaign. Along with counterterrorism, countering disinformation was raised to elevated status in the Reagan-Haig program to strengthen the nation's ability to compete. In deciding to find ways to deal with disinformation, the president exposed himself to the same political hazard that he faced in promising to deal with terrorism: the pathology was uncertain, the cure even more so.

Disinformation may be but is not necessarily false information; it can be "incomplete or misleading information." Haig viewed it as increasingly dangerous to the West as technology made worldwide communications virtually instantaneous.

A private study circulating at high Reagan levels long before the new president took office put it in graphic terms.[4] According to the study, the British in 1973 picked up intelligence that Leonid Brezhnev secretly informed Eastern European Communist leaders at a high-level party meeting that year that détente, then coming into full bloom under Nixon and Kissinger, was "a tactical change to permit the Soviet bloc to establish its superiority in the next twelve to fifteen years." There were two easy interpretations of this intelligence within the U.S. government: high-ranking military officers felt it confirmed suspicions that détente was the Soviet path to disarming the West, permitting the Russians to move out in front and surpass the West in arms with all that would mean; many civilian analysts felt Brezhnev was simply trying to mollify hard-line Communist opposition to his policy of détente by giving it a rationale that would please them.

The British intelligence report describing Brezhnev's assertions to his Eastern European colleagues was not taken into account by the Nixon-Ford Administration or allowed to affect the national intelligence estimates until 1976. CIA Director George Bush then brought in the famed Team B of nongovernment specialists to give his own analysts a competitive reading of Russian intentions. Team B was struck by Brezhnev's reported statements, particularly one to the effect that so long as SALT negotiations were progressing, the United States was unlikely to rearm in response to the Soviet buildup.

The leader of Team B was Harvard's Richard Pipes, who became the National Security Council's Soviet expert in the Reagan Administration. Dr. Marshall Shulman, a liberal scholar deeply committed to détente, had held that position in the Carter Administration (operating out of the State Department rather than the NSC). Pipes understood the real and potential dangers of Soviet disinformation. He had read CIA studies ignored by policy-makers in the days of détente that put the case clearly. Disinformation was run by the KGB, the Soviet intelligence apparatus, and had these objectives: to influence both world and American public opinion against the U.S. government; to isolate the United States; to prove the incompatibility of American goals with the dreams of the developing world; to confuse world public opinion about the aggressive nature of Soviet policy; and finally, to create a favorable environment for executing Soviet foreign policy.

Reagan personally agreed with that CIA finding. He never had softened his conviction that the Soviet Union's goal is world domination. He could never have agreed with the benign interpretation by U.S. civilian analysts of Brezhnev's 1973 remarks to fellow Communist leaders. To accept the benign view was to be "disinformed." That accounts for the unprecedented ideological change at the top of the Reagan bureaucracy in charge of U.S. policy toward the Soviet Union: Haig for Vance, Lefever for Derian, Pipes for Shulman. As much as anything said, done or promised for the future, that defined the policy revolution.

As for carrying out Reagan's promises to stop terrorism and to expose disinformation, one major step was obvious: increased emphasis at the CIA on human intelligence, which included spies but principally meant hard-headed analysis and research that contrasted with the preoccupation of Carter's CIA director, Admiral Stansfield Turner, with nonhuman sources of discovery— not spies but spy satellites and communications intercepts. Reagan also exempted America's worldwide government news and cultural programs—Voice of America, Radio Free Europe and Radio Liberty—from Stockman's economy ax.

The first Soviet disinformation challenge came with disguised but unusual speed: Brezhnev's call for immediate U.S.-Soviet dialogue "at all levels"—which translated into an early summit meeting between him and Reagan. Reagan declined a rush to the altar with his Russian counterpart. Suspecting that the Soviet leader was engaged in an indirect form of disinformation, trying to elevate the Russians as angels of peace and condemn him to purgatory, the president showed minimum interest in the idea. Compared to the haste with which earlier presidents stormed the gilded halls of summitry, that showed the Reagan Revolution was not going to be deflected by the siren song from the Kremlin.

How deeply the Reagan Revolution would penetrate the labyrinth of bureaucratic confusion and competition over the export of American technology was not nearly so clear as the president's intention to clamp down. Reagan's rhetoric during the campaign left few ambiguities. Because of ten years of détente, he said, "the Soviet Union is now fueled by Western capital, run by American computers and fed by American grain." For all this, he went on, there has been "no reciprocity."

The grain embargo, imposed by Carter after the Soviet invasion of Afghanistan, had drastically cut corn, wheat and other grains going into the Soviet Union. As a candidate, Reagan objected to the embargo as demanding an unfair sacrifice by farmers and pledged to end it if elected. Once elected, Reagan at first reneged but on April 24 lifted the embargo, against the wishes of his security advisers and perhaps his own better judgment.

Overall, he had no solid policy on U.S.-Soviet trade. Although his revolution might well produce the same degree of change in U.S. export policy that it had in rebuilding military strength and moving against world terrorism, the problem was slippery and politically dangerous. It needed serious study by the National Security Council, Pentagon, State Department and Commerce Department. At Commerce, however, one early change pointed straight at a drastic clampdown in technological trade with the Russians: the return of Lawrence J. Brady.

Brady had been hounded out of his policy-making post in the department's Export Control Office for telling Congress in 1979 that the Commerce Department had cleared for Soviet export "some of the most sophisticated Western technology" which was then diverted to "military" uses. There was more to Brady's ouster than retaliation for blowing the whistle on technology exports to Moscow. He was also victimized by the pervasive influence of business over the Export Control Office—a hold threatened by the Reagan Revolution. From the early days of the Cold War, business and commercial enterprises had lobbied to get around or under trade restrictions imposed for national security. Big-business pressures plagued the Nixon and Ford administrations, often resulting in softening regulations to satisfy special pleaders eager to make a big sale to a Communist state. As détente blossomed, holding the line on technological trade (often indistinguishable from strategic trade) became almost impossible. The Commerce Department's Export Division, created to promote export business of American companies, lobbied the Pentagon, the State Department and the White House to win licenses for dubious exports to Communist countries.

That's how Brady found himself in trouble with the Carter Administration. In his "whistle-blowing" testimony to the House Armed Services Committee, civil servant Brady attacked business for lobbying the Commerce Department and the State Department for yielding to it. "We should begin to have a little more backbone in this process," Brady said. Pressured into quitting, Brady quickly became a folk hero of the right and a familiar face and name in the pages of *Human Events*, the conservative weekly.

As such, he became the first significant personnel selection for the Reagan Administration—long before Reagan was elected, or even nominated. Returning home to New Hampshire, Brady campaigned for Reagan in that state's 1980 presidential primary and met him the day of the famous Nashua debate, February 23. Reagan, a constant reader of *Human Events*, knew all about Brady and told him: If I'm elected president, you're back in the government. True to his promise, Reagan not only brought Brady back but promoted him to assistant secretary of commerce for trade administration, a job with real authority.

It was in Brady's home state of New Hampshire, in Manchester on January 16, that Reagan delivered his strongest criticism of Western technological trade with the Soviet Union. After proposing suspension of all trade with the Soviets until withdrawal of their forces from Afghanistan, Reagan asked: "Why shouldn't the Western world quarantine the Soviet Union until they decide to behave as a civilized nation should?" Did that mean a "total cutoff" of all Western trade? "Why not?" Reagan replied. "It sure beats war."

Larry Brady was back in Washington, this time with the ideological support of his president. He had allies in this administration, some embittered by business leaders they called unpatriotic and some expert in how the Soviets found military uses for products exported under licenses barring their use for military purposes. His presence symbolized a revolutionary effort not only to take business control out of the Commerce Department's decision-making on strategic trade questions but basically to change East-West trade matters. That posed for Reagan a problem in allied unity no less difficult than the problem caused by his decision to ban SALT negotiations until his military program had been approved by Congress.

New problems for allies and other nations mushroomed in the most unlikely places in the early days of the Reagan Revolution. At Geneva, Switzerland, the shock went deep when the well-known Democrat Michael Novak, a specialist in the politics of ethnicity who was sent there by Reagan as the new U.S. delegate to the United Nations Commission on Human Rights, plugged for—of all things—capitalism in that bastion of Third World states. That, too, was revolutionary, like so much else in Reagan's New Beginning, and it is the habit of revolutions to create problems.

In all the new president's great plans, one was unique not only for its departure from the norm but for its seeming acquiescence in the past trend not to be too tough. That plan was Reagan's refusal even to consider the military draft. In fact, Reagan went one better than that during the campaign; he promised to repeal draft *registration!*

No single act by the new president would have assured U.S. allies and adversaries alike that Reagan meant business in restoring U.S. military strength and thwarting the Soviet Union so much as imposition of the draft. Foreign statesmen who came to Washington from the outset of Reagan's administration made the point privately. If Reagan had only gone to Congress to ask for compulsory military service, there would be no questions asked about the duration or sincerity of the Reagan Revolution; it would be for the long haul. That would have eased European fears about joining Reagan only to find that in 1985, Reagan or his successor might change the game and revert to the America of the seventies, leaving them to face a vengeful Soviet Union. The best insurance policy against that happening would have been Reagan's decision to go to the draft. Because of its political unpopularity, it would have proved the reality of the Reagan Revolution more than any other single decision.

But Reagan went the other way. During the campaign, he had been as unequivocal against the draft as he had been on Kemp-Roth tax reductions. His own inclinations were reinforced by Martin Anderson, his domestic policy adviser who was passionately opposed to peacetime conscription. Thus, Anderson's role as "keeper of the sacred scrolls"—making sure that Reagan in office adhered to his campaign promises—was intensified in this case because of his personal commitment.

Almost all Reagan's advisers in the national security area disagreed with Anderson. They considered the position incongruous with the other defense and foreign policy elements of the Reagan Revolution. For that reason and because of the cost of the volunteer force, they believed the president in years ahead would have to override his own and Marty Anderson's phobia about peacetime conscription.

Two immediate obstacles confronted Reagan. The first was Brezhnev's peace offensive, calculated to weaken Reagan's standing with the allies and to hold before the American people the hope of an alternative to rearmament. The second was public resistance to the speed of his new military planning, such as expanding the Rapid Deployment Force and establishing American military "installations" abroad (the word *base* had become provocative). The election demonstrated that American voters were ready to finance a strengthened defense arsenal, but there was a serious question about public tolerance of the administration's rhetoric that raised the possibility of a naval blockade of Cuba. Shortly after Haig succeeded in making the El Salvador case a daily newspaper headline and the leading item on the evening television news, White House aides ordered a reduced level of rhetoric.

If the new president could keep public acceptance, step by step, for his rising preparedness, there was no reason why he could not succeed in restoring U.S. military strength. If a four-year term did not finish the job, the United States would be put on an irreversible upward track by defense spending plans put in place in 1981 for fiscal years 1984 and 1985. The momentum would carry the defense program forward several years into the future even if spending were cut back after Reagan. "We are putting a long-term program in place," Dr. William Schneider, Reagan's military specialist at OMB, said as the new president's first budget was shaped. "Once it is locked in, we have the insurance we need for the future—even if Teddy Kennedy should happen to win in the 1984 election!"

But Schneider's boss, Dave Stockman, was hunting desperately for new budget reductions and, like his predecessors, thought he saw billions of waste at the Pentagon ripe for the plucking. Inside the White House, there was talk that some rearmament proposals might have to be deferred in the interests of financial stability. Even staunchly pro-defense members of Congress wondered whether inflation of defense costs required a more modest approach to weapons planning. Temptation was strong for this administration, as it had been for its postwar predecessors, to find budgetary savings at the military's expense.

The principal safeguard against this was Ronald Reagan. He made this clear on May 27 in his commencement address to the U.S. Military Academy at West Point. Just eight weeks after the assassination attempt, he spent Memorial Day weekend at his Santa Barbara ranch riding horses, chopping wood and writing the speech in longhand before flying east to West Point. "The era of self-doubt is over," he told the cadets. So, the government, "reflecting the will of the people," has returned to "our longtime tradition of bipartisanship" on military policy. That meant more money for defense, more money for weapons. The president would do his best to make Bill Schneider's forecast a reality.

10

The Moral Majority

His principles were set down concisely in Dallas, Texas, a bastion of Christian fundamentalist and evangelical belief, on August 22, 1980, in a political foray that was both unique and dangerous. Although his political advisers did not like it, Ronald Reagan accepted the invitation to speak to 14,000 Protestant ministers and their parishioners—fundamentalist in religious conviction, very conservative in politics. In his brief talk at the Reunion Arena, the Republican presidential nominee spoke quietly ("tepidly," said one leader of the sponsoring Religious Roundtable) and set down the Reagan credo for rehabilitating the American family and "returning to an older American vision."

He touched every possible issue but purged his words of emotion. He lamented the growth of schools that "educate without ethics"; he warned against public policies that have produced "mounting evidence in crime rates, drug abuse, child abuse and human suffering"; he was saddened that an ever more "morally neutral government" gave its resources to "value-free" institutions, but denied them to citizens "professing religious beliefs"; he criticized the Internal Revenue Service for trying to enforce affirmative action orders against private (mainly religious) schools; he swore to base his policies "on the primacy of parental rights and responsibility," thereby opposing government-financed abortion; finally, he pledged "to keep big government out of the school and the neighborhood and—above all—the home" and return to that "older American vision."

It might have seemed strange that the leader of the party of Wall Street, corporate board rooms and America's country clubs should find so hospitable an atmosphere amid the political heirs of William Jennings Bryan: religious fundamentalism, Southern-based but also with strong support in the rural Midwest, the Far West and the Northern Tier. At the Reunion Arena on that sweltering August day were Republicans of a social class who eighty years earlier followed Bryan: small-town merchants, small farmers, small entrepreneurs—the nonurban masses who felt themselves to be victims of half a century of centralized government perpetually in debt. These were crusaders against crime and sexual license, rejecting governmental interference in their local schools, fighting school busing for racial purposes, opposing gun controls (even after the attempted assassination of Reagan). Their preeminent goal was an antiabortion constitutional amendment.

This was a movement of fundamentalist and evangelical Christians, politicized by disillusion and anger over big government and the welfare state. The fact that Jimmy Carter, a Southern Baptist and fellow born-again Christian, had not disturbed these trends during his presidency hastened that politicization. The movement was called the New Right by its political organizers but more widely referred to as the Moral Majority, after the fundamentalist political action group formed by the Reverend Jerry Falwell. However, its base went well beyond the membership of one organization. Against the judgment of many of his political aides, Reagan was courting it like mad.

The movement that Reagan was courting had been built in hundreds of meetings in 1980 such as one conducted, typically without publicity, on June 24 at the First Baptist Church in Atlanta. Over 200 Protestant preachers from around the state of Georgia had responded to postcard invitations. Those attending were white (except for about a half dozen blacks) and predominantly Baptist, though Methodist, Disciples of Christ, smaller evangelical and even one or two Presbyterian ministers were present. These were the fundamentalist and evangelical clergymen who were fighting for the soul of the Protestant Church in America against the National Council of Churches, fighting humanistic theology and liberal ideology.

On this summer day, the Georgia preachers had not come to

Atlanta to pray. What they had come for was political instruction and political inspiration, exemplified by two of the morning speakers at the First Baptist Church: Paul M. Weyrich and Dr. William W. Pennell.

Weyrich, a thirty-seven-year-old political organizer who had flown down from Washington for the day, was no preacher and not even a Protestant. Born and raised as a Roman Catholic, he had left to join the Eastern Rite Catholic Church when Rome liberalized the liturgy—dramatizing his rigidity in theology and politics. Six years earlier, financed by Joseph Coors, the beer baron and conservative activist from Golden, Colorado, Weyrich had formed the Committee for the Survival of a Free Congress— a New Right political action group—to finance and organize conservative campaigns for Congress. Starting in 1979, Weyrich traveled the country to organize fundamentalist and evangelical preachers on behalf of conservative candidates from the courthouse to the White House. His role at Atlanta was to tell the preachers how to organize themselves and their flocks.

Dr. Pennell told them *why* they should and, implicitly, *whom* they should oppose. Pastor of the huge Forrest Hills Baptist Church in Decatur, Georgia, Pennell had passively supported fellow Georgian and born-again Christian Jimmy Carter in 1976. So had a vast majority of the other Georgia preachers present that day in Atlanta. But they and their fellow fundamentalist clergymen around the country felt they had been betrayed by Carter, on the appointments to his administration and even more so on the issues by taking the humanistic side of every issue that concerned them.

"I've had about all the born-again diplomacy I can stand," Pennell declared (reaping a chorus of "amens" in response). "Diplomacy" meant foreign policy, national security and defense— looming large on the New Right's agenda. To the fundamentalists, the great Satan abroad was godless Communism, centered in Moscow. At home, Satan was the antifamily counterculture of drugs, pornography and godlessness. Carter failed the test of the preachers on these social questions as badly as on his foreign policy. They felt the president had sold them out on abortion, the Equal Rights Amendment, private schools, homosexuals and school prayer. On these "pro-family" issues, it was no contest. Reagan supported them on each issue. To nail down that point, pamphlets were passed out at the First Baptist Church: "Ronald Reagan: A Man of Faith." The economic questions that so engrossed Reagan and were the cutting edge of his political revolution interested these preachers and their followers scarcely at all. They were attracted by Reagan's clear superiority on the "profamily" issues to either Carter or John Anderson, another born-again Christian, that led them to preach politics from the pulpit for the first time (doing what their black brethren had been doing for the past century).

The intense concern over the nation's future coupled with disillusionment over Jimmy Carter was enough to bring the preachers into politics, thanks to two coincidental developments. The first was the increasing expertise and energy of nonclerical New Right political organizers and fund-raisers such as Richard Viguerie, Howard Phillips and especially Paul Weyrich. The other was the increasing prominence of the "electronic church."

These were the fundamentalist preachers bringing their message—an increasingly political message—to millions of Americans through television (including their own cable network). The new breed of electronic preachers had abandoned the reticence of their pioneer, the Reverend Billy Graham, about political endorsements. The Reverend James Robison in Dallas preached a politically muscular Christianity. The Reverend Pat Robertson, son of the late Senator A. Willis Robertson of Virginia, made closely reasoned arguments against Carter Administration policy. But the electronic preacher who to the world was the symbol of the fundamentalist ministry's lunge into politics was the Reverend Jerry Falwell of Lynchburg, Virginia.

Falwell's earthy preachments had attracted a national television audience of 12 million for his weekly *Old-Fashioned Gospel Hour*. They formed the basis for the Moral Majority, Inc., with the Reverend Bob Billings, a veteran evangelist-politician, as its executive director. There was no question where they stood. Had he ever taken the liberal side of any issue? Falwell was asked in late 1979. "No," he replied. "I guess there is no way you are going to clean me up."[1]

The Moral Majority made no explicit presidential endorsement. But in the summer of 1980, two successive issues of *Moral Majority Report* made plain what Falwell wanted on November 4: The first issue put Jimmy Carter on its cover in a stilted, unflattering pose; the second depicted a smiling, handsome Ronald Reagan with Jerry Falwell proudly at his side. There could be no doubt that Moral Majority and other believers in their movement had given their heart to Reagan. But had Reagan given his heart to them?

The "Ronald Reagan: Man of Faith" pamphlet distributed by fundamentalist preachers during the 1980 campaign quoted Reagan as saying: "The time has come to turn to God and reassert our trust in Him for the healing of America." Some aides even claimed that Ronald Reagan, too, was a born-again Christian, at least as much as Jimmy Carter and John Anderson. In truth, however, Reagan never sought the ecstasy of spiritual rebirth claimed by his two rivals. But there was some evidence of faith.

During a particularly tense period during his second term as governor, Reagan complained of an upset stomach and asked aide Mike Deaver to get him some Maalox the next day. But when the next day came, he told Deaver to forget it: "I won't need the Maalox, Mike. I've been praying." He meant it just the way it sounded.

He frequently expressed a nearly fatalistic belief in divine control, as in a letter written during his 1976 run for the presidential nomination that perfectly matched the Moral Majority political rhetoric four years later:

> I have come to realize that whatever I do has meaning only if I ask that it serves His purpose. . . . I believe that in my present undertaking, whatever the outcome, it will be His doing. I will pray for understanding of what it is He would have me do. . . . I have long believed there was a divine plan that placed this land here to be found by people of a special kind, that we have a rendezvous with destiny. Yes, there is a spirit moving in this land and a hunger in the people for a spiritual revival. If the task I seek should be given me, I would pray only that I could perform it in a way that would serve God."[2]

Some two years later, on March 1, 1978, when a Methodist minister wrote him expressing doubt about the divinity of Christ, Reagan responded in statements fully compatible with fundamentalist Christianity. Statements that Christ had made about Himself, Reagan wrote, "foreclose, in my opinion, any questions as to His divinity."

It doesn't seem to me that He gave us any choice; either He was what He said He was or He was the world's greatest liar. It is impossible for me to believe a liar or charlatan could have had the effect on mankind that He has had for 2,000 years. We could ask, would even the greatest of liars carry His life through the crucifixion when a simple confession would save Him? Did He allow us the choice you say that you and others have made, to believe in His teachings but reject his statements about His own identity?[3]

Reagan's own religious background was sketchy. His father, Jack, was a Roman Catholic, who followed that faith indifferently and eventually left it; his mother, Nellie, was a devout member of the Disciples of Christ, the faith that Reagan followed. He later said he attended Eureka College partly because of its Christian Church affiliation and listed himself as a member of that denomination for much of his adult life. There is no record, however, of intense church participation during his long Hollywood career.

By the time he was governor, Reagan was a member of the Bel Air Presbyterian Church, a congregation neither fundamentalist nor evangelical and considered a society church. Its pastor, the Reverend Donn Moomaw, a handsome former all-American lineman from UCLA who was chosen by Reagan to deliver the invocation at his inaugural, evoked Hollywood more than Lynchburg, Virginia. Reagan continued his eclectic churchgoing habits as president, attending the National Presbyterian Church, but on one Sunday during the campaign he attended services at the Episcopal church in Upperville, Virginia, near his rented estate, Wexford. There, Reagan took communion for the first time in his life and had to be shown how by Deaver, a deeply religious Episcopalian.

Whatever the depth of Reagan's faith, he displayed none of the surface characteristics common to many fundamentalists, including both his new political allies and Jimmy Carter. Reagan did not offer prayers in public. While he was a light drinker himself, hard liquor was always offered to guests in his home. No marital infidelity had ever been charged against Reagan (and played no part in the breakup of his first marriage), but he was well known as a ladies' man about town in his Hollywood bachelor days— particularly between his two marriages. As a devoted connoisseur of humor, he did not flinch from the off-color story. Thirty years in

Hollywood also had left him more tolerant of aberrant sexual behavior than Jerry Falwell could have been.

Given those superficial characteristics, it is not surprising that Reagan's history on the pro-family issues was mixed. While he now gave 100 percent support to every issue on the Moral Majority agenda, these issues were not in the forefront of the Reagan Revolution. Unless asked, he seldom spoke about school prayer or pornography.

He was even more out of tune with the Moral Majority on the question of homosexuality. The greatest internal crisis of his governorship, coming in 1967 less than a year after he took office, involved the question of homosexuals in political office. Reagan fired two aides for homosexual behavior but publicly denied it to protect the individuals. Because he felt obliged to protect them despite circumstantial evidence of homosexual behavior, he created a credibility gap for himself. Lou Cannon, an expert and sympathetic chronicler, felt that as a result "the Reagan Administration never recovered its exciting . . . charisma of those first few months in 1967."[4] Certainly it did not help his presidential prospects in 1968.

More than a decade later, Reagan infuriated the California right by publicly opposing a state referendum to remove homosexual teachers from the state's classrooms. "What if an overwrought youngster," asked Reagan, "disappointed by bad grades, imagined it was the teacher's fault and struck out by accusing the teacher of advocating homosexuality? Innocent lives could be ruined." This was a matter of fair play and reverence for the law. But Reagan also revealed attitudes toward homosexuals not in keeping with the Moral Majority's: "Whatever else it is, homosexuality is not a contagious disease like the measles. Prevailing scientific opinion is that, in individuals, sexuality is determined at an early age and that a child's teachers do not really influence him." One biographer traced this attitude to Reagan's Hollywood background: "Reagan and his wife had spent many years in the film business, where gays are an important force; colleagues and, no doubt, friends from those days were gay."[5] That view was concurred in by state senator John Briggs, sponsor of the defeated antihomosexual referendum. Blaming Reagan for the sudden shift in public opinion against his proposal, Briggs charged that "the Hollywood crowd has gotten him to take that kind of position."

Support or nonsupport for the Equal Rights Amendment to the U.S. Constitution guaranteeing equality for women was a much more important litmus test for the Moral Majority and its allies; fervent though unsuccessful efforts to win ratification of ERA lost Carter their support irrevocably. Here, too, Reagan's past was cloudy. In his first term as governor he endorsed ERA as it was being adopted by the California legislature. He later reversed that position as conservative opposition to ERA mounted. But his daughter Maureen was an ERA activist and Reagan himself felt less than passionate on the issue. He kept proposing statutory changes to end discrimination against women. However, political reality for a presidential candidate whose natural constituency overwhelmingly opposed ERA led to unequivocal statements of opposition to ERA whenever Reagan was asked.

It was on abortion, the most emotional and important of the pro-family issues, that Reagan's past was shakiest. In 1967, Governor Reagan, in his first elective office for less than six months, signed a new law liberating California women from a century-old antiabortion law. The new law permitted "therapeutic" abortions, supposedly to save the mother grave physical or mental impairment or to end pregnancies resulting from rape or incest. Signing that bill was one of Reagan's most excruciating decisions, even though the pro-life, antiabortion lobby had nowhere near reached the white heat of intensity that would later characterize it. His doctor father-in-law's advice to sign the bill conflicted with opposition from the right. Only two hours before the California legislature was scheduled to give final passage to the bill, Governor Reagan switched positions, disavowing an earlier pledge to sign it and asserting that he had become "neutral" on the issue. For previous weeks, his agents had sought to derail the bill entirely so that it would not come before him and he could avoid making a decision. But Republican legislators protested that they had voted for the bill only after the governor's endorsement and would be politically devastated by a veto.

"He signed that bill because he thought the doctors would take its provisions seriously," Lyn Nofziger, Reagan's communications director at the time, said early in 1981. "Instead, it became a substitute for abortion on demand." By the time Reagan's second term ended in January 1975, 608,691 California women had undergone legal abortions under the new law. Yet the governor never did ask the legislature for the "corrective amendments" he promised on signing the bill "if the measure fails to carry out the intent of the legislature" for only rare exceptions.

By the time of his first full-scale race for president in 1976, Reagan was unequivocal in supporting abolition of abortion through a constitutional amendment. In 1978, the increasingly effective pro-life political apparatus had helped defeat liberal Democratic senators in Minnesota, Iowa, Colorado, Maine, and New Hampshire and was ready to score similar 1980 triumphs in New Hampshire, Indiana, Idaho, South Dakota and Iowa. The movement's enhanced political influence was in the background when on February 15, 1980, Reagan sent a telegram to the National Pro-Life Political Action Committee promising to pick only a "pro-life running mate." Some two months later, Reagan confirmed to a reporter that this standard ruled out Senator Howard Baker, the Senate Republican leader, as vice presidential nominee on Reagan's ticket.

That was enough to keep the antiabortion movement on his side to November 4, 1980, and beyond. But the marriage seemed more one of convenience than passion. "We couldn't take any more from Jimmy Carter," said Nellie Gray, an antiabortion leader. But she said it without much enthusiasm for Reagan.

Nellie Gray's unenthusiastic endorsement reflected the fact that Reagan walked a high wire on pro-family issues. While eager for Moral Majority help, his political managers feared the impact of the Moral Majority imprimatur.

So Reagan's managers took an essentially passive stance on Republican national platform drafting at the Detroit convention. Within the platform committee, leadership on pro-family issues came from Senator Jesse Helms and Phyllis Schlafly, the militant antifeminist. The result was not only planks opposing abortion and ERA but an unexpected plank calling for the president to select only antiabortionists as federal judges. The backlash against Reagan came as expected from organized women's groups and the liberal news media, but less predictably from nonactivist women (including wives of Republican corporate executives) and a surprising number of male voters. In retrospect, some of Reagan's closest advisers felt they should have intervened more actively in the platform fight, supporting the antiabortion plank but killing the judges plank and pushing through a routine Republican endorsement of ERA of the kind included in the party's platforms since 1940.

Such a course would have enraged the New Right, which was not entirely happy as things were. Weyrich was so disturbed by the selection of George Bush as Reagan's running mate that he withdrew his personal support from the ticket (a step he later conceded was a mistake). There was no sign that either the preachers or the parishioners of the Moral Majority were nearly that upset about Bush. But there was just enough uneasiness about their support to lead Reagan to attend that August 22 rally in Dallas, against the wishes of his political advisers, in order to pin down their backing.

He did so at Dallas in an unexpected way that led most of his backers to believe he had committed a blunder of potentially disastrous proportions. During the question period, Reagan was asked a question most Americans thought had been disposed of at the Scopes trial in Dayton, Tennessee, fifty-five years earlier. What did he think of the theory of evolution? His reply set off political repercussions of far-reaching significance:

> I have a great many questions about it. I think that recent discoveries down through the years have pointed up great flaws. . . . It is a theory, it is a scientific theory only, and it has in recent years been challenged in the world of science and it is not yet believed in the scientific community to be as infallible as it once was believed.

The immediate reaction was delighted chortles from television network newsmen, gasps of despair from Republican politicians and renewed hope by Jimmy Carter's political agents. The sixty-nine-year-old candidate was coming over like a buffoon from the past, insistent on fighting William Jennings Bryan's lost crusade.

In fact, Reagan was entering an ongoing debate over whether evolution or "creationism" should be taught in the schools, a debate renewed some fifteen years earlier that was raging fiercely in several states as Reagan went to Dallas. His claim of "great flaws" in evolutionary theory was hooted at editorially by the *New York Times*, reflecting scientific opinion.

But the merits of the case mattered little. Reagan would say nothing more about evolution versus creation for the balance of the campaign, and almost surely would never have to deal with the controversy as president. Politically, he had in one statement irrevocably secured the Moral Majority types for the balance of the campaign. He had, by risking the sneers of the secular world, made clear to the fundamentalists that he was one of *them*, as nothing else could have. What made it such a political master stroke was that Reagan's statement cost him far less than at first imagined. The evolutionists scarcely constituted a well-organized political bloc, and ordinary voters forgot about the issue once Reagan stopped talking about it—as he immediately did. Unlike ERA and abortion, there was neither a militant opposition group nor a postelection demand for action.

But by striding in the footsteps of William Jennings Bryan, Reagan ensured that fundamentalist preachers through the South and elsewhere in rural America would treat his election campaign as a holy crusade.

Even after the battle was won on November 4, however, the question remained: How much difference had they really made?

Exit polls and samples taken after the election failed to prove that, despite their fervor for Reagan, Moral Majority activists added more than marginally to the Reagan tidal wave that rolled across the South, the Midwest and the West. The fundamentalists themselves saw it differently. *Conservative Digest,* a major New Right organ, published statistics shortly after the election that showed Carter had carried only 16 of 100 representative "evangelical" congressional districts in 1980, as compared to 58 districts in 1976, and took only 49 counties with a "very high percentage" of Southern Baptists in 1980, as against 80 four years earlier.

An even bigger swing to Reagan in districts where the Moral Majority and kindred spirits were especially strong was shown in samples by pollster Louis Harris. Of all the national pollsters, Harris had concentrated most closely on the significance of overt pulpit politics. His survey one month before the election reported an amazing 29 percent of all likely voters as being part of "the evangelical church movement," with Reagan preferred almost 2-to-1 over Carter and Anderson by these voters.

It was on the social issues that Harris found extraordinary identity between evangelicals and Reagan. Although voters rejected the Republican platform demand for a constitutional amendment banning abortion by a 61 percent to 34 percent margin, white evangelicals favored it, 55 percent to 42 percent. Similar departures were evident on other social issues raised by Harris, such as the teaching of religion in public schools, sex education and others. The pollster concluded that "evangelist political preachers and their churches could prove to be decisive in tipping states in the South and the rural Midwest into the Reagan column."

One week after the election, Harris issued a new study that he claimed validated the pre-election prediction. Reagan won, he said, not because the country as a whole went conservative "but because the conservatives—particularly the white Moral Majority—gave him such massive support." The central reason for this support, he said, was the work of "the so-called Moral Majority TV preachers." Thus, Carter won the white Baptist vote in 1976 by 56 percent to 43 percent, "but this time he lost the white Baptists by a 56 percent to 34 percent margin."

If such support from the pro-family movement was indeed so major a factor in Reagan's election, his political aides were curiously unaware of it. That included Reagan's pollster, Dr. Richard Wirthlin (whose views on this point were shared by Carter's pollster, Patrick Caddell). Reagan's camp perceived the Moral Majority as providing strong emotional support for the Reagan candidacy but mainly buttressing voters already strongly trending against Carter. These pro-family voters would have backed Reagan with or without pulpit politics. The political forces unleashed by the fundamentalists, according to this Reaganite thesis, were an important but only tangential part of the 1980 Reagan constituency, not nearly so rich a wellspring of pro-Reagan sentiment as of wholesale disaffection with Carter's economic and national security policies. They were to be savored and protected within the much larger confines of the Reagan Revolution but not to be given undue attention.

This difference of opinion as to the real value of the Moral Majority and its social-issue satellites in the election contained the seed for political problems in the new administration. One such seed sprouted two days after Reagan's inauguration. Not surprisingly, abortion was the issue.

After Reagan's disastrous showing in the Iowa caucuses in January 1980, his political operatives contacted Nellie Gray, one of the leading activists in the pro-life movement as organizer of the March for Life, an annual Capitol Hill demonstration by pro-life women against abortion. Facing possible extinction in the February 26 New Hampshire primary, the Reagan camp was looking for help wherever it could be found. Miss Gray wanted a written promise of Reagan's support for a constitutional amendment banning abortion as the price of her help in New Hampshire. Reagan quickly obliged, sending a hand-carried letter dated February 7 promising not only to support the amendment but also stating that "I hope that future Marches for Life will be addressed by a President of the United States who shares the historic respect for life embodied in the Hippocratic oath." The next March was scheduled for January 22, 1981, two days after the inauguration. ("We're *still* hoping," a Reagan aide cracked in March 1981.)

That letter was enough for Miss Gray to start whipping up pro-life workers in New Hampshire for Reagan and, after Reagan swept the primary election, to claim part of the credit. Reagan's camp saw it differently. "They may have given us marginal help," Nofziger said later, "but it was only marginal. After all, New Hampshire is a strong Catholic state and the pro-life sentiment there doesn't have to be ginned up. It exists by nature."

Eight months later when Reagan won the election, Miss Gray sent him a registered letter reminding him of his promise to join her January 22 Right to Life March. Reagan received similar admonitions from pro-life politicians, including Jesse Helms. But he never had any intention of marching with Nellie Gray and would have been universally ridiculed and attacked if he had.

Presidents seldom march for any cause. Yet the affair left a bad taste. To soothe Nellie Gray, the two-day president at the last minute invited her and other pro-life leaders to the Oval Office on the day of the march. Angry and hurt at his refusal to participate in her march, Miss Gray boycotted the meeting and another pro-life leader remarked sarcastically: "Will Reagan be in the Oval Office to see us?" Reagan was there, polite and charming, but there were no apologies.

Reagan's political advisers were split over going even the short distance of inviting Miss Gray to the Oval Office. "This was hardly number one on our agenda," Nofziger said. "These issues are important, but in terms of the economic and national security problems they are less consequential. They can also be highly divisive." Nofziger's appraisal was widely shared by Reagan's other advisers.

Reagan's heart still was not in the constitutional amendment, despite his letter to Miss Gray. That self-distancing removed Reagan from front-line combat on the social issues, making clear they were not in the forefront of the Reagan Revolution. Asked about abortion at his March 6 press conference, Reagan turned what could have been a brief response into the wordiest answer of the entire session with reporters. The president steered away from talk about a constitutional amendment and emphasized another approach to the abortion controversy that had even less chance of succeeding:

> I think what is necessary in this whole problem and has been the least talked of in the whole question about abortion is determining when and what is a human being. Now, I happen to have believed, and stated many times that I believe, [that] in an abortion we are taking a human life. But if this is once determined then there isn't really any need for an amendment because once you have determined this, the Constitution already protects the right of human life. . . . We have a law, for example, in California, a law that says that if someone abuses or mistreats a pregnant woman to the point of causing death to her unborn child, that individual will be tried for murder. We know that the law of the land gives an unborn child the rights to inherit property and the law protects property rights.

Here was no appeal for fast action by Congress on Reagan's long-standing pledge to support a constitutional amendment banning abortions. But he was joined by a substantial portion of a divided pro-life movement that had elected to set aside the constitutional amendment and instead seek a statute.

Reagan's support of the statute was not merely an attempt to sidestep the difficult journey toward the task of amending the constitution. Reagan was more interested in Moral Majority questions than his political aides. While stressing economic and national security issues, Reagan felt government itself was a primary contributing cause to the breakdown of traditional family values and the breakup of the family.

Beyond that conviction by the president, there were two other reasons why social issues eventually would be part of the Reagan Revolution. First, Reagan considered himself a member of the conservative political movement that over the last decade had taken on pro-family questions as part of its agenda. Second, he did feel an emotional commitment to at least one social issue: abortion. His own aides felt Reagan harbored a sense of guilt from the hundreds of thousands of abortions performed in California after abortion was legalized by the statute he had signed as governor.

If Reagan were unwilling to let tangential issues such as abortion—and school prayer and pornography—get in the way of his new economic program and the military rearmament of America, there would have to be palliatives, if not enough to satisfy, at least to quiet political forces driving the social issues. One palliative was obvious: the appointment of leaders in the pro-family movement to posts in the Reagan Administration with some control over federal policies dealing with these social issues. One such post was assistant secretary for "nonpublic" schools in the Department of Education, one of two Cabinet departments (along with Energy) Reagan was committed to abolish.

"Nonpublic" education, the official usage inside the government, was a euphemism for private schools, many run by fundamentalist Protestant denominations and established following public school desegregation orders in the sixties and seventies. The manner in which the Reagan Administration handled the appointment of the Reverend Bob Billings, the first executive director of Moral Majority, to that post provided a primer on how it hoped to keep its pro-family allies on the reservation with wages just above starvation level.

Billings was shepherded to Secretary of Education Terrel Bell by orders of the White House chief of staff, James A. Baker III, who understood the political importance of throwing a few morsels to the Moral Majority. The appointment of Bell himself had angered the evangelicals and fundamentalists. Bell, U.S. commissioner of education in the Nixon-Ford Administration, had been an ardent supporter of establishing the Education Department. High on the list of the pro-family movement's grievances against the federal government was federal intrusion in local schools. That intrusion was embodied by the Department of Education, second only to the Internal Revenue Service's move to curb the new private schools. Besides, Bell was on record in favor of school busing and a strong federal role generally in education.

Now Bell had been named to run the new department by Reagan who passed over one of his oldest supporters, Illinois state representative Donald Totten. Thus the selection of Bob Billings was a pleasant surprise, if not atoning for Bell, at least muting his influence. Billings would be a guardian against IRS attacks on fundamentalist schools.

Billings was a Moral Majority prototype, a graduate of fundamentalist Bob Jones University in Greenville, South Carolina, who took his doctorate at Clarksville (Tennessee) School of Theology and spent ten years as a Baptist missionary in the British West Indies. He had run unsuccessfully for Congress from Indiana in 1976, after which he helped Falwell form the National Christian Action Coalition, forerunner of the Moral Majority. He chaired several right-wing church groups backing the Reagan-Bush ticket during the campaign and was the director of religious participation for the inauguration during the transition period. Billings seemed to fit the part of a Moral Majority protector of local school independence who could halt what the fundamentalists saw as federal harassment. His credentials among the fundamentalist elite in the pro-family, private school movement were excellent. He seemed ideally suited to make Reagan aware of the fertile political soil to be tilled in the fundamentalist private school issue.

The growth potential of those schools had shocked liberal educators and bureaucrats. During the Carter Administration, surreptitious moves were planned to curb that growth. One route was to question tax exemption and federal school aid to new private schools on grounds that they failed to promote affirmative action on admitting minority students (a requirement for any recipient of federal aid) or that they discriminated against minorities.

Senator Paul Laxalt had tried for two years to convince Reagan's political aides that the private school movement was well worth political missionary work for the 1980 election. He argued that Carter's use of the IRS as the government's private eye keeping tabs on the private school movement, looking for ways to cut off federal assistance and tax exemptions, invited Reagan's attention. Laxalt predicted that the private school movement would fertilize Reagan's cause and produce a bumper crop of voters. But because they worried about anti-Moral Majority political reaction, Reagan's men decided not to press for those votes that were headed in Reagan's direction anyway.

After Reagan's August 22, 1980, speech in Dallas, he met with Falwell and other fundamentalist leaders. They told him that one post they deemed highly significant and influential was the assistant secretary for nonpublic schools. Fundamentalist leaders said that at the rate of private school formation in 1980, which they estimated at four new schools every day of the year, private schools would outnumber public schools by 1996. The assistant secretary for nonpublic schools would control a key post from which to influence the department's policies toward private schools.

Not a single transition leader among the innumerable specialists named weeks before the election came from the pro-family movement. Not until after Reagan took office did Jim Baker decide the time had come to give the fundamentalists a nod and ask Secretary Bell to name Billings as assistant secretary for nonpublic education. Billings quickly accepted.

But when he arrived at work on March 5, Billings found the holdover assistant secretary from the Carter Administration still on the job. Bell, he was told, planned to leave him there for a spell to avoid a "difficult situation." Would Billings be willing to have his title changed to special assistant to the secretary and undertake other duties until the nonpublic school job opened up? Billings was stunned. Nevertheless, he agreed to do what Bell asked. He was told that his job would be transcontinental "travel" to advise Bell how to make the Education Department, which was marked for extinction, work better. Later, he was told, he would be moving into the nonpublic school area.

As he left the department that day, Billings picked up an in-house employee bulletin that quoted an unnamed high department official to the effect that Billings had been vetoed for the nonpublic school job for good, and would not be entrusted with any work in that field. He was flabbergasted. Only later did he learn that when word of his appointment swept through the liberal education establishment, Terrel Bell was besieged by traditionalists to change his mind. The potent Catholic parochial school hierarchy protested loudest. Neither the Catholics nor the old-fashioned private Protestant schools could abide the thought of a fundamentalist Baptist and Moral Majority activist dictating policy to the nation's private schools.

With the support of Reagan's top advisers, Bell blocked Billings from the promised job. Reagan's aides knew that no political gain from making the president a hero with the Moral Majority could match the political loss of alienating the Catholics and the liberal private school establishment. That was a graphic demonstration to the pro-family movement of its secondary rank in the Reagan Revolution.

There were, however, many proposals buried inside the budget documents drafted for Congress by Stockman that endeared Reagan to the fundamentalists. They would have been there with or without encouragement from the Moral Majority. More than such "social" issues as abortion and school prayer, they always had been an integral, vital part of the Reagan Revolution.

Even if Bob Billings did not get the job he wanted, Reagan's pledge to get the federal government out of local education went a long way toward the goals of the Moral Majority. Consolidating the myriad confusing educational grants to the states into "block grants" would cut the lines of control between the Department of Education and local school systems. No longer could the feds dictate policy through complex regulations and directives. During 1980, these federal aid moneys were moving out of Washington to the states at a rate of $5.5 billion. When Stockman rolled them up into block grants, he cut that by almost $1.5 billion. The balance would have to be made up from local and state sources, and cost-cutting.

The rationale was spelled out by Bell for Congress on March 10 in words most pleasing to the pro-family movement. "In proposing these reforms, the administration assumes that families and students—not the federal government—should be the first source of funds for educational expenses." Earlier, the White House itself had explained the new rationale. Block grants would "shift control over education policy away from the federal government and back to state and local authorities—where it constitutionally and historically belongs." The new approach would "eliminate unneeded federal rules," limiting Washington "to supply necessary resources, not to specify in excruciating detail what must be done with those resources."

Few words could have been more pleasing to the Moral Majority than this promise to return policy over education to local control. But that was not the only nonlegislative initiative by

Reagan pleasing to the movement. The end of federal financing of legal services for the poor terminated what the New Right long had believed was a government subsidy for radical left activities. Reagan also was moving, without legislation, in an area that neither he nor the Moral Majority talked about much: special advantages for the black minority. They were agreed in opposition both to forced busing for the purposes of school desegregation and to compulsory affirmative action in hiring, promotions and school enrollment that in effect had developed a government-imposed quota system for blacks.

Although several pro-family groups listed racial questions on their questionnaires used for the basis of candidate support, few had much to say about it publicly. While the Moral Majority opposed busing and the quota system, it did not list these goals on its priority list. The reason was a matter of political prudence. Jerry Falwell, James Robison, Pat Robertson and their colleagues were white Southern fundamentalist preachers whose predecessors for generations had upheld racial segregation in the South. Consequently, they wanted at all cost to avoid a white racist label for a movement whose leaders were so predominantly Southern whites. By the same token, Reagan did not want to give the impression of declaring total war against the race that had given him so few votes against Carter. Since his cuts in social welfare affected blacks disproportionately anyway, he did not want to be seen taking action against the advantages won by blacks in the sixties and seventies.

There was no concerted legislative action on either busing or affirmative action, and the New Right did not complain on this point. But behind the scenes, Reagan was inexorably changing the nature of the bureaucracy. When, after six months or so, his own appointments were in place and civil servants had been shifted, the emphasis of the Carter Administration in pressing for busing and for quota systems would end. In short, the U.S. government would change sides, a revolutionary development much faster and perhaps just as significant as changes coming from the legislative track.

The change of sides was formally announced by William French Smith in an address to the American Law Institute in Philadelphia on May 22. "Rather than continuing to insist in court that the only and best remedy for unconstitutional segregation is pupil assignment through busing," the attorney general said, "the Department of Justice will henceforward propose remedies that have the best chance of both improving the quality of education in the schools and promoting desegregation." Smith added that government would return to the stance of "color-blindness" in opposing busing and also in ending "discrimination by establishing racial quotas." That was a signal to holdover lawyers in the Justice Department, still filing affirmative action suits based on quotas. Smith's speech, given scant attention in the next day's Saturday newspapers, began another major policy reversal of the Reagan Revolution.

Reagan's feeling of warmth, tinged with a certain distance, was expressed on January 5, 1981, when an interviewer asked him what "role" the pro-family organizations and their leaders would play in the new administration. Reagan replied:

> The president is the only one in Washington elected by all the people. I think therefore that constituents, whether individuals or groups, who have a particular bond or interest should have a method of access, and I will provide that for them. They have taken an awful lot of criticism and I think much of it is undeserved. I have found them to be good people who have some specific problems in their dealings with government, just as all Americans do today.[6]

"Access" to minor employment in his administration, yes. But not "access" to administration backing for the Moral Majority's special legislative dreams. Realization that this was Reagan's meaning, plus the lack of Moral Majority figures in high administration offices, immediately drew criticism from New Right leaders. Reagan had barely taken the oath of office before Richard Viguerie indicated his patience was at an end, and Paul Weyrich was not much less impatient in calling the new administration's record "cause neither for outrage nor celebration."[7] That did not bother Reagan's political aides. They had not forgotten either Viguerie's support for John Connally against Reagan or Weyrich's withdrawal of support from the Reagan-Bush ticket. They felt the millions of fundamentalist and evangelical Christians who had been attracted to Reagan would stay there, if only for the lack of anywhere else to go.

But the problem could not be talked away as a matter of pure politics, as Reagan's aides tended to do. An insightful analysis of the depth behind the pro-family movement came from an unexpected source: Representative Bob Michel of Illinois, the newly elected Republican leader of the House. He seemed typical of the orthodox conservative Republicans who looked down their noses at the Jerry Falwells and their embarrassing issues and, even if they did not, preferred to let the new Republican president set the priorities. Accordingly, an article by Michel published in the February 20, 1981, edition of the *Washington Post* surprised both the White House and the New Right leadership.

Michel began by denying that the primacy of economic and national security questions meant that Congress could forget forever such "sticky issues" as abortion, busing, quotas and school prayer. "The social issues are not going to go away, and Congress is going to have to come to grips with them."[8] People concerned with these issues are not just activists affiliated with the Moral Majority or New Right and certainly are not limited to conservatives, much less Republicans. "Just because most of us in Congress do not relish dealing with questions of abortion or school prayer doesn't mean we can turn our backs on those who say these issues should be discussed and, yes, voted on." Even abortion, so long bottled up in House committees, must be considered, because "the issue can no longer be ignored."

Michel concluded with what purportedly was a guide for Congress but was actually a warning to the president:

I agree with President Reagan's initial emphasis on trying to solve our economic problems. But I also agree with him that these problems that directly affect the values of family, school and community are also major concerns and that we must not pretend they do not exist just because they are difficult. There are, in short, two mistakes Congress can make concerning the social issues. The first is to treat them as if nothing else matters. The second is to treat them as if they don't matter at all.

But at best, Michel was talking about 1982. That was made clear by Michel's Senate counterpart, Howard Baker, when he breakfasted with Washington political correspondents a month later, on March 26. Claiming to speak for all fifty-three Republican senators, Baker said that pro-family issues would be postponed until 1982 at the earliest. "They are important issues, emotional issues, but they are next year's issues. I want this year to be

Ronald Reagan's year." Baker said the postponement was his own idea but that the entire Senate Republican Policy Committee—that is, all eighteen Republican senators—agreed with him, and Reagan had no objection.

Several conservative Republican senators were incensed. Leaders of the Republican Steering Committee, an informal alliance of about two dozen conservatives headed by the increasingly powerful Helms, forced Baker to admit that he had not sampled the entire Policy Committee after all. But Baker's embarrassment did not last long.

On March 29, Ronald Reagan underwrote his plan in forceful language, settling once and for all his real intentions when it came to doing the work of the Moral Majority.

> I can't quarrel with that [Baker's plan]. Right now, we're concentrating on this [economic] package and I don't think Congress in my memory has ever been faced with anything in quite the dimensions of this. This doesn't mean that we've drawn back from our position on many of these social goals. It just means that these are things that we think must wait while we dispose of this [economic] problem and once we get that out of the way and get economic recovery underway, then we can discuss priorities with these other measures.[9]

Nine days earlier, on March 20, Reagan had received a tumultuous ovation when he went to the Mayflower Hotel to address the Conservative Political Action Committee and turned the meeting into a tearful homecoming. The audience was sprinkled with Moral Majority believers who deeply felt the emotional vibrations. Reagan deftly touched the bases with just the right firmness: "We seek to protect the unborn, to end the manipulation of school children by utopian planners and permit the acknowledgment of a Supreme Being in our classrooms."

When they considered the alternatives, the Moral Majority conservatives, the pulpit politicians and the restless voters worried about the social issues would stay in Reagan's corner even though their issues were clearly given a low priority in the Reagan Revolution. They knew Reagan was with them in spirit as no other president of the last half century had been. Yet, as Bob Michel said, the issues at stake transcended both the revolution and the Moral Majority itself. They would not go away. In time, they would have to be frontally addressed by Ronald Reagan, but that time would not come until 1982.

11

Reagan on the Record

On Monday, March 23, 1981, Ronald Reagan had been president of the United States for two months and was obviously having the time of his life. Nobody since John F. Kennedy had enjoyed it so much—attending the theater, going to dinners, selling his program to the nation. There was no malaise in the land, certainly no foreboding that just one week later he would be shot by an unsuccessful assassin.

On March 23, Reagan had met alone in the morning with Alexander Haig, the first of a series of thrice-a-week meetings—with no White House staff present—requested by the secretary of state. Haig was protesting a proposal he had just learned about in Sunday's *Washington Post* that would put Vice President Bush in charge of national security "crisis management," instead of the secretary of state. He and Reagan discussed the issue inconclusively, but the next day Reagan selected Bush.

The tension between Haig and senior White House aides Edwin Meese and James Baker, which would explode into public view the next day, did not outwardly affect Reagan when he submitted to a special interview for this book in the Oval Office starting promptly at 4 P.M. on that Monday.

He had always seemed a person fully at ease with himself, and never more so than this brisk, sunny early spring afternoon. He was putting into action a philosophy of government he had long espoused and he enjoyed talking about it.

Our questions were designed to elicit philosophical responses that would transcend such momentary difficulties as the Haig problem. In his answers, the president reaffirmed the manifold aspects of the Reagan Revolution—even the Moral Majority issues that he had by then decided to postpone in favor of his economic program. In explaining and defining his positions on the issues, he was exploring familiar ground. He spoke without notes. His defense of his tax program gave a historical and theoretical case for supply-side economics. His argument that smaller companies outdo the big corporations in the entrepreneurial spirit seemed straight from George Gilder's *Wealth and Poverty*, a book he had given an ailing Senator Robert Dole as a gift but that aides said he had not had a chance to read himself. In citing thirty-year-old budget figures without the help of notes, he was precisely on the mark.

The cadence of his remarks was natural and conversational, not lifts from those 5 × 8 speech cards that he once relied on not only in formal interviews but even in casual conversation with reporters. There was an occasional stray from an old speech segment—the woman writing him to ask, "Who the hell do they think they are?"

But most of Reagan's comments were drawn from his daily life as president—his experience in attending the theater in New York the previous week and in going to Ford's Theater in Washington two nights earlier. His comments on the need for young girls to seek parental approval for an abortion were surely influenced by a Supreme Court decision that very day affirming laws requiring such approval.

The full forty-minute interview is printed verbatim, except for clarifying changes of syntax, to get the full flavor of Ronald Reagan, at ease, talking on the record about issues and philosophy. The White House did not seek approval of the transcript.

EVANS: Mr. President, you told Bill Moyers during a show—I think it was nineteen seventy-nine—that Americans pulled together to help each other a great deal during the Depression, but they don't seem to do that as much anymore. Can you explain what you meant by that?

REGAN: Well, yes, I think that spirit and that feeling is still there. As a matter of fact, in the complete conversation, I remarked that a story pops up in a [small] town newspaper about something terrible happening to some individual, and almost overnight, they form a local committee to go to work to help. What I meant is that the danger is that the necessity of people doing that has been taken away by government—you might say, *preempting* that whole field. There's not only a danger of that happening, I think it *has* happened to a certain extent. People just assume that government will do things that we used to think was our responsibility to our neighbors.

NOVAK: Do you think that has diminished not only the altruistic spirit, but also the entrepreneurial spirit in America?

REAGAN: Well, I don't think the spirit has been dimmed but the ability to be an entrepreneur has been lessened by excessive regulations—punitive tax policies and so forth. The inability to find people who will go with risk capital—I'm kind of ambivalent on this. I think, on the charity side, the feeling is still there among our people. They don't see the opportunity as much, again because of the preemption by government. I think people kind of hunger, they hunger—as we saw in the recent thing with the hostages—to have a feeling of patriotism and service to their country again.

I'll give you two examples. One example was just the other night—one's enough here—the other night at the Ford Theater—

EVANS: Saturday night.

REAGAN: That announcement of the sudden outpouring of contributions [for the theater's operating budget]. And I have heard of other, similar instances where, in our cutting back government and with all the publicity that's been given that, the people didn't even wait for it [the budget] to be passed, but suddenly have come marching in with contributions, in effect saying, "We'll take care of it."

NOVAK: What about the entrepreneurial side, Mr. President? Do you think there are still as many people as there were, say, fifteen years ago in this country, who are willing to risk their fortunes, risk their careers for the sake of trying to build a business, trying to build something from nothing?

REAGAN: Well, I think they're *there*, if the *odds* are right. By that I mean if the reward [is there] if they're successful, [there] is the inducement to them to do it. But some years ago, not too many, but if you remember back—was it nineteen sixty-nine?—when they raised—I know there's been a reduction *since* in the capital gains tax—but when the capital gains tax was raised, virtually doubled, the decline almost immediately in the number of small business and capital-raising ventures in the stock market, something like a drop from hundreds and millions and millions of dollars down to literally the *thousands* of dollars. It was clear-cut—and it *stayed* down there. Now an increase began again when you cut that capital gains tax.

It seems to me—and there's sufficient evidence—that if you lower the odds, *lower* the payoff for a winner, the people then turn to the safer things. There was, at the same time, an increase in the investments in tax-free municipals.

EVANS: Mr. President, on a slightly different question—what philosophical thinkers or writers most influence your conduct as a leader, as a person? I know it's not an easy question.

REAGAN: Oh, boy, Rowly.

EVANS: You know, Jimmy Carter used to talk about Reinhold Niebuhr, et cetera. Is there anybody that—

REAGAN: Well, the thing is, I've always been such a voracious reader—I have read the economic views of Von Mises and Hayek, and . . . Bastiat, back a hundred years ago in France.* I think that part of my reading—for all those years that I was on the "mashed potato" circuit speaking, I was almost compelled to. I have to say that I don't know where I could put a finger on someone as having had a—

EVANS: For example, Adam Smith or Thomas Hobbes or Spinoza—

REAGAN: Oh, I know about Cobden and Bright in England—and the elimination of the corn laws and so forth, and the great burst of economy or prosperity for England that followed.†

---

*Ludwig von Mises (1881–1973), Austrian economist and social philosopher, a champion of laissez-faire economics who argued that the socialist system cannot function because it lacks a coherent price system. Friedrich A. Von Hayek (1899–   ), Austrian political economist of the laissez-faire school who offered solutions to problems posed by the business cycle and economic controls. Frederic Bastiat (1801–1850), French political economist who published works against protectionism and socialism.

†John Bright (1811–1899), British radical statesman and orator who led the fight for free trade in Great Britain beginning with the repeal of the corn laws. Richard Cobden (1804–1865), British economist and politician who advocated free trade along with John Bright.

As I say, Bastiat has dominated my reading so much—ideas of that kind—I often think back to when I was getting my degree in economics, and how the professor had to literally force you to read outside reading and now I do it . . . he'd be very happy to know that maybe he'd planted a seed.

NOVAK: What about the last fifteen years since Vietnam and Watergate? Do you think the American people have lost their will for world leadership? Do you think they've lost the will to bear that burden?

REAGAN: No. I think there's been a great resurgence of it now. I think that some of the things we get in the mail that have to do with our economic program—[for example,] I've received letters from men who were unemployed, who've been laid off and write and say, "I'll give up my unemployment insurance if it will help." But we're not asking them to do that or anything of the kind.

We got a letter the other day from a civil service retiree, enclosing his entire month's pension check endorsed over to the Department of the Treasury. The same thing is true [in other places]—I think we're seeing it. I think we saw it, actually, with regard to the hostages. The same thing is true on that scale. The American people—it has finally reached them, and I think the whole meaning of what has happened in the past year is that the people finally were convinced in their own minds that we weren't where we had been with regard to [our] strength, that we *were* able to be pushed around, and they're making it plain—they don't want that.

The other night in the theater in New York—Mickey Rooney—we went to see *Sugar Babies*—was taking the curtain calls and —I don't know whether it was security that asked him or whether it was his own idea—he asked them [the audience] to please remain in their places until we left—we were right down in the front row or *near* the front row—and as we started up the aisle, not from the stage but from the *audience*, the audience in a New York theater began to sing *America the Beautiful*. And, I'll tell ya, I was all choked up by the time I got to the head of the aisle and so was Nancy—

EVANS: Spontaneous?

REAGAN: *Yes*, they just started singing.

EVANS: Mr. President, do you think our foreign policy has tended, in the recent past, certainly, to be guided too much by humanistic philosophy—human rights, moral goals—and not enough by the fact of military and economic strength that we need and by a willingness to accept strong allies, even if they're not perfect?

REAGAN: I think, yes, I think there was a great inconsistency with regard to human rights; the inconsistency being that we were virtually silent about their violation by potential adversaries like the Soviet Union. But we really caught any deviation from our philosophy on human rights in those countries that were otherwise friendly to the West, to free enterprise and hostile to the Communist bloc. And that, I think, has lost us a certain esteem and respect in the world and among our allies, [who] see us so one-sided in that approach. And the, ah, the thing of allowing our military strength to diminish put us at such a disadvantage when we went to the [negotiating] table.

Now, I believe in trying to negotiate, certainly, a reduction in strategic arms, to reduce the threshold of danger—and there's never been anything like it in the world before, weapons that can literally destroy civilization—but to go to a table to bargain, you gotta have something to give. When you sit down opposite someone who has the superiority that could lead—if they continue this increase—toward the delivery someday of an ultimatum, what do you have to say to persuade them to reduce that strength? But if, on the other hand, you've embarked on a course of saying, "We're not going to let you have that superiority," now they have to weigh, strained as they are to provide—we know they can't provide consumer goods for their people—now, there would be some *reason* for them to listen. Because we can say to them, "We can go one of two ways: We can both keep on straining in this direction [arms buildup] or we can mutually agree to some reductions in strength."

NOVAK: You have placed very heavy emphasis on family as a very important factor in American life—the cement of American life. Why has the family weakened? Do you think it's because of television or the permissive society and what can you, as a president, do about that?

REAGAN: Well, I think some of it can be attributed, again, to the great social reforms of government—the seeming interference with the family's right regarding the education of a child. You know, the school board once was far more conscious of little Willie's or little Mary's momma and poppa than what to say about how he or she was being educated. And it's moved further and further away from them. Ah, legislation that again put the government in between the family, the parent and the child—the type that I've had to veto when I was governor—legislation that, had it passed, would have allowed underage children to go to a doctor and seek advice on contraception, and so forth, without their parents' knowledge. The very laws—social programs—the combination of Aid to Dependent Children and Medicaid which will allow a girl, if a young girl gets in trouble, by way of those two programs, to remove her trouble through abortion—provided by the government and, again, kept secret from her parents.

Now, an underaged girl—or an underaged child of any kind—I don't think a doctor can take an *appendix* out without getting the parents' consent. But through the combination, [the government] allows them [unwed mothers] to go on Aid to Dependent Children. The privacy laws regarding welfare prevent anyone in their family from knowing they've done this.

Being on Aid to Dependent Children automatically makes them eligible for Medicaid and they then have the abortion. And when I tell you, we had cases when I was governor, that we know of—there's no means test—young ladies, whose family is *most* affluent, but they would choose that route and thus never have to face that old trauma—which was at the heart of the family—of having to go before their parents and ask their help.

NOVAK: What do you think as president you can do in this office about strengthening the family?

REAGAN: Well, I've said before that Teddy Roosevelt called it a "bully pulpit." I think there is *that*. I think there is a moral suasion from here. But I think also that the very reform of some of the government programs—I keep remembering a letter that I received from a mother once and the opening line and the closing line were, "Who do they think they are?" I cleaned that up a little. She said, "Who in the *hell* do they think they are?" And then she said that it is my right to carry my child for nine months and to give birth and then to walk the floor with her at night as a baby, wondering if she's sick and loving her so much I could squeeze her to death. She said, to watch her grow up and then one day she's a fifteen-year-old young lady and may be in deep trouble and they tell me I have no right to know. She said, I repeat, "Who the hell do they think they are?"

A father who called me one day to tell me his income, which was in six figures—back when six figures meant more than it does today. And he said, "How dare you put my son on welfare?" He said, "I'm sending my son to your state to be educated. He's going to college there." And I said, "Well, what do you mean by 'welfare'?" "Food stamps." And I said, "Look, under the federal rules, if your son is a student and asks for food stamps, I have no choice. He gets food stamps."

EVANS: Let me ask you a related question, Mr. President. In the election—last November—do you think the Moral Majority, and all its intended influences, really helped you? And do you now see the Moral Majority and the movement that it represents as a permanent fixture in American politics?

REAGAN: I don't know—no one can foresee how permanent something might be. But I think that the Moral Majority—oh, I'm *sure* it was helpful—

EVANS: How helpful was it?

REAGAN: Eh?

EVANS: How helpful was it, sir?

REAGAN: Well, I've got no way of analyzing that or knowing, uh, but I'm sure I had support from a great many people that were influenced by that movement. But I think that the Moral Majority is a reflection of another hunger on the part of the people. And that is a hunger for a return to more spiritual things. Uh, a rebellion against a period in which the humanistic philosophy—materialism, and so forth—well, I think it's the same thing that makes us find that there has been a decrease in the membership of some churches that adopted [humanistic] social philosophy; the fundamentalist churches are having an increase in membership.

EVANS: Which churches? Can you, could you specify for me, sir, have adopted the, what you called, that "social philosophy"?

REAGAN: Well . . .

EVANS: For example—

REAGAN: Ah, I'd rather not do that [chuckle]. But let me just say that this is one of the things that bothers me. We have seen certain splits occur in some major religions when some dogma persisted and others broke away. You could go clear back— and I remember one day in a speech *long* before I was ever governor, talking about a man named Reichenbach. Now Reichenbach was one of the most revered teachers in Protestant theology in the seminaries.* I had quoted him once in a speech, when he had written that what they needed to do was to get into government employment and he *openly* said, "One socialist on the inside of government is worth a thousand on the outside." I quoted this, and I had a man who I knew was a solid clergyman but whose memory of the greatness of Reichenbach [was gained] years before in the seminary—he said, "I revered that man. I just can't go along . . ." And I said, "Well, look, *I* didn't say it. I'm quoting—*he* said it" [chuckle].

What I call the social philosophy is this thing that churches believed—and I'm sure, sincerely—or clergymen believed—that they were meeting their responsibility to be their brother's keeper by advocating and endorsing the governmental takeover of so many of these things.

NOVAK: Mr. President, if your economic plan is not adequately enacted by Congress, or if it's enacted and it doesn't perform adequately, what do you think the alternative is for the American economy? Where would this country go for an economic philosophy?

REAGAN: Well, it's hard for me to imagine it not succeeding, and I think all previous history that we look at in our own country indicates that it will. But how could we not be better off if our program has bounced back to a balanced budget, reduced the excessive power of the federal government and transferred more authority and autonomy to state and local governments? Now, you go clear back to 1932 and Franklin Delano Roosevelt ran for *election* on the pledge that the federal government had *then* seized too much authority of state and

*Hans Reichenbach (1891–1963), German philosopher who was a member of the "Vienna Circle" of logical positivists.

local government. And we have to agree that the New Deal then—with the Great Depression and with World War II—instead of reducing [government], further centralized it to a great extent.

But let's move up to the time of Eisenhower. Eisenhower, in 1953, inherited a budget of some 78 billion dollars or so—I have the figures—for nineteen fifty-four, just as *I* have inherited the nineteen eighty-two budget left by the previous administration. Eisenhower reduced that budget, when he took office, by almost 14 percent. He brought it down by—it was only a 78-billion-dollar budget—he brought it down by more than ten billion dollars; brought it down into the 60-billion range. He then, the following year, actually *reduced* the budget. It was *smaller* than the year before. Here, all we're trying to do is reduce the *increase* in spending. The budget will still be bigger than it was the previous year. But he [Eisenhower] actually reduced it. *Then*, five years later—by 1959—his budget began increasing, but his 1959 budget was 3 billion dollars smaller than Truman had left him for 1954. And, we have to say, with the exception of one recession there, of brief duration, there was virtually no inflation in those Eisenhower years. There was great prosperity—and peace.

This again is an indication that clear back to the turn of the century, the classic economists back then had a philosophy or belief that many of the business cycles—the ups and downs—that the downs were occasioned any time that *government* went beyond a certain point in the percentage of the revenues from the private sector that it took for itself. Now, if we get what we're after, we know that the rate of increase in spending, and then revenue, are going to come together to a balanced budget. We know that we're going to reduce the percentage of the Gross National Product that the government is taking for itself. And we know also—particularly with George Bush's task force on the regulations—that we're going to return authority and through our combining of the block grants instead of categoric grants, we're going to return authority to the state and local government.

This gets us back, you might say, to the figures and to the

system that we had before we had this present economic crisis that's been building for several generations, or for several decades now. But I also believe that it is going to create jobs. I believe that, on all the evidence of the past, that the investment that will be possible in business and industry to increase productivity and modernization of plant and equipment, that those things *are* going to take place. Because they have before—even without such a comprehensive program as ours. We found out that when there was—when we lowered, after the war, the 90 and 94 and the 91 percent brackets down to 77 and then to 70 percent—and that was Kennedy's plan that was implemented after his tragic death—but we know in that plan that there was an immediate stimulant to business investment; investment by way of the market in stocks, in industrial development. And we know also that when the rate was decreased in capital gains, the same thing followed. And what really happened was money came out of tax shelters. Those people who have that ability to choose what they're going to do with investment capital—if you tax too high, they're in tax shelters. If you lower that, they will go back to "risk capital" again.

EVANS: Let me ask you on that, Mr. President, about big business. Do you feel that you have so-called big business behind you today or that big business expects its own safety net? Witness the whole Chrysler problem, witness the auto import problems today—and they're going to insist on special treatment from you.

REAGAN: Well now, at the risk of blanket indictment—and recognizing that you can't do that, there are some who don't fit what I'm going to say—big business has been far less active in opposing big government than has what I think is really the basis of capitalism in our country, which is the independent businessmen and women. And I do know that I have their support. Uh, I've been told so [chuckle].

Now, these are the people who create 80 percent or more of the new jobs that are created. *Big* business is pretty much static in its employment. It's those smaller businesses seeking to get bigger, and to increase, that create the new jobs that we must have for our increasing population.

EVANS: Do you mean by that that big business does not accept the free market system as much as you think it should? By big business I mean with the distinction you put on the difference between big business and—

REAGAN: I think there's been a tendency to go along with some of this—to accept that well, maybe some of the regulation reduces competition and—

NOVAK: *Why* are you so convinced, Mr. President, that your tax rate reduction will work as a means of reviving the economy?

REAGAN: 'Cause it always has. It did when Kennedy did it. It did in the time of Coolidge. Andrew Mellon has written about the tax cuts, and they worked. So I just—I take my own personal experience in pictures. I was in that excessively high tax bracket after World War II and I know what *I* did. I would be offered scripts of additional pictures and, once I had reached that bracket, I just turned 'em down. I wasn't going to go to work for six cents on the dollar.

EVANS: Let me—are you through with that? Let me turn to a foreign policy question, Mr. President, for a moment. If your rearmament program works—you get the money from Congress, the military services produce, you get an industrial base and we really *do* rearm and can maintain strong alliances with Europe and Japan—how will the U.S.-Soviet relationship look at the end of four years?

REAGAN: I think, I think it [rearmament] offers the best opportunity for improved relations.

EVANS: And what are those relations between us and the Soviets if these things work?

REAGAN: Well, I think that . . . first of all, I believe that when you sit at the table with the Soviets and make these plans— you've never done this before—that you don't just discuss the level of your armaments. I think you have to sit at that table and take into account, uh, their activities and what they're doing with regard to stirring up the pot in the emerging countries—what they're doing in using the surrogate troops of East Germany and Cuba, Afghanistan as an example, the threat to Poland as an example. I think they've got to recognize this, because they are not totally self-sufficient—and part of this they've brought on themselves with their own militarism.

But here is the most planned, controlled economy in the world and it can't feed its people if it is unable to buy from capitalist countries the food they need to eat. Now, I think over these coming years I certainly want to do my best to convince them—if there is still a fear on their part that somehow we mean [to be] a *threat* to them—I want to alleviate—*eliminate*—that fear and concern but, at the same time, I want them to know that there is a line beyond which the free world cannot be pushed and . . . that those things that they need from the free world—*must have*—they're going to have a better opportunity to get them if they give up the pattern, the imperialism that they've been following—and I think that that should lead to a better world and a better understanding between us.

NOVAK: Mr. President—Jim [Brady] says I've got one more question—I want to ask you something that's bothered a lot of us and that's on the question of environmental standards. How much protection is it necessary to give up in the interest of productivity and economic growth?

REAGAN: I don't think very much. I think we've got the technology now to enable us to make better use of coal, for us to make, certainly, far better use of nuclear power. I think here the hysteria—if anything, Three Mile Island—now . . . should be looked at as proof of what the pro-nuclear people have been saying because *there* was the worst disaster and now we look back and, after all the hysteria is gone, we find the safety system worked. No one died. We know now that all the rumors about radioactive leaks [weren't true]—there was less radioactivity emitted in that whole disaster than you get from flying a jet from here to Los Angeles—just *once*. So . . .

NOVAK: You think this country's going to look a lot different at the end of four years?

REAGAN: I'm sure gonna try.

EVANS: You hope so.

REAGAN: Yes . . . I would have wasted a lot of time if it doesn't.

But, uh—let me just [say] this on the environment. I think, I think *I'm* an environmentalist. I think we've been dictated to by what I call environmental extremists—let's take one thing. Let's take the . . . recently—and I won't name him, but he's no longer a governor—but a governor of one of the Great Lakes [states] was determined that he was going to reduce thermal pollution—or it had to be within two degrees of the lake water temperature. How do you say this when you've got a lake that changes about thirty degrees temperature just from, from spring—or from *summer* to *winter*.

It's like in California, forced under the environmental thing for a power plant to lay, at a cost of 18 million dollars, a line on the bottom of the ocean—this was for thermal pollution, not any other kind—so that heating water by the time it was released from this pipe would have reached ocean temperature, and you then find out from the most reputable of scientists in our universities out there that if [you] turned that warm water—just spilled it in at the water's edge—the total effect would have been that two acres of sea bottom would have become uninhabitable for shellfish. Now, 18 million dollars to protect just two acres of the whole Pacific Ocean sea bottom [laughter]—when you look at the size of that ocean.

It reminds me of a man—[in] the food industry—once, one terribly hot summer up near Sacramento and he had access to all the ice in the world . . . and his swimming pool got so warm he decided to cool off his swimming pool . . . and he just filled it with 300-pound blocks of ice—and it didn't make an impression in changing the temperature of that pool [laughter]!

EVANS: I heard your story about the imported car distributorship the other day—

REAGAN: Oh, the—

EVANS: Guy is shipwrecked and finds a bottle. The genie comes out and gives him one wish—I was told this was your story. His *wish* is to have a foreign car distributorship—in a big city— and woke up, and he had the Chrysler distributorship in Tokyo [laughter]. I was told this was your story.

REAGAN: No, uh—

EVANS: I've been attributing it to you all over town.

REAGAN: No, I was in the group where it was told—but—Lord, I'd love to have taken credit for it [laughter].

12

The Last Chance

Within hours after an assassin's bullet lodged perilously close to his heart, Ronald Reagan was transformed from an amiable father figure to a folk hero. He was the first president ever to survive a bullet wound in an assassination attempt and he did it with the grace under pressure that Hemingway defined as courage. In the public perception, he was transformed when he walked into the George Washington University Hospital under his own power with a bullet in his lung, then fired off a succession of one-liners. "Honey, I forgot to duck," he told Nancy Reagan, using Jack Dempsey's famous line. For his doctors, he used the old W.C. Fields line: "All in all, I'd rather be in Philadelphia." Those two lines were instantly memorialized into the nation's history books, but a less-publicized one-liner that convulsed the nurses after surgery was more original and more typical of Reagan's show-business humor. "I'd like to do this scene again, starting at the hotel." So did the grisly events of March 30, 1981, bestow upon the former Hollywood actor a mythic quality that, whatever the future, he would never lose.

The shooting also ended the illusion, cultivated by political opponents and the news media but accepted even by some supporters, that this was a figurehead president—a long-haired Merovingian king of sixth-century France exhibited to the public on an oxcart, while the business of the realm was conducted by a modern mayor of the palace, Ed Meese. What happened after the assassination attempt erased that widespread image.

The twelve days of Reagan's hospitalization interrupted the momentum that had been building under his economic program. A presidential speech prepared at the Treasury and all but approved at the White House, giving a supply-side lesson on the necessity of marginal tax reduction, went undelivered. The supersalesman in an administration shy of salesmen had been silenced.

But more than salesmanship was lost. While his two months in office showed Reagan to be as much a delegator of duties and responsibility as Eisenhower, he was also a decision-maker of critical importance. Cabinet members complained that crucial decisions went unmade during those twelve days of hospitalization. A temporary setback in the Republican-controlled Senate Budget Committee, caused by arcane disagreements over budget estimates two years in the future, was attributed by Stockman to the absence of command decisions by Reagan.

Beyond salesmanship and decision-making, however, Reagan also embodied the spiritual essence of his administration to a degree that made his presence indispensable. The Eisenhower Administration traveled its uneventful course without discernible setbacks during three protracted illnesses of the old general. That was impossible in the Reagan Administration. The old movie actor was its fount of philosophical dynamism: while Eisenhower's was an administration of continuity, Reagan's was one of radical change.

This reality sank into the consciousness of the president's supporters that dreadful early evening of March 30, when nobody could be certain whether the president would survive the day. If he died, all would be different. His death would have changed the course of history, even more than did William McKinley's (followed by Theodore Roosevelt's progressivism, which ultimately split the Republican Party) and John F. Kennedy's (followed by Lyndon B. Johnson's zeal to outdo his glamorous predecessor) and perhaps even as much as Abraham Lincoln's (which was followed by the tragedy of Reconstruction and the attendant Jim Crow laws to begin a century of racial animosity).

Vice President Bush, the old Yale baseball captain, was a loyal team player who supported Reagan's policies—even the supply-side tax cuts that he had denounced as "voodoo economics" when battling Reagan for the presidential nomination. But did Bush embrace these programs with enough conviction to carry them out if he succeeded to the presidency? Bush could in all sincerity say that he would, but the truth was he lacked the ideological intensity to promote a program of revolutionary change. The rare involvement of Bush in a policy dispute during the early weeks of the administration, successfully battling Stockman's effort to end the Federal Trade Commission's traditional antitrust function, was a symbolic choosing of sides, with Bush joining respectable opinion against those elements of the Reagan Revolution that most opposed the conventional wisdom.

Without Ronald Reagan, the Reagan Revolution would end. The succeeding Bush Administration would avoid the instability and excesses of the Nixon Administration but would closely resemble the Eisenhower and Ford administrations in avoiding radical solutions and seeking consensus.

George Bush, certainly, was no radical. But then hardly anybody else was in the administration. Ed Meese was more interested in process than policy. Reagan's other Cabinet-level aide, Jim Baker, was only slightly more ideological than Meese. Most of the Cabinet members could have fit neatly into the administrations of Eisenhower, Nixon and Ford. None went so far as Sam Pierce at HUD in catering to his department's constituency. But John Block at Agriculture, Richard Schweiker at Health and Human Services, Malcolm Baldridge at Commerce and even Ray Donovan at Labor sometimes forgot the nature of Reagan's mandate and argued for the narrow interests of their departmental constituents.

But never Jim Watt. Although the Department of the Interior had an army of militant constituency groups (spearheaded by the environmentalists), Watt's gaze was fixed on the objectives of the Reagan Revolution without regard to traditional concerns of a secretary of the interior. Watt was the only member of Reagan's Cabinet as radical as Reagan. Its only other member who might qualify as radical was Stockman. But Stockman himself within three months regretted that he had succumbed to establishment conventionality on policy issues such as the depth of budget cuts and wished he had taken a *more* radical approach.

To the radical triumvirate of Reagan, Watt and Stockman might be added a quiet fourth partner: Dr. Martin Anderson, Reagan's assistant for domestic policy. As a protégé of Arthur Burns, Anderson was distrusted by supply-siders as a disciple of conservative economic orthodoxy. But in his role as "keeper of the sacred scrolls," Anderson zealously advocated Reagan's commitment to the Kemp-Roth tax bill and, beyond that, to radical change in government. As Burns's young aide, Anderson in 1969 suffered as President Nixon, for the sake of social stability, rejected Burns and accepted the advice of Pat Moynihan to continue the liberal consensus and not dismantle the Great Society's social welfare legislation. When Nixon finally chose Moynihan over Burns and proposed family assistance payments, a disillusioned Marty Anderson left Washington to return to Stanford.

Back in Washington a decade later at a more exalted level in the White House, Anderson was determined that Reagan should not fall into the trap that ensnared Nixon. To prevent that, he quietly exercised a veto on anybody who had been closely associated with Moynihan. That eliminated Checker Finn, a former Moynihan aide, for assistant secretary of education after he had been all but selected for the post.

Anderson worked stealthily behind the scenes to prevent Reagan from veering away from his revolution by bowing to proposals such as a quota on Japanese auto imports. The outside council of economic elders, an Anderson creation, was brought in to argue against quotas. Only Charls Walker supported quotas. In his inimitable manner, Bill Simon pounded the table to make his point against quotas. But the most telling argument came from Milton Friedman. When Reagan stressed that the plan was only for *voluntary* quotas, Professor Friedman interrupted the president of the United States to instruct him that, voluntary or involuntary, the destructive impact of quotas on all Reagan's dreams would be the same. Reagan nodded his head, but added that there were political reasons for advocating the quota. Friedman retorted that politics usually was the worst reason for making a decision.

Friedman lost. Without any formal decision by the divided Reagan Cabinet, quiet pressure from the Reagan Administration forced the Japanese into a "voluntary" quota agreement. Special Trade Representative Brock was sent to Tokyo in April and negotiated a "voluntary" quota, much to the consternation of Stockman and the Treasury free traders. They considered it the worst decision of the first hundred days, opening the door to pleas for help from Washington by other distressed industries.

Others felt the worst decision was the lifting of the Soviet grain embargo, against Haig's recommendations and the wishes of Senate conservatives, to redeem a campaign promise. In giving a wrong signal to Moscow, Reagan was violating the foreign policy premises of his own revolution. These two decisions, on auto imports from Japan and grain exports to Russia, had a similarity: policymaking based on political strategizing, the common practice under recent presidents (particularly Nixon) that eroded their credibility and ultimately their authority. Reagan in his first hundred days proved so successful because, almost always, he truly followed the precept that he put forth a few hours before he was shot: "We'll do the job as if there will never be another election." Japanese autos and Soviet grain were exceptions to that rule.

Why was it that Reagan had named so few radicals to high position? Why was it that William Simon, William Van Cleave, Laurence Silberman and Lewis Lehrman had found no place in this most radical administration? One radical so excluded put that question this way after the assassination attempt: "Why is it that Reagan doesn't want anybody around him as radical as he is?"

The question almost surely misunderstood Reagan's self-conception. Closer to the truth was the analysis of one Cabinet member: "Ronald Reagan is a radical by any reasonable measurement, but he does not *perceive* himself to be one." Therefore, he flinched from surrounding himself with radical administrators, preferring and choosing assistants, typified by Ed Meese, who naturally recommended still more nonradicals for high office.

A clue to this fact surfaced at the end of an hour-long interview of Reagan by Bill Moyers shown over the Public Broadcasting Service on May 14, 1979. Moyers mentioned the slogan, "Reagan in 1980: It's Our Last Chance," and asked Reagan: "Last chance for what?" Here was an opportunity to explain his revolution, but instead Reagan rambled into a discourse on inflation deriving from the diminished value of the dollar. "So, it's the last chance to . . ." Moyers interjected, trying to get Reagan back to the subject. Reagan interrupted: "It's the last chance to get back some common sense . . . and that's what I believe in in government. It's common sense, and I found that it worked in our own California state government." At that point Reagan again digressed, repeating a description he had given earlier in the interview of how as governor of California he had distributed government surpluses as tax rebates—all of which justifiably ended up on PBS's cutting-room floor. Moyers thereupon gave up efforts to find out: "Last chance for what?"

That Reagan could think only of "common sense" suggested his self-perception; in fact, he was pursuing radical goals but using nonradical language. It was perhaps a major asset that politicians in Washington incorrectly saw in him a pragmatist and consequently were not alarmed. He was the mirror image of Richard Nixon. While Nixon spoke in the contentious rhetoric of hyperbole, his policies as president were moderate if not downright liberal, careful not to disturb the national political consensus dating back to Franklin Roosevelt. In contrast, Reagan spoke in moderate language while pursuing policies whose only intent was to destroy that consensus.

In three months, he had done more to change the direction of policy than any president since Roosevelt. Only one year earlier, in the spring of 1980, Jimmy Carter had shocked the Democratic Congress by proposing a $15 billion cut in the budget for the 1981 fiscal year. Despite strenuous efforts and a crash in the bond market, Carter was able to achieve only little more than half of his reduction. By the spring of 1981, however, Reagan was within reach of a budget reduction for fiscal 1982 four times that level, a stunning turnabout.

Indeed, the Reagan Revolution was in some ways even more remarkable than the New Deal in that Roosevelt faced a stricken land nearing financial collapse and yearning for radical change, while in 1981 the American people, though troubled, did not see themselves as perched on the brink of disaster as Reagan did. Reagan was convinced it was indeed "the last chance for America"—the last chance to revive its leadership in the world, the last chance to halt pervasive growth of government, the last chance to revive the free market.

If measured in overall governmental change rather than the journalistic standard of legislative accomplishment, Reagan's Hundred Days could be compared to Roosevelt's. What was so quickly started then in regulatory relaxation, spending cuts and tax cut proposals was just the beginning. Removing the regulatory wedge was a continuing process; Stockman was making plans for further and deeper budget cuts in years ahead; Reagan saw tax rate reduction as a process that would not cease so long as he was president. Even the Moral Majority's social issues would be pursued in due time.

This was the Reagan Revolution. Doubts that Reagan was serious about it disappeared in the first weeks in office. By spring, it was clear that most of it would be put into effect.

The larger question remained: Would it work?

Source Notes

As in our previous books, much of the material is based on confidential conversations with news sources who cannot be identified. In addition, we have not listed the sources for public statements, speeches and official documents, which are readily available. Consequently, the following notes are limited to secondary references containing material that cannot be found elsewhere.

1. A NEW BEGINNING

1. John Sears, "A Man Who Knows Himself," *Washington Post*, July 13, 1980.
2. Rowland Evans and Robert Novak, " 'Meanness' Backlash," *Washington Post*, October 13, 1980.
3. Louis W. Koenig, "The Presidency Today," *Current History*, June 1974.
4. Ibid.
5. George H. Skau, "Franklin D. Roosevelt," *Current History*, June 1974.
6. George Reedy, "On the Isolation of Presidents," *The Presidency Reappraised*, eds. Thomas E. Cronin and Rexford G. Tugwell (New York: Praeger, 1977).
7. Ibid.

2. HOLLYWOOD TO SACRAMENTO

1. Ronald Reagan (with Richard G. Hubler), *Where's the Rest of Me?* (New York: Karz, 1981), p. 74.

2. Ibid.
3. Ibid.
4. Ibid., p. 301.
5. Lou Cannon, *Ronnie and Jesse: A Political Odyssey* (Garden City, N.Y.: Doubleday, 1969), p. 39.
6. Edward Langley, "Reagan: He Got It Right from America's People," *New York Daily News*, November 18, 1979.
7. Reagan, p. 29.
8. Lee Edwards, *Ronald Reagan: A Political Biography* (Houston, Texas: Norland, 1980), p. 74.
9. Stephen Shadegg, *What Happened to Goldwater? The Inside Story of the 1964 Republican Campaign* (New York: Holt, Rinehart and Winston: 1965), pp. 252–3.
10. Bill Boyarsky, *The Rise of Ronald Reagan* (New York: Random House, 1968), pp. 107–8.
11. George Gilder, *Wealth and Poverty* (New York: Basic Books, 1981), p. 121.
12. Bill Boyarsky, *Ronald Reagan: His Life and Rise to the Presidency* (New York: Random House, 1981), p. 136.
13. Ibid.
14. Rowland Evans and Robert Novak, "The New Messiah, " *New York Herald Tribune*, June 14, 1965.
15. Ibid.

3. 1976: DEFEAT

1. "The Impact of '74," *U.S. News and World Report*, November 18, 1974.
2. Rowland Evans and Robert Novak, "Reagan's Self-Destruction," *Washington Post*, July 30, 1976.
3. Ibid.
4. Jules Witcover, *Marathon: The Pursuit of the Presidency 1972–1976* (New York: Viking, 1977), pp. 84–86.
5. Ibid.

4. 1980: VICTORY

1. Jude Wanniski, *The Way the World Works* (New York: Simon & Schuster, 1978), p. x.
2. ———"The Mundell-Laffer Hypothesis—a New View of the World Economy," *Public Interest*, Spring 1975.

3. Rowland Evans and Robert Novak, "Pupil Defers to Master," *New York Post*, June 3, 1978.
4. ———, "Reagan Talks Out of School," *Washington Post*, October 12, 1979.

5. THE SUPPLY SIDE

1. Steven Rattner, "Reagan Is Lowering Extent of Tax Cut for the Affluent," *New York Times*, February 17, 1981.
2. Paul A. Samuelson, *Economics* (New York: McGraw-Hill, 1980), p. 788.
3. Ibid., p. 335.
4. Jude Wanniski, *The Way the World Works* (New York: Simon & Schuster, 1978), p. 157.
5. Ibid., p. xi.
6. Ibid., pp. 85–86.
7. Jack Kemp, *An American Renaissance: A Strategy for the 1980s* (New York: Harper & Row, 1979), p. 53.
8. Wanniski, p. 158.
9. "Tax the Rich!" *Wall Street Journal*, March 8, 1977.
10. George Gilder, *Wealth and Poverty* (New York: Basic Books, 1981), p. 59.
11. Ibid., p. 63.
12. Ibid., p. 45.
13. Will Durant, *Caesar and Christ* (New York: Simon & Schuster, 1944), p. 641.
14. Ibid., pp. 643–44.
15. Ibid., p. 668.
16. Wanniski, p. 173.
17. Andrew Mellon, *Taxation: The People's Business* (New York: Macmillan, 1924), p. 13.
18. Arthur Schlesinger, Jr., *A Thousand Days: John F. Kennedy in the White House* (Boston: Houghton Mifflin, 1965), p. 630.
19. Wanniski, p. 72.
20. Kemp, p. 98.
21. Suzanne Garment, "Liberal Openers: Mr. Frank Comes to Washington," *Wall Street Journal*, February 27, 1981.

6. AVOIDING AN ECONOMIC "DUNKIRK"

1. Rowland Evans and Robert Novak, *Nixon in the White House: The Frustration of Power* (New York: Random House, 1971), pp. 41–43.

2. Jude Wanniski, "The California Tax Revolt," *Wall Street Journal*, May 24, 1978.
3. George Gilder, *Wealth and Poverty* (New York: Basic Books, 1981), p. 227.
4. Jack Kemp, *An American Renaissance: A Strategy for the 1980s* (New York: Harper and Row, 1979), p. 83.
5. Ibid., p. 84.
6. David A. Stockman, "The Social Pork Barrel, *The Public Interest*, Spring 1975.
7. Wanniski, *The Way the World Works* (New York: Simon & Schuster, 1978), p. 75.
8. Gilder, p. 112.

7. NOT ON OUR BACKS

1. Murray L. Weidenbaum, *The Future of Business Regulation* (New York: AMACOM), p. 28.
2. ———, *Government-Mandated Price Increases: A Neglected Aspect of Inflation* (Washington: American Enterprise Institute, 1975), p. 6.
3. George Gilder, *Wealth and Poverty* (New York: Basic Books, 1981), p. 170.
4. Weidenbaum, "Reforming Government Regulation," *Regulation*, November/December 1980.
5. "Toward a 'Neutral' OSHA," *New York Times*, March 29, 1981.
6. Weidenbaum, "Reforming Government Regulation."
7. ———, *Government-Mandated Price Increases*, p. 34.
8. ———, *Future of Regulation*, p. 172.

8. REAGAN VERSUS THE KREMLIN

1. "Reagan's Prescription for Beating Inflation," *U.S. News & World Report*, August 14, 1978.
2. "Reagan and Human Rights," *Newsweek*, December 15, 1980.
3. Ernest Lefever, "The Trivialization of Human Rights," *Heritage Foundation Policy Review*, Winter 1978.
4. Bernard Gwertzman, "Haig Favors Stand Against Violations of Rights Abroad," *New York Times*, April 21, 1981.
5. "Reagan's Prescription," *U.S. News*.

9. RESTORING THE BALANCE

1. George Wilson, "The Missile Gap the MX Can't Close," *Washington Post*, December 14, 1980.
2. Ibid.
3. Claire Sterling, "Terrorism: Tracing the International Network," *New York Times Magazine*, March 1, 1981.
4. Joseph D. Douglass, Jr, "Soviet Disinformation," *Strategic Review*, Winter 1981.

10. THE MORAL MAJORITY

1. "Politicizing the Word," *Time*, October 1, 1979.
2. Helene von Damm, *Sincerely, Ronald Reagan* (New York: Berkley, 1981), p. 88.
3. Ibid., p. 90.
4. Lou Cannon, *Ronnie and Jessie: A Political Odyssey* (Garden City, N.Y.: Doubleday, 1969), p. 188.
5. Bill Boyarsky, *Ronald Reagan: Life and Rise to the Presidency* (New York: Random House, 1981), p. 178.
6. "Ronald Reagan: The President Talks About His Health, His Children and His Divorce," *People*, January 5, 1981.
7. "Shortages of Reaganites in Administration Concerns, Surprises Supporters of Reagan," *Conservative Digest*, February 1981.
8. Bob Michel, "Social Issues *Won't* Go Away," *Washington Post*, February 20, 1981.
9. Lee Lescaze and Lou Cannon, "Delay is Found on the Social Issues," *Washington Post*, March 29, 1981.

Index

"At 8:30 A.M. on March 30, 1981, departmental assistant secretaries appointed by President Reagan and known collectively as the subcabinet filed into the Roosevelt Room in the White House for a rare meeting with the fortieth president. The administration was seventy days old, but many of the subcabinet officials, some barely in office, had not yet met Ronald Reagan.

"Reagan was smiling, confident and soft spoken. 'I'll tell you what I told the Cabinet at the first meeting,' he began.

We'll all do the job as if there will never be another election. In other words ... we'll take no actions or make no decisions that are based on how they might bear on or affect an election. Whatever we do will be based on what we believe, to the best of our ability, is best for the people of this country.

"Shortly after one of the assistant secretaries returned to his office from lunch, he learned that the seventy-year-old president had been rushed to the George Washington University Hospital with a bullet in his lung. Remembering the Roosevelt Room lecture, the official was struck by the importance of Ronald Reagan to the fulfillment of his administration."

It comes as no surprise to the writers of this book that Mr. Reagan's White House reveals a driving ideology that informs his every action and demands compliance by his colleagues in government. As Evans and Novak, intimates of the most revolutionary presidential admin-